MYTHOLOGY OF THE
AZTECS AND MAYA

MYTHS AND LEGENDS OF ANCIENT MEXICO AND NORTHERN CENTRAL AMERICA

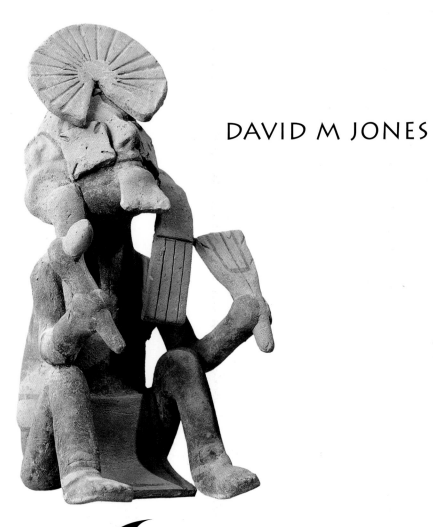

DAVID M JONES

southwater

I dedicate this book to Anne, my flower-skirted travelling companion in Mesoamerica.

This edition is published by Southwater

Southwater is an imprint of
Anness Publishing Limited
Hermes House
88-89 Blackfriars Road
London SE1 8HA
tel 020 7401 2077;
fax 020 7633 9499
www.southwaterbooks.com; info@anness.com

This edition distributed in the UK by The Manning
Partnership Ltd, 6 The Old Dairy, Melcombe Road,
Bath BA2 3LR; tel. 01225 478 444; fax 01225 478
440; sales@manning-partnership.co.uk

This edition distributed in the USA and Canada
by National Book Network, 4501 Forbes Boulevard,
Suite 200, Lanham MD 20706; tel. 301 459 3366;
fax 301 429 5746; www.nbnbooks.com

This edition distributed in Australia by
Pan Macmillan Australia, Level 18,
St Martins Tower, 31 Market St, Sydney,
NSW 2000; tel. 1300 135 113; fax 1300 135 103;
customer.service@macmillan.com.au

A CIP catalogue record for this book is available from
the British Library

Publisher: Joanna Lorenz
Managing Editor: Helen Sudell
Project Editor: Sue Barraclough
Design: Mario Bettella, Artmedia
Map Illustrator: Stephen Sweet
Picture Researchers: Veneta Bullen (UK),
    Anita Dickhuth (US)
Editorial Reader: Richard McGinlay
Production Controller: Nick Thompson

Previously published as part of a larger compendium
The Mythology of the Americas

10 9 8 7 6 5 4 3 2 1

Page 1: *TOLLÁN (ANCIENT TULA)*
Frontispiece: *BAS-RELIEF PORTRAYING QUETZALPAPÁLOTL AT TEOTIHUACÁN*
Title page: *AZTEC GOD, XÓLOTL*
This page: *CUP WITH HANDLE DEPICTING COQUI BEZALAO MIXTEC GOD OF DEATH*
Opposite page: *EAGLE AND JAGUAR WARRIORS*
Page 8: *CREATION OF THE WORLD INSPIRED BY THE TEXT OF THE POPUL VUH
(PAINTING BY DIEGO RIVERA, 1886–1957)*
Page 16: *RECONSTRUCTED DETAIL QUETZALCÓATL, TEOTIHUACÁN*

PUBLISHER'S NOTE: The entries in this encyclopedia are all listed alphabetically. Names in italic
capital letters indicate the name has an individual entry. Special feature spreads examine specific
mythological themes in more detail. If a character or subject is included in a special feature spread
it is noted at the end of their individual entry.

MYTHOLOGY OF THE

AZTECS AND MAYA

CONTENTS

PREFACE

This encyclopedia describes the religious beliefs developed by the Aztecs, the Maya, their contemporaries, and predecessor cultures and civilizations from the earliest village-farming peoples of central America, now known as Mesoamerica, from about 4,000 years ago.

People migrated into the New World from the far north-east of Asia from at least 15,000 years ago. There is some evidence to suggest that they came both by land, following an ice-free corridor between the great glacial sheets of Canada, and by sea, travelling along the western coast. By about 9,000 years ago, at least, the descendants of these migrants had populated the continents of North and South America, right down to the tip of Tierra del Fuego.

The word myth is derived from the Greek word *mythos*. It originally meant "word" or "story", but later came to be juxtaposed to the word *logos*, meaning "truth", and over time came to mean "fiction", or even "falsehood". These meanings form a Western point of view, and are popularly, and often subconsciously, applied to what is called the "mythology" of an ancient, and especially pre-Christian and pre-Islamic, culture, and even more especially of a "non-Western" culture.

When considered from the point of view of the peoples and cultures who created the myths, however, the stories and their characters described here constitute, in fact, the religion of the ancient peoples of Mesoamerica.

Myths are about gods and goddesses, and about divine or semi-divine heroes. The mythology of a people or culture is part of a coherent system of beliefs. The myths themselves are sacred to those telling them or recording them, and are almost always linked to ritual. The sacred stories are re-enacted – usually through a regular cycle of specified days or other time periods, in specially designated or constructed places – and involve elaborate preparations. A culture's mythology is usually intimately linked to and endorsed by the élite of society – rulers and priests, who might be one and the same group. In ancient cultures, the mythology usually forms part of the élite's reason for being and part of its power base. The myths give the élite their power by explaining how it has been given to them as part of the divine scheme of life.

Scholars have analysed the mythologies of cultures throughout the world in an attempt to discover universal themes and a single cause for myth-making. They have approached the subject as external, trying to find common themes in mythological stories – for example divine rulership, or the nature of an afterlife – and as internal, attempting to identify universal features of the human psyche – for example the reason for human existence, or a perceived universal nature in the relationship between children and their parents. Complex meanings in mythological themes are said to be for the purpose of explaining and resolving apparent contradictions in the human experience. Universality has even been sought by constructing elaborate checklists of functions common to all world myth.

Such scholarly pursuits continue to be a basis for debate. Returning to the point of view of the peoples who created the myths, however, it seems clear that their purpose when the culture and mythology were concurrently active was to provide an explanation for their world and everything in it. Every culture has a need to explain the vastness and power of the cosmos and the natural world around it. All peoples need to explain not only how they came into being as a tribe, village, city, state or larger political entity, but also how the universe itself came into being, how the land in which they live was formed, and their own origins within it. The nature of human desires, fears, likes and dislikes, capacity for doing good and evil, and selfishness and altruism needs to be explained. Thus "mythology" enables a people and culture to find meaning, balance and a sense of place in the world they inhabit.

Mythology is not just a miscellaneous collection of old tales and legends. To the people and culture concerned, myth embraces all of what we now call religion, science and philosophy (natural, moral and metaphysical). It asks fundamental questions – how the world began, how it will end, where humans fit in and how they can influence it, and how individuals and communities should interact on a variety of levels. As such general ideas have universal underpinning and application, the questions asked are the same.

Thus we see common threads running through the mythology of Mesoamerican peoples and successive archaeologically defined cultures. A modern division of religion and politics was unknown to ancient Mesoamericans. The entire basis of political power was derived from divine development and designation. In Aztec, Maya and contemporaneous societies rulers and priests were

THE CREATOR GOD, *Quetzalcóatl, and the rain god, Tláloc, alternate along the tiers of the temple-pyramid at Teotihuacán. The gods were believed to be vital to the wellbeing of the city. The stone retains traces of the brilliant colours in which they were originally painted.*

often one and the same. Although certain specializations prevailed, the two groups were intimately entwined in ruling, governing and regulating every aspect of daily life. Rulers, for example, often performed sacrifice and ritual. Not only this, but the very landscape itself was regarded as sacred, and as a sacred manifestation of the stories in the myths.

There was a long sequence of traditional development among Mesoamerican peoples and cultures, such that we can identify a pantheon of gods and goddesses that was almost universal, but whose gods and goddesses were simply called by different names by different peoples. The Mesoamericans themselves recognized this commonality, and the Aztecs in their conquests were eager to incorporate others' deities to expand their pantheon. There were also favoured "tribal" deities for different cities and kingdoms, and deities specific to certain groups within society, such as the merchants or the warriors, or even stages in human life, such as childbirth or death. We can recognize deities sculpted, carved and painted by the predecessors of the Aztecs, Maya and their contemporaries, and on this basis reconstruct the earlier development of Mesoamerican mythology. From the Aztecs, especially, we have descriptions and a declared reverence for early civilizations whom we can identify archaeologically – for example the Aztec "incorporation" of Toltec civilization.

The appeal of "mythology" from all of the approaches outlined above appears self-evident. The popular appeal of story-telling as pure entertainment forms one end of a continuum of interest that progresses through the analysis of myth itself as a universal human product. At the same time it is the particular character, the imaginative invention in explanation, and the richness of expression and physical depiction of their religion/"mythology", as well as its "alien" appeal – at least to Western readers – that makes Mesoamerican mythology so fascinating.

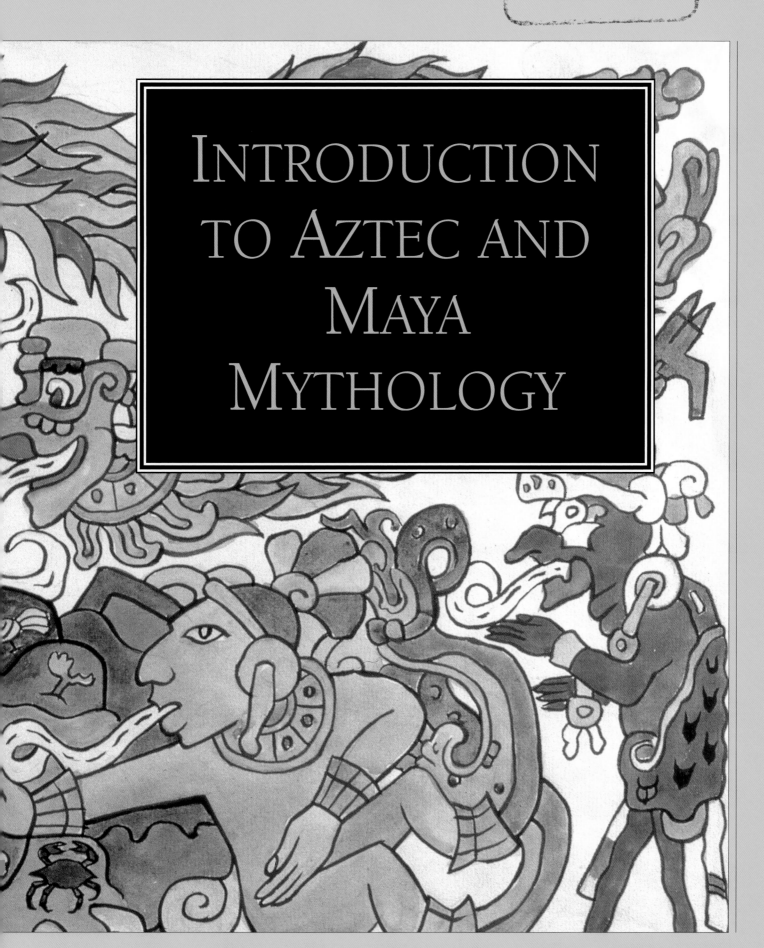

INTRODUCTION TO AZTEC AND MAYA MYTHOLOGY

INTRODUCTION

MESOAMERICA IS BOTH a cultural concept and a geographical area. The geographical area includes both drier highlands and more humid lowlands, and is defined by mountain chains and plateaux within, deserts to the north, and tropical rain forests, grasslands and marshes to the south and east, and by the Pacific Ocean to the west and the Caribbean Sea and Atlantic Ocean to the east. The ancient native peoples of this vast area shared a general cultural cohesion that has been defined and refined by archaeological evidence – comprising artifacts, architecture, technology, economy, settlement patterns and social organization – since the term Mesoamerica first came into use in the 1920s.

A long list of cultural traits is recognized as common to peoples and cultures who lived in what are now central, southern and eastern Mexico, Guatemala, Belize and El Salvador, and parts of Honduras, Nicaragua and Costa Rica. One principal trait was an economy based on corn (maize) agriculture (both irrigation and slash-and-burn). The northern limit of Mesoamerica was defined by the limit up to which irrigation agriculture was possible, corresponding approximately to the Sinaloa, Lerma and Pánuco rivers in northern Mexico. This boundary shifted somewhat over the course of time, especially in the northwest region, as climatic change limited or expanded the area in which agriculture was possible with the technology of the time. A southward shift of the northern boundary in the Postclassic Period (see below) was a major cause for the migration of peoples southwards into central Mesoamerica, and of much military conflict.

The southern boundary of Mesoamerica is less well defined. Nevertheless, there is a noticeable "fading" of the full set of Mesoamerican traits, although individual characteristics were present in parts of the isthmus of Central America. Conversely, this area was the northern limit of the penetration of some South America cultural traits and therefore constituted a cultural "buffer zone".

Within its vast area, the peoples and cultures of Mesoamerica had distinct characteristics and languages, both through history and as co-existing cultures and civilizations. At the same time, they also shared a wealth of primary cultural characteristics and comprised a "diffusion sphere", within which important events in one region eventually affected the whole area. Making use of natural communication routes between regions, intricate networks of long-distance trade were established, which endured through the development and passing of civilizations. In addition to corn agriculture and long-distance trade, the principal Mesoamerican cultural traits included ball courts with ring goals, stepped pyramid-platforms, *codices* (books of bark paper and deerskin), hieroglyphic writing, human sacrifice, position numerals and an acute understanding of mathematical principles, a solar year of 18 months of 20 days each plus 5 extra days, and sophisticated socio-political structures encompassing complex social hierarchies, market systems, urbanism on a vast scale and complex religious beliefs with a large pantheon of gods, goddesses and concepts.

As in the southern intermediate zone, the diffusion of certain Mesoamerican cultural traits accompanied long-distance trade contacts, both in commodities and as a result of Mesoamerican prospecting for raw materials, particularly into the far north. The most prominent examples are the adaptations of the ball game in the Southwestern cultures of the US and in the Caribbean Antilles, and the construction of ceremonial complexes of earthen mounds in the Southeastern cultures of the US.

THE CREATION *of the world and its creatures and inhabitants, inspired by the mid-16th-century Quiché Maya text of the* Popul Vuh. (PAINTING BY DIEGO RIVERA, 1886–1957.)

Languages and writing

Before about 4000 BC all Mesoamerican languages were probably closely related. Soon after that, several large language groups developed. In central and northwestern Mesoamerica numerous Uto-Aztecan languages were spoken, the most important of which are Nahua, its close

la insignia

llamále tea pay tegal

Elscavatl

dias del fuego Xuo tecutl

Elscava

relative Nahuatl, and Cora and Uto-Aztecan dialects to the far northwest. Nahuatl was the language of the Aztecs, and almost certainly of the Toltecs before them, but was probably not spoken by the still earlier Teotihuacanos. As the Aztecs built their empire in the Late Postclassic Period, they spread the use of Nahuatl as a sort of *lingua franca*. Another language group in the north was Otomí, several dialects and languages of which were spoken by peoples north and west of the Basin of Mexico.

A second group was Macro-Mayan, comprising numerous related languages spoken throughout the Gulf Coast lowlands and the Yucatán Peninsula and highlands to the far south. It includes Huastec in the northeast Gulf Coast region, Totonac in the central Gulf Coast, and various Maya languages east and south of these. Lowland Maya languages include Mixe, Zoque and Chontal in the southern Gulf Coast region, Yucatec Maya in the Yucatán Peninsula, and Mame, Pipil and Quiché in the far southern highlands east of the Isthmus of Tehuantepec.

A third language group was the Mixtecan languages in the highlands to the south of the Basin of Mexico, west of the Isthmus of Tehuantepec. The most important are Mixtec and Zapotec, which, with several other languages, developed from a more ancient Oto-Zapotecan stock.

One language, Tarascan, represents a sort of "Basque" among these groups. It is unrelated to any of the Uto-Aztecan or other languages, although it sits in the midst of the former, and was spoken by the arch-rivals of the Aztecs on their northwestern frontier.

Several writing systems were developed by ancient Mesoamericans. For the most part these consist of hieroglyphs carved on stone monuments, stelae and walls, carved in plaster, and on bone, shell and jade objects, sometimes on wood, and painted on murals and in the *codices*. Thus most early Mesoamerican writing did not progress beyond pictographs.

Aztec and Maya writing, however, was more sophisticated. Aztec writing in the *codices* and other media comprised a close association of text and images, combining pictographs directly depicting objects with ideograms (glyphs, "ideographs", with meanings of a more abstract concept or action). The Aztecs employed some phoneticism by using homonyms, and were on the verge of a truly phonetic writing system at the time of the Spanish conquest of Mesoamerica in 1519.

Maya hieroglyphs are even more advanced. They were carved primarily on stone, but also on stucco and wood, and were painted on pottery and cloth as well as in *codices*. They could be read fully only by an educated elite. Like Aztec writing, Maya hieroglyphs must be used in combination with pictographic images and with the entire pictorial scene to fully appreciate the "embedded text". For example, the verb or the activity might be provided by the image, while the nouns and objects are provided by the glyphs. Many glyphs were phonetic, for while some represent whole words, others represent single syllabic sounds – a consonant plus a vowel. Thus Maya writing was nearly fully phonetic, and was certainly fully functional as a writing system.

Cosmology

Mesoamerican "mythology", a somewhat suggestive term from a Western religious point of view, was based on religious naturalism. Ancient American peoples, like all peoples, felt compelled to explain the important things in their universe, beginning with where they came from and their place in the larger scheme of things. They developed accounts of their observable cosmos to help them to understand what things were important, and how and why things were the way they were. These beliefs constituted their religion.

These accounts, which we refer to here as "myths", did for the ancient peoples of Mesoamerica what science and/or the Christian religion does for Western society today, or indeed any other religion or belief structure does elsewhere in the world: they provided people with a conceptual framework for living and for the comprehension of, and relation to, the mysteries of their observable universe. Their myths sanctified the universe and humankind's place within it, at the same time eliciting or inciting direct experience of the sacred.

Religion permeated virtually every aspect of Mesoamerican life, and cosmology was completely bound up within Mesoamerican religious concepts. Religious themes were important from very early times, and ritual symbolism was made manifest in art and architecture. Physical expressions of religious practices became prominent first among the Olmecs of the central-southern Gulf Coast, and only a little later in the central and southern highlands. As well as architecturally complex ceremonial centres, there were many figurines and symbols on pottery, and carved stone stelae. The details of the nature of worship at these early ceremonial precincts are unknown, but many of the deities can be identified.

Several themes can be detected within Mesoamerican religion, more detail on which is given in the feature pages and alphabetical entries. These include the concept of duality, death and the underworld, a large pantheon of gods and goddesses with specific characters, functions and manifestations for different occasions and meanings, sacrifice – including animal, human, and autosacrifice – and cyclical time, together with a progression of creation episodes.

Mesoamerican worship was focused on public display and a certain amount of communal participation. At the same time there was a distinct élite body of trained priests, and the most sacred rites were performed only by them. In addition, there were cults and semi-secret societies, such as those of the Jaguar and Eagle Warriors. The function of ceremonial centres and their precincts was public display, to which the populace of the cities and of the surrounding countryside could gather on religious festival dates. Private and small-group worship was also practised to images of the major deities and to lesser household deities. There were also many sacred sites, such as caves or mountains, some of which had temples. Some locations were clearly sacred from a very early time, even

though, much later, the actual original site was hidden under the multi-layered building episodes of a huge temple-pyramid. Perhaps the two most famous examples are the cave and spring beneath the Pyramid of the Sun at Teotihuacán and the Sacred Cenote (a natural water hole) at the Maya site of Chichén Itzá, into which sacrifices and offerings were made over a long period of time.

Sources of information

There are many sources of Mesoamerican religious beliefs, verbal, written and archaeological. Native verbal accounts were recorded by Spanish chroniclers and priests, and much information about their cultures and religions was written down by native Mesoamericans who had been taught by Spanish missionaries. In addition to such written sources, there are the monuments and artefacts of the cultures themselves. Gods, goddesses, religious themes and ceremonial rites were depicted in stone – and in a few cases wooden – sculptures (both as free-standing figures and as architectural embellishment), on ceramics and in jewellery, in wall murals, in featherwork and textiles and in metalwork. Temple edifices and ceremonial precincts can also tell us something about the nature of religious worship through their layout, room divisions, and the use of open and

JAGUARS were an essential and prominent feature of Mesoamerican religious iconography. They were painted in murals and on pottery, carved in plaster and stone, and depicted in the codices. These stone jaguar heads decorate a platform at Maya-Toltec Chichén Itzá. (EARLY POSTCLASSIC PERIOD.)

enclosed, sunken and raised spaces between and within them.

For Mesoamerica, only 18 native screenfold *codices* that pre-date the Spanish conquest, survive. From central Mesoamerica a group of five manuscripts, often referred to as the "Borgia Group", are concerned primarily with the sacred ritual calendar and divination: the codices *Borgia*, *Cospi*, *Fejérváry-Mayer*, *Laud* and *Vaticanus B*. Nine other central Mesoamerican codices describe the myths and historical legends of the Aztecs and their Late Postclassic Period near neighbours. From the Maya area, only four Late Postclassic codices survive: the *Dresden*, *Grolier*, *Madrid* and *Paris* codices. Like the Borgia Group, they are principally manuals of divination for use with the ritual calendar.

The most important sources of Aztec and late Maya mythology are post-Spanish-conquest manuscripts written by Spanish priests and Spanish-trained natives. Some of these manuscripts even appear to be transcriptions of lost pre-conquest books. Two of the most famous examples of the former are by the priests Fray

Bernardino de Sahagún and Fray Andrés de Olmos. From the prolific efforts and studies of Sahagún we have the massive *Historia General de las Cosas de Nueva España*, an encyclopedia of Aztec culture, written in both Nahuatl and Spanish in 12 books and with more than 1,850 pictures. From Olmos we have the *Historia de los Mexicanos por sus Pinturas*, one of the most complete accounts of the Aztec creation myths. Perhaps the most important example of a transcription from a lost ancient book is the highland Guatemalan Quiché Maya *Popul Vuh*, an account in three sections of the origins of the Maya world, the mythical tale of two sets of hero twins and of the origins of humans and corn, and the legendary history of the Quiché people.

Archaeological material speaks for itself in as much as it represents the physical manifestations of Mesoamerican beliefs – how they depicted their gods and goddesses, and the physical spaces within which they practised their religion. Our knowledge of Aztec and Maya religion from the written sources provides the backdrop on to which we project a picture of the religious practices of their contemporary neighbours, and into the past. The Aztecs and Maya had an all-embracing religious philosophy, and the Aztecs especially, in their empire building, maintained an open capacity for absorbing

the deities and ceremonies of their predecessors and contemporaries. Similarities between the artifacts of Aztec and Maya religion and earlier ones provide a sound basis for deducing the strong themes in Mesoamerican religion that began with the Olmecs and most ancient Maya, and were developed, added to and remoulded by the civilizations that followed.

Mesoamerican history

Archaeologists organize the chronology of Mesoamerica into several periods. The first, the Palaeoindian or Archaic Period, began with the migration of humans into the New World across the Bering Strait land bridge, provided by a lower sea level when much water was locked up in glacial ice. Evidence for this migration is dated about 15,000 years ago, but migrations might have taken place as early as 40,000 years ago. The earliest incontrovertible evidence of humans in Mexico is dated *c.* 7500 BC at Iztapan.

Incipient agriculture and the development of early village life began in the sixth millennium BC and continued in some areas into the first millennium BC.

SERPENT IMAGERY, alongside that of the jaguar, permeated Mesoamerican religious iconography. Many ceremonial precincts – as at the pyramid-platform of Tenayuca, north of the Aztec capital at Tenochtitlán – were defined by a Coatepantli *("serpent wall") of writhing stone serpents.*

MONTE ALBÁN, the Zapotec capital, was established deliberately by the expanding, and probbaly rival, urban centres in the valleys overlooked by the plateau. The ceremonial precinct was built on the partly artificially levelled ridge between two hilltops.

The first cultural developments to warrant the term civilization began in the Preclassic Period or the Formative Period (*c.* 2500 to 100 BC). Villages grew in size and population, and the construction of special buildings among ordinary dwellings indicates the beginnings of religious ceremony. In about 1200 BC the Olmecs of the central and southern Gulf Coast began to construct ceremonial architecture and to erect monumental sculptures with iconography that depicted deities, cosmology and symbols of rulership. A little later, similar activities began among the Zapotecs in the southern highlands, where calendrical symbols were used from 600 BC, and in the Maya area of the Isthmus of Tehuantepec, Yucatán, Guatemala and Belize. The Zapotec mountain city and ceremonial centre of Monte Albán was established about 500 BC, apparently as a deliberately co-operative effort by the towns of the valley.

In the Protoclassic Period (*c.* 100 BC–AD 300), complex urban-based cultures began to flourish all over Mesoamerica. Long-distance trade and diplomatic and military contact spread pan-Mesoamerican religious themes, raw materials and artefacts among these cultures. In the Basin

of Mexico, the sites of Cuicuilco in the south and Teotihuacán in the northeast Basin began to grow at increasing rates. In the Oaxacan highlands, Zapotec civilization remained focused at Monte Albán. At Maya sites such as Izapa, Kaminaljuyú, Abaj Takalik, El Mirador, Tikal and Uaxactún, monumental architecture and art were erected in large centres loosely spread over large areas. At Izapa, in particular, stone monuments were carved with mythological scenes.

In the succeeding Classic Period (*c.* AD 300–900), Maya ceremonial cities flourished throughout eastern and southern Mesoamerica. Maya hieroglyphic writing reached a high level of complexity and, now that it has been deciphered, reveals the names of Maya cities, rulers and deities. Classic Period Maya cities were never united into a single empire or confederation, but hieroglyphic inscriptions record the conquests and temporary alliances of numerous rulers and cities (for example Uxmal, Río Bec, Palenque, Yaxchilán, Tikal, Copán and Kaminaljuyú). Their calendrical system, writing, art, architecture and religious iconography were shared. In Oaxaca, Monte Albán continued to dominate the southern highland region.

In the Basin of Mexico, Teotihuacán grew under a strict authoritarian plan to cover more than 20 sq km (8 sq miles), with some 200,000 inhabitants, around an immense ceremonial centre whose main avenue stretched 2 km (1.5 miles) north to south. Near the centre, the walls of élite palaces were painted with religious scenes, gods and goddesses. Teotihuacán's rulers were ambitious and dominated the whole of central Mesoamerica economically, if not militarily, and traded and prospected for raw materials far into the northern regions. Teotihuacán and Monte Albán rulers established and maintained diplomatic and economic contacts, and even kept enclaves of their respective peoples in each other's cities. Diplomatic and economic ties were also maintained between Teotihuacán and Maya Tikal and Kaminaljuyú, both of which might have been conquered by Teotihuacán.

Other Classic cities included Gulf coast El Tajín and, around the Basin of Mexico, Teotenango, Cholula and Xochicalco dominated local regions, but seem to have been restricted by the power of Teotihuacán. At Xochicalco, the iconography of the Pyramid of the Serpents and other monuments indicates that, in the seventh century, there appears to have been a gathering of priests and "astronomers" from the Maya, Zapotec and central Mesoamerican cities to synchronize and standardize their calendars.

The Postclassic Period (*c.* AD 900–1521) began with the virtual abandonment of many Classic Period Maya cities, and Monte Albán and Teotihuacán, many of which had suffered periods of decline in the century and a half before AD 900. In the Early Postclassic Period (*c.* AD 900–1250) new cities arose to dominate the regions of Mesoamerica. Northwest of the Basin of Mexico,

Tula (ancient Tollán) dominated northern and central Mesoamerica, as climatic change shifted the northern limits southward. About the same time, Chichén Itzá in Yucatán rose as a ruling city remarkably similar to Tollán in what appears to be a sort of Toltec "Empire" of strong military alliance between north and south. Nevertheless, in the intervening area, cities such as Teotenango, Cholula and Xochicalco reasserted their local power, and new centres, such as Mitla and Yagul, Tututepec and Tilantongo were established in the Oaxacan highlands to replace Monte Albán.

In the final, Late Postclassic Period (*c.* AD 1250–1521), Toltec and Chichén Itzán powers waned, while the Aztecs rose to power in the Basin of Mexico from their capital at Tenochtitlán, and began their conquests of central Mesoamerica. At the same time, new Maya city-states, such as Mayapán and Tulum, were established throughout Yucatán. Northwest of the Basin of Mexico, the Kingdom of the Tarascans, from their capital at Tzintzuntzan, held out staunchly against Aztec attempts to conquer them. Similarly the Tlaxcaltecan state, to the east of the Basin, resisted and held the Aztecs at arms length.

In 1519 Hernán Cortés and about 500 Spanish soldiers, with a few firearms, cannon and horses, landed at Veracruz on the Gulf Coast. Despite its wealth and power, the Aztec Empire was only about a century and a half old. Many of its subjects resented Aztec domination and were eager to rebel. Taking advantage of this internal ferment and using knowledge of the predicted return of Quetzalcóatl, the plumed serpent god, in the guise of a bearded man from the east, Cortés was able to ignite this turmoil into open rebellion, to gain hundreds of thousands of native allies and overthrow the Aztec Empire.

MESOAMERICA

HUASTECS

CHICHIMECS

TLAXCALLÁN/
TLAXCALTECANS

*Gulf
of
Mexico*

MAYA
STATES

OTOMÍ

Tenochtitlán

TARASCANS

AZTECS

TOTONACS

TLAHUICAS

*Pacific
Ocean*

MIXTECS

*Extent of
Aztec Empire*

QUICHÉ
STATE

Aztec Empire and
Neighbouring States

UNITED STATES
OF
AMERICA

R. Rio Grande

0   Kilometres   500

0   Miles   300

N

MEXICO

La Quemada

CHICHIMECS

L. Cuitzco

L. Chapala

Zacapu
Tzintzuntzan

L. Pátzcuaro

Calixtlahuaca

Teotenango

Malinalco

Xochicalco

Huaxtepec

Tepoztlán
/Tepozteco

Chalcatzingo

TOLTECS

Tollán/Tula

TEOTIHUACANOS
Teotihuacán

Cholula

Mexico
City

Tilantongo

Monte
Albán

Yagul

Mitla

ZAPOTECS

El Tajín

Cempoala

OLMECS

Tres Zapotes

La Venta

San
Lorenzo

*Gulf
of
Mexico*

*Northern and
southern extents of
Mesoamerican cultures*

Dzibilchaltún

Mayapán

Chumayel

Uxmal

Chichén
Itzá

Puuc

Tulum

*Yucatán
Peninsula*

LOWLAND
MAYA

R. Usumacinta

Petén

Palenque

Yaxchilán

Tikal

*Caribbean
Sea*

Belmopan

BELIZE

*Pacific
Ocean*

HIGHLAND
MAYA

Izapa

Copán

Kaminaljuyú

HONDURAS

Tegucigalpa

GUATEMALA

Guatemala
City

San
Salvador

EL SALVADOR

NICARAGUA

Managua

Basin of Mexico

0   Kms   10

0   Miles   6

*Limits of
ancient lakes*

Teotihuacán

Tenayuca

Azcapotzalco
Tlacopán
Chapultepec

Tlatelolco
Tenochtitlán

Texcoco

*Present limits
of Lake
Texcoco*

Culhuacán

Xochimilco

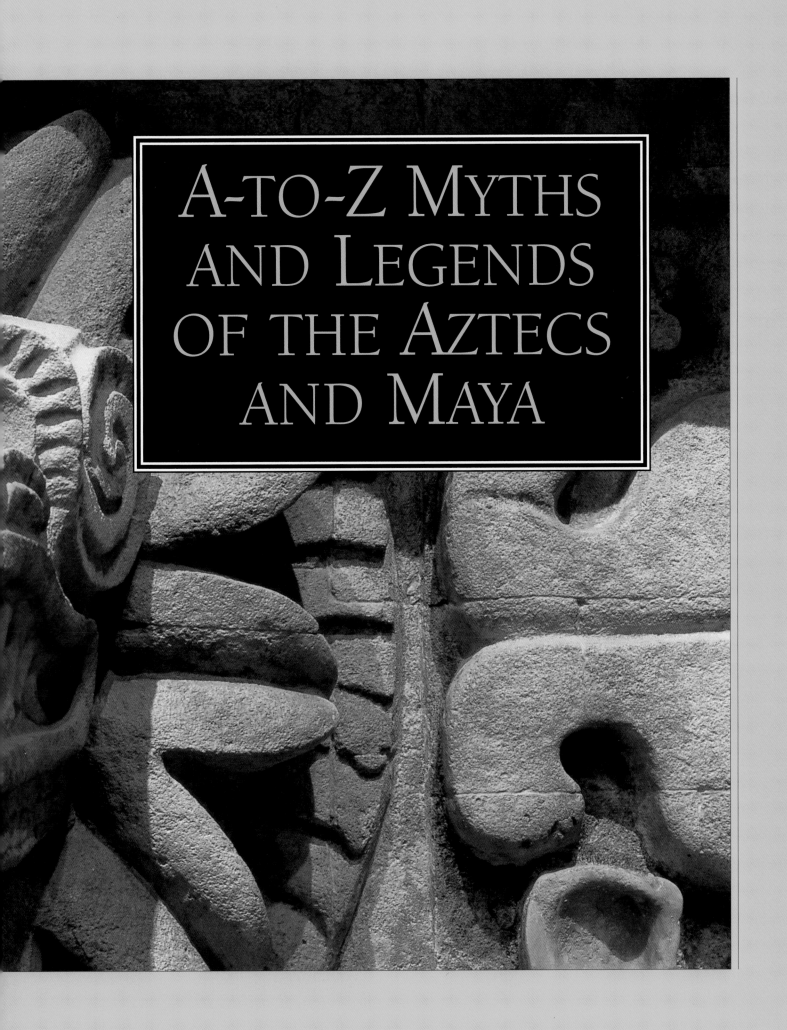

A-to-Z Myths
and Legends
of the Aztecs
and Maya

A

THE ACANTUN were four demons, each one associated with a colour and a cardinal direction. They figured in *MAYA* new year rites and in ceremonies associated with the carving of idols. They are frequently mentioned in the *RITUAL OF THE BACABS*.

ÁCATL ("reed") was the 13th of the 20 *AZTEC* day-names and one of the year-bearing days – there were 13 *Ácatl* years in a 52-year cycle (see also *CALLI*, *TÉCPATL* and *TOCHTLI*). It had an unfavourable augury and its patron deity was *TEZCATLIPOCA* or *ITZTLACOLIUHQUI*; its orientation was east. The *MAYA* and *ZAPOTEC* equivalent days were *BEN* and *QUIJ*.

It is depicted in the codices as a bundle of cane arrows bound with leather straps. Calendrical dates and deity associations included: *1 Ácatl*, the mythical birth date of *QUETZALCÓATL*; *2 Ácatl*, the mythical death date of Quetzalcóatl; *7 Ácatl*, the dedication date of the Templo Mayor in *TENOCHTITLÁN*; and *13 Ácatl*, for the calendrical representation of the sun.

ACHE ("lizard") was the fourth of the 20 *ZAPOTEC* day-names; the *AZTEC* and *MAYA* equivalent days were *CUETZPALLIN* and *KAN*. (See also *BEYDO*)

ACPAXACO was an *OTOMÍ* water goddess, an aspect of or equivalent to Aztec *CHALCHIÚHTLICUE*.

AH CHICUM EK was an alternative name for *XAMEN EK*, the *MAYA* god of the North Star.

AH KINCHIL see *KINICH AHAU*.

AH MUCEN CAB was the *MAYA* "honey" god, patron of bee-keeping. Honey figured prominently in Mesoamerican cuisine and was an important item in Maya trade, along with *cacao* (see *EK CHUAH*). (See also *THE BACABS* and *XMULZENCAB*)

AH MUN, *MAYA* God E, also known as Yum Kaax, was the corn (maize) deity and god of agriculture in general. His alternative name Yum Kaax meant "Lord of the forests". He is always represented as a youth, to personify growth and well-being, and frequently has a corn plant sprouting from his head, or a corn-ear headdress. In the Maya codices he is portrayed with a deformed head, the forehead sloping or flattened.

He was patron of *KAN* ("ripe corn"), the fourth day of the Maya 20-day month, and associated with the south and with the colour yellow. He was symbolized by the number eight, and his name glyph is his own head merging into a conventionalized corn ear and leaves. He was a benevolent god and, as such, was associated with, or under the protection of, *CHAC*, god of rain, but was also controlled by wind, drought and famine; he is sometimes shown in combat with *AH PUCH*, god of death. In the Classic Period, Maya rulers were sometimes depicted in the guise of Ah Puch/Yum Kaax scattering grains of corn. (See also *CREATION & THE UNIVERSE*)

AH MUN, Maya god of corn (maize) (God E), is typically portrayed as a beautiful youth to personify ripe corn, the silk tassel forming his hair. (LATE CLASSIC PERIOD, COPÁN TEMPLE 22.)

AH PUCH, *MAYA* God A, also Hun Ahau, also Yum Cimil, was the god of death and principal rival of *ITZAMNÁ*. In the Yucatán he was frequently called *YUM CIMIL* ("Lord of Death"). He was portrayed with a death's-head skull, bare ribs and long spine with projecting vertebrae, or sometimes as a bloated figure, with black spots on his clothing, suggestive of decomposition, and sometimes adorned with bells (see *CIZIN*).

As a principal deity – Hun Ahau – he ruled *MITNAL*, the lowest level of the nine Maya underworlds. He was patron of *CIMI* ("death"), the sixth day of the Maya 20-day month, and of the number ten, and was associated with the south and with the colour yellow. His connection with death made him a close ally of the gods of war and of sacrifice, and he was often accompanied by a dog, a tropical *Muan* (or *Moan*) bird and/or an owl – a

bird generally associated with unfavourable events and a portent of death in Mesoamerica. Glyphs that signify him included a sacrificial flint knife and a motif that resembled a % sign. In form and domain he was the equivalent to Aztec *MICTLANTECUHTLI*.

The Maya in particular, and in contrast to central Mesoamericans, were highly fearful of death, and the bereaved expressed extreme mourning, weeping silently by day and giving out shrieks of grief at night. For them, Yum Cimil stalked the houses of the sick in search of more victims. Ordinary members of society would be buried beneath house floors, or behind the house, their mouths filled with ground corn (maize) and their hands holding jade bead "money". Nobles were cremated and their ashes deposited in special urns; sometimes shrines were built over them.

AHAU ("lord") was the last of the 20 *MAYA* day-names; it was the day of the sun god *KINICH AHAU* and was associated with the number four. *1 Ahau* was the Maya calendrical name for the planet Venus as the morning "star" and *7 Ahau* was the name for Venus as the evening "star". The *AZTEC* and *ZAPOTEC* equivalent days to *Ahau* were *XÓCHITL* and *LAO*.

AHAU KIN see *KINICH AHAU*.

AHUIATÉOTL, or Ahuíatl, the *AZTEC* god of voluptuousness, was one of the five *AHUIATETEO*. He was one of several manifestations of *XOCHIPILLI* and an alternative name for *MACUILXÓCHITL*.

THE AHUIATETEO were the five *AZTEC* spirits of the south, who were companion deities of voluptuousness. *AHUIATÉOTL* was one of their number.

AHUÍATL see *AHUIATÉOTL* and *MACUILXÓCHITL*.

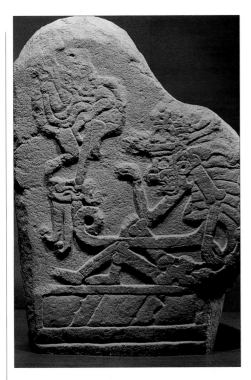

AH PUCH, the Maya death god (God A), or Yum Cimil ("Lord of Death") is depicted in this unprovenanced stone relief as having skeletal features and projecting vertebrae. He is also clutching an umbilical cord.

AKBAL ("darkness") was the third of the 20 MAYA day-names; it was associated with darkness and the night. The AZTEC and ZAPOTEC equivalent days were called CALLI and GUELA.

ANALES DE CUAUHTI-TLÁN, also known as the *Codex Chimalpopoca* or as the *Historia de los Reinos de Culhuacán*, is a late 16th-century source of Aztec history, myth and legend written in NAHUATL, the language of the Aztecs. In particular, it relates the story of how corn (maize) and other edible plants were given to humankind in the world of the Fifth Sun.

APE ("cloud") was the 19th of the 20 ZAPOTEC day-names; the AZTEC and MAYA equivalent days were QUIÁHUITL and CAUAC.

ARARÓ, the Springs of, see SICUINDIRO.

ATEMOZTLI ("the water falls") was the 17th (or, in some sources, 16th) of the AZTEC 18 months in the solar year. The rain god TLÁLOC was the principal deity worshipped during this month.

ATL ("water") was the ninth of the 20 AZTEC day-names; it had an unfavourable augury and its patron deity was XIUHTE-CUHTLI. The MAYA and ZAPOTEC equivalent days were MULUC and NIZA or Queza. Calendrical dates and deity associations included: *1 Atl*, for CHALCHIÚHTLICUE; and *4 Atl*, for the Fourth Sun of the Aztec CREATION MYTH.

ATLATONAN, an earth and water goddess, was one of four AZTEC goddesses who were impersonated by virgins and were symbolically married to a young warrior, himself impersonating the god TEZCATLIPOCA. For a year Atlatonan and her companions – HUIXTOCÍHUATL, XILONEN and XOCHIQUETZAL – served and attended to the warrior, until the festival of TÓXCATL, the sixth of the 18 Aztec months, held in honour of Tezcatlipoca. At the end of the month, the warrior was abandoned by his wives and all five were then ritually sacrificed.

ATLCAHUALO ("they leave the water") was the second (or, in some sources, the first) of the 18 months in the AZTEC solar year, in which the rain deities, especially TLÁLOC and CHALCHIÚHTLICUE, were propitiated by the sacrifice of children. QUETZALCÓATL, who, as ÉHECATL ("wind"), blew the rains away, was also honoured. It was also called *Cuauhuitlehua* ("raising of the poles") and *Xilomanaliztli* ("offering of the tender corn/maize ears"). (See also ETZALCUALIZTLI)

AZCATL, the red ant, was the messenger who led QUETZALCÓATL to his grain store inside TONACATÉ-PETL ("sustenance mountain"). As told in the *ANALES DE CUAUHTITLÁN*, he was running along the ground carrying a corn (maize) kernel, when he was discovered by Quetzalcóatl, who was searching for food to feed the newly created human race of the Fifth Sun (see CREATION MYTHS). Quetzalcóatl asked where such wonderful food could be found, but only after much bullying would Azcatl agree to reveal the source. He led Quetzalcóatl to Tonacatépetl, where Quetzalcóatl transformed himself into a black ant and followed Azcatl through a narrow entrance deep into the mountain. Inside Azcatl had stored corn and many other types of seeds and grains, some of which Quetzalcóatl took back to TAMOANCHÁN, where the gods chewed the corn and fed some of the resulting mash (*maza*) to the infant humans, giving them sustenance for growth and strength.

THE AZTECS were comprised of seven tribes, usually recognized to be the Acolhua, the Chalca, the Méxica, the Tepaneca, the TLALHUICA, the TLAXCALTECA and the Xochimilca, all of

THE MÉXICA Aztecs were the last to arrive in the Basin of Mexico. Several codices depict the scene of the "sign" sent to the Méxica priests through their war god Huitzilo-pochtli, to settle on the island where they witnessed an eagle sitting on a nopal cactus devouring a serpent, here depicted in the Codex Aubin.

whom migrated into central Mesoamerica from somewhere in the northwest of present-day Mexico. The Méxica were the last to make their way into the Basin of Mexico, and were the tribe that is now generally referred to as "the Aztecs".

After serving other tribes in the Basin as mercenaries, they angered the Culhua-Toltec tribe by sacrificing to HUITZILOPOCHTLI a Culhua-Toltec princess offered to them in a marriage alliance. Banished to an island in the westernmost lake of the Basin, they built their capital city, TENOCHTITLÁN, from which they proceeded, through alliances and conquests, to built their empire. In the mid-15th century their ruler Moctezuma I Ilhuica-mena formed and led the Triple Alliance between Tenochtitlán, Texcoco and Tlacopán against the states of Tlaxcala and Huexotzingo east and southeast of the Basin. Later, as Aztec ambitions increased, they began to subdue their allies and other city-states throughout the Basin and beyond.

They were eventually overthrown by the Spanish adventurer Hernán Cortés in 1521, who used their legend of QUETZALCÓATL's return against them.

B

The Aztec gods formed a large pantheon, which was acquired both by inheritance from, and participation in, a long tradition of deities in earlier Mesoamerican civilizations, and also through the propensity of the Aztecs to adopt the deities of peoples they conquered. The mythologies of the Aztec tribes and their contemporaries included some 1,600 deities, many with overlapping attributes and functions. They can be grouped into several general thematic categories.

The *Principal deities* were HUITZILOPOCHTLI, QUETZALCÓATL, TEXCATLIPOCA and TLÁLOC.

Creator deities included CIPACTONAL and OXOMOCO, OMECÍHUATL and OMETECUHTLI, OMETEOTL, TLOQUE NAHUAQUE and Tonacacíhuatl and Tonacatecuhtli.

Deities of fertility included AHUIATÉOTL, Ahuiatl, CENTÉOTL, CHALCHIUHCÍHUATL, CHICOMECÓATL, CIHUACÓATL, COATLÍCUE, ILAMATECUHTLI, IXCUINAN, MACUILXÓCHITL, QUILAZTLI, TETEOINNAN, TLAZOLTÉOTL, TOCI, TONANTZIN, Xilmen, XIPE TOTEC, XOCHIPILLI and XOCHIQUETZAL.

Fire deities included AHUIATETEO, CHANTICO, CUAXÓLOTL, HUEHUETÉOTL and XIUHTECUHTLI.

The *PULQUE deities* included CENTZÓNTOTOCHTIN, MAYÁHUEL, OMETOCHTLI, PATÉCATL, TEPOZTÉCATL and TEZCATZONTÉCATL.

Sky or heavenly deities included CAMAXTLI, the CENTZONHUITZNAHUAC, the CENTZONMIMIZCOA, CITLALICUE, CITLALINICUE, CITLATONA, COYOLXAUHQUI, ITZPAPÁLOTL,

TWO OF the most important Aztec deities were one of most ancient in the Mesoamerican pantheon and one of most recent: Tláloc (above), the ancient god of rain and agriculture was vital to Mesoamerican existence; and the war god Huitzilopochtli (left), unique to the Aztecs and the god who sent a sign to the México priests about where to found their capital, Tenochtitlán.

MEZTLI, MIXCÓATL, NANAHUATZIN, OMEYOCÁN, PILTZINTECUHTLI, TECUCIZTÉCATL, TLAHUIZCALPANTECUHTLI, TONATIUH and the TZITZIMIME.

The *Deities of the underworld* included CHALCHIUHTECÓLOTL, CHALMECATECUHTLI, Huahuantli, MICTECACÍHUATL, MICTLANTECUHTLI, TEOYAOMIQUI, TEPEYOLOHTLI, TLALTECUHTLI and YOHUALTECUHTLI.

The *Weather deities (rain, wind, storm)* included CHALCHIÚHTLICUE, ÉHECATL, HUIXTOCÍHUATL, NAPPATECUHTLI, the TEPICTOTON and the TLÁLOCS.

Miscellaneous other deities are ATLATONAN, CHALCHIUHTOTOLIN, CHIMALMAN, the CIHUATETEO, HUEHUECÓYOTL, ITZTLACOLIUHQUI, ITZTLI, IXTLILTON, MATLALCUEITL, Matlalcueye, OMÁCATL, OPOCHTLI, PAYNAL, TLALCHITONATIUH, TLALTÍCPAC, XÓLOTL, YACATECUHTLI and YÁOTL.

AZTLÁN ("place of the cranes") was the legendary land in northwest Mesoamerica in which the caves of CHICOMOZTOC were located,

and from which the seven Aztec tribes originated; sometimes associated with La Quemada in Zacatecas.

THE BACABS were the sons of the supreme god ITZAMNÁ. They supported the four corners of the earth in the MAYA cosmos. (In another version of the myth, they were said to have been placed at the four corners of the earth by HUNAB KU to hold up the sky.) Each Bacab was named, was a "year-bearer" in the Maya calendar, and was associated with a world colour and a cardinal direction: thus Can Tzional was white (*zac*), associated with north, and bore MULUC years; Hozanek was yellow (*kan*), associated with south, and bore CAUAC years; Hobnil was red (*chac*), associated with east, and bore KAN years; and Zac Cimi was black (*ek*), associated with west, and bore IX years. (See also THE CHACS and THE PAUAHTUN.) As year-bearers they influenced the luck of the year. In addition, the Bacabs were the patron deities of bees and of apiaries (see also AH MUCEN CAB).

The Maya sacred book, the CHILAM BALAM of Chumayel, describes the creation of the world, when the 13 Lords of the Sky (the OXLAHUN TI KU) were defeated by the nine Lords of the Underworld (the BOLON TI KU) and the four Bacabs were set to support the four corners of the earth. At the Toltec-Maya site of Chichén Itzá, small, carved stone "atlantean" figures

with upheld arms, that support stone shelves, lintels and benches, are thought to represent Bacabs.

THE BAT-GOD figures prominently in the ZAPOTEC, MAYA and AZTEC pantheons. At Zapotec Monte Albán, the Bat-god was portrayed as a god of corn (maize) and of fertility generally. In the Maya pantheon bats were especially associated with the underworld (see CAMA ZOTZ, XIBALBA and ZOTZ). The Aztec Bat-god, Tlacatzinacantli, is shown with similar associations in several codices.

BEN ("growing corn/maize") was 13th of the 20 MAYA days and was associated with growing corn (maize) plants. The AZTEC and ZAPOTEC equivalents were ÁCATL and QUIJ or Ij or Laa.

BENELABA, or Pilalapa Caache, with his wife Jonaji Belachina, were the special deities of Southern ZAPOTEC Coatlán. Benelaba was the sun god and god of war, while his wife was goddess of the dead and of the underworld. A *relación* (native history) tells us that these deities were brought to the city by one of its rulers after a visit to the MIXTECS, and that he also brought back with him the Mixtec practice of animal and human sacrifice, which had not been practised previously in Coatlán. Worship of Benelaba was exclusive to men, who sacrificed dogs, turkeys, quail and male war captives. Worship of Jonaji Belachina was exclusive to women, who offered similar sacrifices to her. The alternative name for Benlaba was – Pilalapa Caache ("seven rabbit" in Zapotec), and for Jonaji Belachina, Xonaxi Peochina Coyo ("three deer").

BETAHOXONA was the Sierra ZAPOTEC creator god; see COZAANA.

THE BACABS supported the sky at the four corners of the Maya cosmos. They were frequently depicted as old men.

(CLASSIC PERIOD COPÁN TEMPLE 11)

BETAO YOZOBI was the Sierra *ZAPOTEC* for the corn (maize) god *PITAO COZOBI*.

BEYDO ("seeds" or "wind") was a *ZAPOTEC* deity of the southern highlands of Mesoamerica. He was fourth of the nine Southern Zapotec day names (known as *ACHE* to the Central Zapotec), associated with objects considered to be sacred, and with natural forces.

BEZELAO see *COQUI BEZELAO*.

BOLON DZ'ACAB, or Bolon Tz'acab ("he of the nine generations"), *MAYA* God K, also called Kawil, was the Maya god of lineage and descent. Sculptures and depictions of him in the codices portray him with a reptilian face and an extended upper lip, or with a long upturned snout – and he is therefore called the "long-nosed god" by archaeologists – usually with an axe or smoking cigar in his forehead, holding a mirror, and sometimes with serpent feet. In carvings on stone stelae the image of Bolon Dz'Acab often appeared on a manikin sceptre, the symbol of rulership and power, grasped by Maya kings. For example, at the Maya city of Palenque (on the Usumacinta River in Chiapas, Mexico), Bolon Dz'Acab's mythical birthdate is carved on the Temple of the Foliated Cross, which itself was built to commemorate the birth and origins of the authority of the ruling lineage of the city.

In Classic Period Maya texts he is also called Kawil. Like the *BACAB* Hobnil, he was associated with the east and with years that began with the Maya day *KAN* ("ripe corn/ maize"). He is frequently shown in association with *ITZAMNÁ* or with *CHAC*, and is possibly the equivalent of Aztec *TEZCATLIPOCA*.

THE BOLON TI KU were the nine *MAYA* Lords of the Underworld, identified as distinct glyphs but whose names are otherwise

BOLON DZ'ACAB, *Maya God K of descent and lineage, is the incised effigy at the end of this ceremonial stone bar of rulership, depicted with his characteristic extended upper lip.*

unknown. They were arch rivals of, and were beaten by, the 13 Lords of the Sky (*OXLAHUN TI KU*) at the creation (see *CREATION MYTHS*). Their Aztec equivalent were the Yohualteuctin (see *LORDS OF THE NIGHT*).

BOOK OF THE DAYS see *TONALAMATL*.

BULUC CHABTÁN ("11 faster"), *MAYA* God F, was an earth deity, a god of war and of human sacrifice (see also *EK CHUAH* and *ETZ'NAB*). In the Maya codices he is distinguished by a black line partly encircling his eye and extending down his cheek. The glyph for 11 appears at his head, and he was patron of the Maya day *Manik* (a grasping hand). Sometimes he is shown accompanying *AH PUCH* – or Yum Cimil – but he is more often depicted on his own as a god of war, torching houses with one hand and stabbing people with a spear in the other.

CABAN ("earth") was the 17th of the 20 *MAYA* day-names; it was associated with the number one

and with the young earth goddess, the moon and corn (maize). The *AZTEC* and *ZAPOTEC* equivalent days were *OLLIN* and *XOO*.

CABRACÁN, giant and mountain destroyer in the Maya *POPOL VUH*, was the second son of *VUCUB-CAQUIZ* and brother of *ZIPACNÁ*, and was destroyed with them by hero twins *HUNAHPÚ* and *XBALANQUÉ* in *XIBALBA*. The twins offered him a dish of poisoned fowl, which made Cabracán so weak that they were able to bury him alive.

CALLI ("house") was the third of 20 *AZTEC* day-names and one of the year-bearing days – there were 13 *Calli* years in a 52-year cycle (see also *ÁCATL*, *TÉCPATL* and *TOCHTLI*). It had a favourable augury and its patron deity was *TEPEYOLOHTLI*; its orientation was west. The *MAYA* and *ZAPOTEC* equivalent days were called *AKBAL* and *GUELA*.

Calendrical dates and deity associations included: *1 Calli*, one of the *CIHUATETEO*; *2 Calli*, for *XÓLOTL*; *3 Calli*, for the gods of fire; *4 Calli*, for *MICTLANTECUHTLI*, god of death; *5 Calli*, god of lapidaries and husband of *9 Itzcuintli* as *CHANTICO*, patroness of metalworkers; *6 Calli*, also for Mictlantecuhtli; *7 Calli*, regarded as a good day for merchants; *8 Calli*, for the year of the creation of the *macehual* (Aztec commoners); and *10 Calli*, the mythical birth date of the wind god *ÉHECATL*.

A TERRACOTTA figurine of a warrior from the island of Jaina, off the Gulf Coast, is probably meant to represent Buluc Chabtán, Maya God F of war and human sacrifice.

CAMA ZOTZ, portrayed with a sharp obsidian knife, was the killer *BAT-GOD* of Maya *XIBALBA*, the underworld. As described in the sacred *POPOL VUH* text, Cama Zotz challenged the hero twins *HUNAHPÚ* and *XBALANQUÉ* in *ZOTZIHÁ* (the "House of Bats", one of the levels of *XIBALBA*), and tried to prevent their passage. In the fight that ensued, Hunahpú was beheaded by Cama Zotz, but later retrieved it through a ruse during a ball game against the gods who ruled the underworld.

CAMAXTLI was the *TLAXCALTE-CAN* god of the hunt and of war. He had aspects corresponding to Aztec gods *MIXCÓATL*, *HUITZILOPOCHTLI* and *TEZCATLIPOCA*.

CAN TZIONAL see *THE BACABS*.

THE CANEQUES, probably of *OLMEC* origin, were *MAYA* dwarf-like "poltergeists" and minor rain and thunder deities, possibly the assistants of the Maya god *CHAC*. They lived in the forests and caused mischief to residents and travellers.

C

CANNIBALISM in Mesoamerica, although widespread among the cultures, was neither casual nor common. It was a solemn under-taking and a religious act only engaged in by selected, high-ranking members of society, usually priests, but also kings and nobles. The practice is well attested in Spanish Colonial native documents.

There is some suggestion of ritual cannibalism among the Pre-classic Period *OLMECS* at the site of San Lorenzo, where fractured human bones were found in spe-cial deposits. The best evidence for cannibalism, however, is confined to the Postclassic Period. Among the *MAYA* the flesh of human sacri-fice was considered sacred food; among the *TARASCANS* the bodies of sacrificial victims were divided between the gods and the chief priests – the portion for the gods being sacrificially burned and the remaining parts eaten by the priests. For the *AZTECS*, the con-sumption of the flesh of human sacrificial victims constituted a communion with the gods. The gods demanded human sacrifice and were "fed" the bodies of the victims in ritual burnt offerings. At the same time, the victim was per-ceived to embody the god (through deity impersonation), and therefore consumption of the victim's flesh was a partaking of divine being.

CAUAC ("rain" or "storm") was the 19th of the 20 *MAYA* day-names and one of the year-bearing days – there were 13 *Cauac* years in a 52-year cycle (see also *IX, KAN* and *MULUC*). It was associated with the south cardinal direction and the colour yellow, with the number three, and it had an unfavourable augury. *AZTEC* and *ZAPOTEC* equiv-alents were *QUIÁHUITL* and *APE*. (See also *DUALITY & OPPOSITION*)

CE ÁCATL TOPILTZIN QUETZALCÓATL ("One Reed Sacrificer Plumed Serpent"), to the *AZTECS*, was both a manifestation

CANNIBALISM was a religious act in Mesoamerica, undertaken only by priests and nobles after ritual sacrifice. This gruesome scene from the Codex Magliabecchiano *shows the death god Mictlantecuhtli presiding over such a feast.*

of the god *QUETZALCÓATL* and the legendary human founder and ruler of ancient Tollán (modern Tula), the new *TOLTEC* capital to the north-west of the Basin of Mexico. In his human guise, he was the son of the Toltec-*CHICHIMEC* tribal ruler *CE TÉCPATL MIXCÓATL* and a Nahua woman (other versions suggest that he was the son of Mixcóatl and the goddess *CHIMALMAN*), born after his father's death at the hands of a rival faction. The boy was raised in exile and brought up to revenge his father. Later, after becoming ruler of the Toltecs, he led them out of the Basin of Mexico and founded Tollán (in AD 968, according to Aztec tradition). He was himself defeated in further factional rivalry, however, and departed Tollán with his followers for the Gulf of Mexico.

Intriguingly, the Maya tradi-tional date of AD 987 for the establishment of Maya-Toltec Chichén Itzá by the invading leader *KUKULKÁN* coincides roughly with the traditional Aztec dates for the departure of Quetzalcóatl from Tol-lán (see also *TEPEU*) – although there is incomplete agreement with the historical and archaeological evidence. The Aztecs regarded the Toltecs as the fount of civilization and strove to emulate them in their warlike and expansionist demean-our, so there is ample reason to suspect that they tampered with

Toltec legend themselves. Indeed, we have several renditions in three principal post-Spanish conquest documents: the *ANALES DE CUAUHTITLÁN*, the *Relación de Genealogía*, and the *Memoria Breve de Chimalpahin*. Some scholars even argue that the events in the Toltec legends have been com-pressed, and therefore record in a formal way events and situations that occurred more than once dur-ing Toltec history.

For more on this complicated figure, see under *KUKULKÁN, MIXCÓATL, QUETZALCÓATL* and *TAMOANCHÁN*.

CE TÉCPATL MIXCÓATL ("One Flint Cloud Serpent") was the legendary *TOLTEC-CHICHIMEC* tribal ruler whom the Aztecs regarded as the founder of the Toltec dynasty. He led his people from somewhere in northwest Meso-america into the Basin of Mexico, where they established the city of Culhuacán. After his murder by a rival faction his son, the future king *CE ÁCATL TOPILTZIN*, was born to his wife, a Nahua woman from the Basin, but she died giving birth to him. Ce Técpatl Mixcóatl was sub-sequently deified as *MIXCÓATL*.

CENTÉOTL, or Cintéotl, was the central Mesoamerican god of the corn (maize) plant; he also had sev-eral feminine forms. He was the son of the earth goddess

CENTÉOTL, the Aztec corn (maize) deity, is seen here in feminine form as a young maiden wearing a corn-cob headdress. (LATE POSTCLASSIC PERIOD.)

TLAZOLTÉOTL and possibly origi-nated in the Olmec *GOD II*. He was often portrayed wearing a head-dress of corn ears and, in contrast to *XILONEN* (young, tender corn) and to *ILAMATECUHTLI* (old and dried-up corn), represented the mature, ripe plant. He was fourth of the nine Aztec *LORDS OF THE NIGHT* and, in the guise of Xochip-illi-Centéotl ("corn-flower prince"), seventh *LORD OF THE DAY*.

In some sources he was the son of *CHICOMECÓATL* and closely related to *XOCHIPILLI*, the flayed flower god of souls. Thus, peni-tence to Centéotl was thought to ensure a regular supply of corn. In April he was given offerings of blood, dripped on reeds and placed at the doors of the houses, to solicit a favourable planting sea-son. Also in connection with the spring planting, Centéotl was pro-tected by *TLÁLOC*, god of water.

CENTZONHUITZNAHUAC AND CENTZONMIMIZCOA (both from *NAHUATL centzontli*, "400"), were the stars of the south-ern and northern constellations respectively, and the brothers and sisters of *HUITZILOPOCHTLI*, the *AZTEC* god the sun and of war. The Centzonmimizcoa were the "cloud serpent" (the Milky Way; see also

CITLALÍCUE, CITLATINÍCUE and MIXCÓATL). Both of the groups were dispersed into the sky by Huitzilopochtli as a punishment for plotting to kill their mother (sometimes named as OMECÍHUATL, and sometimes as COATLÍCUE) who they thought had conceived them in sin.

THE CENTZÓNTOTOCHTIN
("400 rabbits (tochtli)") is a collective term in NAHUATL for the gods of PULQUE and drunkenness. The maguey plant goddess MAYÁHUEL and the pulque god PATÉCATL were their figurative mother and father.

CHAC
CHAC, MAYA God B, was the god of rain, and the equivalent of Aztec TLÁLOC, Mixtec DZAHUI, Totonac TAJÍN and Zapotec COCIJO, and possibly also to Tarascan CHUP-ITHIRIPEME. He was portrayed with a long, hanging nose, often up-turned at the tip, a lolling tongue and scrolls (probably tears) beneath his eyes. He was sometimes fanged, sometimes toothless. Chac was depicted singly and in stacks of heads at Copán and at Chichén Itzá, and at many other Maya sites throughout the Petén and Puuc regions of Yucatán.

Despite his somewhat fierce appearance, Chac was benevolent and brought rain and fertility to crops, but also wind, thunder and lightning. He was symbolized by the number six and patron of the day IK ("wind"). In some texts Chac has four manifestations who, like the BACABS, were each associated with a cardinal direction and a colour – north/white, south/yellow, east/red and west/black. Other texts refer to these CHACS as his four assistants.

CHAC PAUAHTUN
see PAUAHTUN.

CHAC XIB CHAC
see THE CHACS.

CHACMOOL
CHACMOOL, a life-size or near-life-size reclining carved stone figure, was associated with temples.

CHAC was the Maya rain god (God B). His stone head, with curled nose, decorated the platforms and buildings of numerous Classic Period Puuc-style sites, as here at Kabah in central Yucatán.

Its legs are half bent and its head is turned to one side, and the figure grasps an open stone box, resting on its abdomen, to receive offerings. The name – MAYA for "red jaguar" – was applied to this type of figure by archaeologists because the first example was discovered at the Maya-Toltec city of Chichén Itzá in Yucatán, but the origins of such figures were in fact in north-central Mesoamerica, at the TOLTEC capital of Tollán (Tula). Chacmool figures have also been found at sites in the Basin of Mexico, in the TARASCAN cities to the northwest of the Basin, and among the TOTONACS in the central Gulf Coast.

Some scholars consider the chacmools to be representations of TEZCATZONTÉCATL, who was one of the Aztec PULQUE gods of drinking

and inebriation. (See also DEATH & SACRIFICE)

THE CHACS
THE CHACS, in some MAYA texts, are portrayed as the four assistants of the rain god CHAC. Each ruled a cardinal point, or corner, of the earth and a colour: Zac Xib Chac was white (zac) and ruled the north; Kan Xib Chac was yellow (kan) and ruled the south; Chac Xib Chac was red (chac) and ruled the east; and Ek Xib Chac was black (ek) and ruled the west. They are closely related to the four year-bearing BACABS. (See also THE PAUAHTUN)

CHALCHIHUITLICUE
see CHALCHIÚHTLICUE.

CHALCHIUHCÍHUATL
CHALCHIUHCÍHUATL was an AZTEC goddess of the harvest.

CHALCHIUHTECÓLOTL
CHALCHIUHTECÓLOTL ("precious owl") was, appropriately, the AZTEC god of the night, one of the many aspects of "black" TEZCATLIPOCA, a major deity of the Postclassic Period.

CHACMOOL figures, designed to receive offerings in the "box" held on their abdomens, were first found at Maya-Toltec Chichén Itzá, but their origin was later realized to be from the Toltec culture of north-central Mesoamerica.

CHALCHIÚHTLICUE
CHALCHIÚHTLICUE ("she of the jade skirt"), or Chalchihuit-licue (an alternative spelling), the AZTEC goddess of water, was the sister and female counterpart of TLÁLOC. Her name incorporates the NAHUATL term chalchíhuitl, meaning "jade" or "green stone", and, thus by extension, anything precious; and by further analogy still to the colour of jade, it also means "water".

Chalchiúhtlicue was the goddess of rivers, oceans and floods, patroness of the fifth day Cóatl ("serpent"), third of the 13 LORDS OF THE DAY and sixth of the nine

CHALCHIÚHTLICUE, the Aztec water goddess, suitably bedecked with jade – the symbol of water – depicted in the pre-Spanish conquest Codex Vaticanus B.

LORDS OF THE NIGHT. She presided over the Fourth Sun of the Aztec CREATION MYTH. She was often portrayed as a river, beside which grew a nopal (prickly pear) cactus bearing fruit which symbolized the human heart. The Gulf of Mexico, whose coastal waters were so important in Mesoamerican trade, was known as Chalchi-uhcueyecatl, meaning "water of the goddess Chalchiúhtlicue" in Nahuatl. She was related to the goddesses CHICOMECÓATL and XILONEN.

23

CHALCHIUHTOTOLIN
("precious turkey") was an aspect of the *AZTEC* god *TEZCATLIPOCA*. As such he was a deity of the night and of mystery. He ruled the Aztec day *TÉCPATL* ("flint knife").

CHALMECATECUHTLI,
an *AZTEC* god of sacrifice and of the underworld, was an alternative for *MICTLANTECUHTLI* as the 11th of the 13 *LORDS OF THE DAY*.

CHANTICO
was an *AZTEC* earth goddess and special deity of Xochimilco, in the Basin of Mexico. She was goddess of the hearth (see also *CUAXÓLOTL*) and patroness of metalworkers, especially of goldsmiths. She bore the calendrical name *9 ITZCUINTLI* and was related to *MICTLANTECUHTLI*, god of death.

CHEBEL YAX
see *IX CHEBEL YAX*.

CHICCAN
("serpent") was the fifth of the 20 *MAYA* day-names; it was associated with the number nine and with the rain god. The *AZTEC* and *ZAPOTEC* equivalent days were *CÓATL* and *ZEE* or *Zij*.

CHANTICO, the Aztec goddess of the hearth and of metalsmiths, is depicted in the early post-Spanish conquest Codex Borbonicus wearing a jade nose ornament .

CHALCHIUHTOTOLIN, the "precious turkey" god of night and mystery – one of the many manifestations of Tezcatlipoca – is depicted in the early post-Spanish conquest Codex Borbonicus.

CHICCHAN,
MAYA God H, was the rain god of the Chorti Maya of eastern Guatemala, Honduras and El Salvador. He was patron of Chicchan ("serpent"; the fifth day of the Maya 20-day month) and symbolized by the number nine.

CHICHÉN ITZÁ
see *TOLTECS*.

CHICHIMECA
was the general term used by the *AZTECS* to refer to the nomadic hunter-gatherer peoples of the northern deserts, beyond the fringes of the civilized societies of Mesoamerica. They were regarded as "barbarians".

The term was also applied to all groups who originated in the north and migrated south after the fall of Tollán (Tula), including the *TOLTECS*, whom the Aztecs regarded as the fount of civilization.

One of the most important Chichimec groups entered the Basin of Mexico in the 12th century AD, led by the legendary chief Xólotl. They founded the city of Tenayuca in the north Basin, and their descendants later joined the Acolhua Aztecs on the eastern lake shores to establish a capital city at *TEXCOCO*. In keeping with their background, a prominent Toltec-Chichimec god was *MIXCÓATL*, god of the hunt.

CHICOMECÓATL,
or Chicomolotzin, ("seven serpents", derived from *chicome* "seven" and *cóatl* "serpent") was a central Mesoamerican goddess of corn (maize) and vegetation generally, who was closely related to *CENTÉOTL*. She was usually portrayed in the codices with a red face and body, and wearing a paper mitre-like headdress adorned with rosettes, or, in sculpture, holding ears of corn in each hand. She was also known as Chicomolotzin or "seven ears of maize" (*olotl*) and, in her manifestations as a goddess of fertility, as *CHALCHIÚHTLICUE* and *XILONEN*. Her feast day was 7 *Cóatl*, and she was honoured at the festival of *OCHPANITZLI*, an *AZTEC* harvest festival held during the 12th month of the 18 months that made up the Aztec solar year.

CHICOMOLOTZIN
see *CHICOMECÓATL*.

CHICOMOZTOC
("seven caves") were the legendary caves from which the seven *AZTEC* tribes originated. They were located in *AZTLÁN*, a land somewhere to the northwest of the Basin of Mexico. The seven tribes are usually recognized as the Acolhua, the Chalca, the México, the Tepaneca, the Tlal-huica, the Tlaxcalteca and the Xochimilca, all of whom migrated southeastwards to settle in or near the Basin of Mexico.

CHICOMOZTOC, the seven caves located in Aztlán ("place of the cranes") – somewhere in the northwest of Mesoamerica; in legend the seven Aztec tribes emerged from them, depicted here as an island in the Codex Boturini.

THE CHILAM BALAM
(literally "prophet jaguar") are 18 post-Spanish-conquest Yucatecan *MAYA* sacred texts, written in European script. They relate the Maya calendar, traditional histories and myths (including the Maya *CREATION MYTH*), along with advice and medicinal recipes. The most informative texts are the so-called *Pérez Codex* and those that came from the Yucatecan towns of Chumayel, Tizimín, Maní, Kaua and Ixil.

CHILLA
("crocodile") was the first of the 20 *ZAPOTEC* day-names; the *AZTEC* and *MAYA* equivalent days were *CIPACTLI* and *IMIX*.

CHIMALMAN
was the *AZTEC* personification of female divinity, expressed in several ways. The term was applied to the human female bearers (counterpart of the *TEOMAMAQUE*) of tribal cult objects during the Aztec migration stories. In one myth Chimalman was the Nahua wife of the *TOLTEC-CHICHIMEC* tribal ruler *MIXCÓATL*, who impreg-

nated her with an arrow from his bow. As a result she became the mother of *CE ÁCATL TOPILTZIN QUETZALCÓATL*, the legendary founder and ruler of Tollán (Tula). In other myths she is portrayed as either the mother of *COATLÍCUE*, the Aztec earth goddess, or sometimes of *HUITZILOPOCHTLI*.

CHINA ("deer") was the seventh of the 20 *ZAPOTEC* day-names and one of the year-bearing days – there were 13 *China* years in a 52-year cycle (see also *PIJA*, *QUIJ* and *XOO*). The *AZTEC* and *MAYA* equivalent days were *MÁZATL* and *MANIK*.

CHICOMECÓATL, or "seven serpents", the Aztec corn (maize) and fertility goddess, is depicted wearing an elaborate headdress decorated with rosettes and a phallic-like serpent belt, and holding a corn plant and ears. (LATE POSTCLASSIC PERIOD.)

CHINAMPAS, misnamed "floating islands", were not floating at all. Rather, they were artificial rectangular fields, separated by canals, built out from the shores of the southern lakes and around the island capital of Aztec *TENOCH-TITLÁN* in the Basin of Mexico. In the course of more than a century

aligned rows of *chinampas* extended from the southern lake shores roughly halfway across lakes Xochimilco and Chalco, connecting the island city of Cuitláhuac (modern Tláhuac) and the island of Xico to the mainland. Around Tenochtitlán they extended up to about 500 m (545 yards) from the island's shores towards the mainland.

They were created by constructing a frame of wood and reeds, then filling this with mud from the lake bottom. Trees were planted on the plots to anchor them and to help hold the soil with their roots. New lake mud was dredged periodically and spread onto the islands to maintain fertility.

The use of *chinampas* enabled the scores of city-states throughout the central and southern Basin of Mexico to support dense populations, and encouraged regular trade through market gardens.

CHUEN ("monkey") was the 11th of the 20 *MAYA* day-names; it was associated with the arts and crafts, and with the *MONKEY-FACED GOD* (Maya God C). The *AZTEC* and *ZAPOTEC* equivalent days were called *OZOMATLI* and *LOO* or *Goloo*.

CHUPITHIRIPEME was the *TARASCAN* rain god. He was probably the equivalent in aspect and importance – especially in the semi-arid lands of the Tarascan state – to the *AZTEC TLÁLOC*, the *MAYA CHAC*, the *MIXTEC DZAHUI*, the *TOTONAC TAJÍN* and the *ZAPOTEC COCIJO*.

CIB ("wax") was the 16th of the 20 *MAYA* day-names; it was associated with the *BACABS*, patrons of beekeeping. The *AZTEC* and *ZAPOTEC* equivalent days were *COZCACUAUHTLI* and *LOO* or *Guiloo*.

CIHUACÓATL (meaning "serpent woman") was an *AZTEC* earth goddess associated specifically with the west. Cihuacóatl represented a

passive principle in Aztec religious pluralism: as *TONANTZIN* she was the mother of humankind; as *COATLÍCUE* she was the venerated mother of *HUITZILOPOCHTLI*, god of war; as *QUILAZTLI* she raised the legendary ruler *CE ÁCATL TOPILTZIN QUETZALCÓATL*, founder of the Toltec capital at Tollán (Tula), after his mother, *CHIMALMAN*, died while giving birth to him. Thus Cihuacóatl became the patroness of the *CIHUATETEO*, the spirits of woman who died in childbirth. In reference to her role as companion, Cihuacóatl was the title the Aztecs gave to the co-ruler alongside the *tlatoani* or Aztec king. Following the conversion of the Aztecs to Christianity she became "La Llorana" ("the weeping woman") in Mexican folklore.

Cihuacóatl's role in the creation of humankind followed the escape of *QUETZALCÓATL–ÉHECATL* from the devious attempts of *MICTAL-NTECUHTLI* to stop him in the underworld. Having fetched the bones of the inhabitants of the previous world, turned into fish bones in the destroying deluge, Quetzalcóatl–Éhecatl brought them to Cihuacóatl in *TAMOANCHÁN*, the place of miraculous birth. She ground them up into a flour-like meal and placed the meal in a special clay pot, around which the gods gathered, and into which they shed drops of their blood (or, in another version, just Quetzalcóatl's blood, from his penis). From this paste, men and women were moulded to populate the newly created world.

CIHUAPIPILTIN was the general term used for the souls of deceased *AZTEC* women; see also the *CIHUATETEO*.

THE CIHUATETEO were the spirits of *AZTEC* women who died while giving birth. Their patroness and protector was the earth goddess, *CIHUACÓATL*. They lived in the west in a paradise known as

CIHUACÓATL, "serpent woman" – note her serpent belt – is manifested here as the earth-mother goddess Coatlícue, mother of the war god Huitzilopochtli. (LATE POSTCLASSIC PERIOD AZTEC STONE SCULPTURE.)

Cincalco (*NAHUATL*, meaning "the house of corn/maize"), from which their role was to come to the aid fallen warriors and eventually to convey them to the world of the dead, which was in the east. The warriors were borne across the morning sky by the sun and were met at noon by the Cihuateteo. Death in childbirth was considered to be the equivalent of a man's death in battle, the latter being believed by the Aztecs to be the most honoured way to die. Portrayed with skulls for heads, and feet bearing fierce claws, the Cihuateteo were venerated by sorcerers and witch doctors, but they sometimes descended to earth in order to create mischief and harm amongst humans.

CIHUATLAMPA is the western quadrant of the earth in *AZTEC* cosmography. It was represented by the year sign *CALLI* ("house"), and by the day signs *MÁZATL* ("deer"), *QUIÁHUITL* ("rain"), *OZOMATLI* ("monkey"), *CALLI* and *CUAUHTLI* ("eagle"). It was the location of both *Cincalco* (the paradise for women who died in childbirth) and the world for fallen warriors, and was generally associated with misfortune.

25

CREATION & THE UNIVERSE

THE AZTECS AND THE MAYA both recorded an elaborate sequence of creations preceding their own world. The Aztec creation myth comprised five successive worlds and suns, the first four ending in cataclysm; the Maya creation story comprised three worlds, the first two, being imperfect, also ending in destruction. In both of these cultures the final creation myth ended with humans being formed from corn (maize) dough, the ultimate gift of the gods being the knowledge of how to grow corn and other edible plants for human consumption and survival.

Similarly, virtually all Mesoamericans perceived the earth as the back of a huge reptilian being, a crocodile or cayman, lying in the water. The other parts of the cosmos were above and below the earth, and in both Aztec and Maya sources are described as multi-layered. Maya sources also describe a second concept, in which the earth is a huge iguana house, a reptilian structure whose sides (walls), roof (sky), and floor (earth) were formed by the bodies of iguanas.

The Aztec universe – Teyollocualoyán – comprised a vertical stratification of thirteen celestial and nine underworld layers, with the earth in between as the first layer in both directions. The levels were each ruled by a deity, and the celestial deities were each associated with a bird.

AZTEC CREATION was based on the idea of four successive worlds (left), created and destroyed before the Aztecs' own world, that of the Fifth Sun. Four of these "suns" or "epochs of nature" are depicted here: the people of the Second Sun – destroyed by winds – were turned into monkeys (upper left), those of the Third Sun – destroyed by fire – into birds (lower right), those of the Fourth Sun – destroyed by floods – into fishes (upper right), and those of the Fifth Sun given the gift of agriculture (lower left). (ILLUSTRATION FROM RESEARCHES CONCERNING THE INSTITUTIONS AND MONUMENTS OF THE ANCIENT INHABITANTS OF AMERICA BY FRIEDRICH ALEXANDER BARON VON HUMBOLDT, 1814.)

QUETZALCOÁTL (left), the "plumed serpent", was sent by the gods after the creation of the Fifth Sun, in his guise as the wind god Éhecatl, to collect the bones of the fishes of the Fourth Sun's inhabitants from the underworld. Having completed this task, and humans having been created from a paste of the ground-up bones and blood of the gods, Quetzalcóatl-Éhecatl discovered corn (maize) kernels and seeds of other edible plants in Tonacatépetl ("sustenance mountain"). He gave humans the knowledge of agriculture, scattering the seeds across the land for the rain god Tláloc to water.

THE VIENNA CODEX (below) or Codex Vindobonensis shows a "world tree" with the gods Tezcatlipoca (left, with "smoking mirror" figure above his left arm) and Quetzalcóatl (right, with quetzal bird head above his right arm) to either side of it. Rooted in the earth, the branches of the tree spread into the heavens to support the sky. The concept of a "world tree", planted at the centre of the universe and constituting the fifth of the cardinal directions, was central to both Aztec and Maya thought.

THIS PANEL (above), painted by the artist Diego Rivera (1886–1957), was one of a series inspired by principal episodes in the sacred text – known as the Popul Vuh – of the Guatemalan highland Quiché Maya. The Maya believed in a universe that was the result of a succession of creations. From a world of darkness and water, the gods created the earth and all the creatures on it, and the fish of the seas. Then the gods Tepeu and Gucumatz (or Kukulkán) attempted to fashion humans out of mud, as Rivera shows.

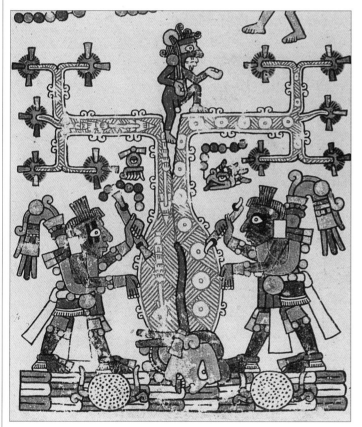

AH MUN (right) or Yum Kaax, the god of agriculture and corn (maize) plants, featured prominently in architectural and portable artefacts, such as this incense burner in the form of the god holding a potted corn plant in his right hand. Maya civilization was as dependent on corn as its contemporaries in central Mesoamerica. The crop was grown in cleared plots of rain forest and on raised, irrigated fields around the ceremonial centres of Maya cities.

(ARTEFACT FROM THE POSTCLASSIC PERIOD MAYA CITY OF MAYAPÁN, YUCATÁN.)

CIMI ("death") was the sixth of the 20 MAYA day-names; it was represented by the owl, portent of death, and its glyph resembles a % sign. The AZTEC and ZAPOTEC equivalent days were MIQUIZTLI and LANA.

CINCALCO see CIHUATETEO.

CINTÉOTL see CENTÉOTL.

CIPACTLI ("crocodile") was the first of the 20 AZTEC day-names; it was a lucky day, a symbol of birth, life and sustenance; its patron deity was TONACATECUHTLI. The MAYA and ZAPOTEC equivalent days were IMIX and CHILLA.

Cipactli was the Earth Monster, the crocodile on whose back the world sits. Calendrical dates and deity associations included: 4 Cipactli, for the fire god XIUHTECUHTLI; 6 Cipactli, for the earth goddess TLAZOLTÉOTL; and 9 Cipactli, for MICTECACÍHUATL, goddess of death.

CIPACTONAL was the "first man" in the TOLTEC and AZTEC CREATION MYTH. He and his wife OXOMOCO were regarded as the first sorcerer and sorceress, who together invented astrology and the calendar. His MAYA equivalent was XPIYACOC.

They were also instrumental in bringing corn (maize) and other edible plants to humankind. When QUETZALCÓATL was unable to shift TONACATÉPETL (literally "sustenance mountain") the two old diviners cast lots to determine how to do this. The signs told them that the weakly and diseased god NANAHUATZIN should do this, by splitting Tonacatépetl open. To do so, Nanahuatzin called upon the help of the four TLÁLOCS, the directional gods of the winds, rain and lightning. The mountain was duly split and the winds blew the grains and seeds across the land while the rains watered them so that they grew where they fell. Humans were quick to take advantage of this renewable source of food.

CITLALÍCUE, or Citlalinícue, literally the "star-skirted" or "she of the skirt of stars" in NAHUATL, was goddess of the heavens and one of the AZTEC names for the Milky Way (see also the CENTZONMIMIZCOA and MIXCÓATL). As Citlalícue she was the ruler of the third of the 13 celestial levels in the Aztec universe (but see also OMECÍHUATL). As the female counterpart of CITLATONA she was one of the feminine aspects of OMETEOTL.

CITLALINÍCUE, another name for CITLALÍCUE; the AZTEC name for the Milky Way. See also THE CENTZONMIMIZCOA and MIXCÓATL).

CITLALTEPEC ("Hill of the Star") was one of the AZTEC names for Cerro de la Estrella in the Mexico City precinct of Ixtapalapa near the ceremonial centre of TENOCHTITLÁN, and the venue for the TOXIUHMOLPILIA, ("the tying of the years") ceremony.

CITLATONA was the masculine aspect of OMETEOTL, the Aztec concept of duality (see OMETECUHTLI).

CIZIN, from ciz, is the MAYA word for flatulence and, by extension, the putrescence of the underworld (see also AH PUCH).

CITLALÍCUE, "star-skirted", was goddess of the heavenly firmament, seen here on the right, below the Milky Way. Opposite her sits Mayáhuel, goddess of the maguey plant. (EARLY POST-SPANISH-CONQUEST AZTEC CODEX BORBONICUS).

CLOUD SERPENT
see MIXCÓATL.

COAÍLHUITL
see TLACAXIPEHUALIZTLI.

THE CÓATL ("serpent") figured prominently in Mesoamerican imagery stretching from the earliest times through to the Postclassic Period. Serpents were associated with both male and female deities and cóatl forms an element of many of their names, for example CHICOMECÓATL, CIHUACÓATL, COATLÍCUE, MIXCÓATL, QUETZALCÓATL and XIUHCÓATL.

Along with feline features, fangs and forked tongues they formed an important element in the art of every Mesoamerican culture. Examples that attest to the endurance and ubiquitous use of serpent imagery include the "Greek Key" patterns that form stylized, sinuous snakelike architectural decorations seen on ZAPOTEC and MIXTEC walls, the writhing serpents on the Temple of Quetzalcóatl at TEOTIHUACÁN, the Pyramid of the Serpent at Xochicalco, the coatepantli (serpent walls) around TOLTEC and AZTEC ceremonial precincts, and the "cloud serpent" image of the Milky Way.

Cóatl was also the name of the fifth of the 20 Aztec day-names; it had a favourable augury and was associated with the number nine; its patron was CHALCHIÚHTLICUE. The MAYA and ZAPOTEC equivalents were CHICCHAN and ZEE or Zij.

COATLÍCUE ("serpent lady"), was the AZTEC supreme earth goddess. She was the mother of HUITZILOPOCHTLI (god of war), of COYOLXAUHQUI (moon goddess)

CÓATL, the serpent, appeared from the earliest of times in Mesoamerican iconography alongside feline imagery. Here, the roof of the Temple of the Jaguars at Postclassic Period Maya-Toltec Chichén Itzá is supported by serpent columns, their heads on the ground, rattles in the air.

COATLÍCUE, "serpent lady", the supreme Aztec earth goddess, embodied the earth-monster. She is shown here with a serpent tongue and fangs, snake-headed arms and a writhing mass of serpents for a skirt.

and of the *CENTZONHUITZNAHUAC* and *CENTZONMIMIZCOA* (the southern and northern stars). She ruled the rainy season and was associated generally with agriculture and sustenance. In one myth she is the daughter of *CHIMALMAN*; other manifestations include *CIHUACÓATL*, *TETEOINNAN*, *TOCI* and *TONANTZIN*.

Coatlícue was wife of the cloud serpent *MIXCÓATL* (god of hunting) but was magically impregnated with Huitzilopochtli by a feathery ball that descended to her as she swept her house. She tucked the ball into her bosom, but later could not find it. It was said that this was what impregnated her "without sin". Nevertheless, her sons and daughters plotted to kill her for her disgrace. They would have succeeded had not Huitzilopochtli been born just in time, fully armed, to decapitate his sister Coyolxauhqui, by mistake, and to kill his other brothers and sisters, dispersing them into the heavens as stars.

The most famous sculpture of Coatlícue (at the Museo Nacional de Antropología in Mexico City) shows her as a hideous monster with a massive head covered in scales, two beady, staring eyes and a wide, scaly mouth complete with four huge fangs and a forked serpentine tongue. Two great spurts of blood, in the shapes of snake heads, issue from each side of her block-like torso to form her arms, and are thought to be representations of Tonacatecuhtli and his consort Tonacacíhuatl (Lord and Lady Flesh), or perhaps less graphically *OMETECUHTLI* and *OMECÍHUATL* (Lord and Lady of Duality). She wears a necklace of alternating severed human hands and hearts, setting off a skull pendant in the middle – all symbolic of the need for blood and human sacrifice to sustain the sun. A scaly snake encircles her waist and her skirt writhes with serpents (the two largest form the ties of her waist band and dangle below the skull of her pendant), the whole symbolizing the human race of which she was Mother. Down her back fall 13 tresses to represent the 13 heavens or levels of Aztec cosmography as well as the gods who control the earth's natural forces. The tresses also symbolize the 13 months of 20 days in the 260-day calendrical cycle – and possibly of the normal human gestation period – and the 13 *LORDS OF THE DAY*. Another skull, the counterpart of that on the front, dangles below her tresses. Beneath her skirt, her legs are covered with plumage and end in "feet", each of which have four vicious talons.

In such hideous guise Coatlícue represented both the womb and the grave of humankind.

COCHANA was an alternative name for *HUECHAANA*, a valley *ZAPOTEC* mother goddess.

COCIJO ("lightning"), or Pitao Cocijo, also called Gozio and Lociyo, was the southern highland Valley *ZAPOTEC* rain god. The evidence of archaeology, and of native histories (*relaciones*) indicate that Cocijo was a principal deity of the Valley Zapotec cities, who ruled the four cardinal directions and the Zapotec fifth direction, the zenith. He was portrayed with a composite body of human, jaguar and serpent features and a forked tongue to symbolize lightning. So numerous were representations of Cocijo, especially on funerary urns accompanied by "companion" urns set in a semi-circle around his effigy, that it is thought that there was a special cult devoted to him. One *relación* (from the Southern Zapotec city of Sola) states that rites performed to *PITAO COZOBI* (god of corn/maize) were also offered to Cocijo at the harvest cutting of the first chilli plant.

To the Southern Zapotec he was Lociyo and, to the Sierra Zapotec, Gozio. Other Mesoamerican equivalents deities were *MAYA CHAC*, *MIXTEC DZAHUI*, *TOTONAC TAJÍN* and *AZTEC TLÁLOC*, and possibly also *TARASCAN CHUPITHIRIPEME* (see also *COQUENEXO*).

Cocijo (or *tobicocij*) was also the name for a period of 65 days, a full quarter of the Zapotec ritual calendar (*piye*), which served as the Zapotec equivalent to the Aztec Tonalpolhualli (see *ORDERING THE WORLD*). Each *cocijo* was further subdivided into five periods of 13 days each.

CODEX CHIMALPOPOCA see *ANALES DE CUAUHTITLÁN*.

COPIJCHA, or Pitao Copijcha, also sometimes called Xaquija, was the Valley *ZAPOTEC* sun god and the god of war, and was the patron deity of the city of Xaquija (modern Teotitlán). He was associated with the macaw, a sun bird, who was believed to fly down from the sky to enter his temple. He was equivalent to the Aztec *TONATIUH*.

COQUEBILA was the *ZAPOTEC* lord of the centre of the earth. His name glyph was apparently the same as that for *QUIABELAGAYO* ("five flower").

COQUECHILA, who was the Southern *ZAPOTEC* Lord of the Underworld, was an alternative name for *COQUI BEZELAO*.

COQUEELAA was the Southern *ZAPOTEC* god of the cochineal harvest, and a deity worshipped especially in the city of Sola. Fowl were sacrificed to him at the planting of the nopal cactus, which harbours the insect, and at the cochineal harvest.

COQUENEXO was the "Lord of multiplication" (probably a permutation of *COCIJO*), and was the principal deity to the Sierra *ZAPOTEC* city Zoquiapa.

COCIJO was the Zapotec god of rain. This stone sculpture from the southern highlands of Oaxaca shows him with a human body, jaguar face and forked tongue to represent lightning,

made the journey to the top of a nearby mountain in order to practise autosacrifice, by piercing and letting blood from their tongues and ears, and to pray for the city's well being and prosperity. These rites were always begun at night, when the sacrifices were performed, and ended at the same hour of the following night.

To the Southern Zapotec Coqui Bezalao was known as Bezalao, Pezalao or Pitao Pezalao – in the city of Ocelotepec – and Leta Ahuila.

COQUI XEE, also called Leta Aquichino, Liraaquitzino, Pijetao and Pije Xoo, was the Valley *ZAPOTEC* abstract concept of infinity, the unknowable – "the he (or it) without beginning or end" – and in this sense the creator god. He (it) was the supreme "force", the "above" and, as Pije Xoo, "the source of time". All the seemingly baffling and complex pantheon of Zapotec gods and goddesses were in essence merely aspects, attributes, manifestations, permutations, or refractions of this supreme being. In this, he was similar to the Aztec concept of *TLOQUE NAHUAQUE*. The Southern Zapotec knew him as Leta Aquichino or Liraaquitzino.

COQUIHUANI, a *ZAPOTEC* deity, was god of light, and was special to the city of Tlalixtac in the Mesoamerican southern highlands. Men and boys were sacrificed to him, along with offerings by the priests of quetzal feathers, dogs and blood. These rites were accompanied by excessive *PULQUE* drinking and dancing before the idol.

COQUIXILLA see *COQUI XEE*.

COSANA NOSANA see *COZAANA*.

COQUI BEZELAO, or Bezalao, also called Coquechila, Pezalao, Pitao Pezalao and Leta Ahuila, was the special god of the Valley *ZAPOTEC* city of Mitla, along with his wife *XON-AXI QUECUYA*. They were the gods and goddesses of death and of the underworld and were worshipped throughout the Oaxaca Valley around

Mitla, sometimes under their Southern Zapotec names of Coquechila and Xonaxi Huilia, respectively. Mitla itself was known among the Zapotecs as the "city of death", "place of rest", or "the underworld" and, indeed, passages and tombs beneath palaces and monumental staircases at the site lend credence to this epithet.

Coqui Bezalao was also a patron deity to the Sierra Zapotec city of Teocuicuilco, and only the priests were permitted to enter the temple in which his idol was kept. Special rites were held every 260 days; the residents brought quail, brightly coloured feathers and precious green stones to the priests, who

COYOLXAUHQUI was the Aztec moon goddess. Her name means "golden bells" and she was frequently shown, as here, with bell ornaments on her cheeks and also depicted on her cap.

COYOLXAUHQUI

("golden bells") was the *AZTEC* moon goddess and daughter of *COATLÍCUE*. She is easily recognized in sculpture and various portrayals in the codices by her ornaments of bells. According to the Aztec myth, her brothers and sisters the stars (see *CENTZONHUITZNAHUAC* and *CENTZONMIMIZCOA*) conspired to kill their mother, because they believed that Coatlícue had conceived a child in sin. Coyolxauhqui attempted to warn her mother but, as she approached ahead of her brothers and sisters, her new brother *HUITZILOPOCHTLI* (sun and war god), who emerged fully armed from his mother's womb, decapitated her in his haste to defend his mother. Only afterwards was Coatlícue able to tell Huitzilopochtli of his sister's good intentions. Huitzilopochtli threw Coyolxauhqui's head up into the heavens to become the moon, where the bells on her cheeks still shine in the night sky. In Aztec myth, the scene of her decapitation recurs each day as the moon sets and the sun drives away the darkness, and this daily brother-sun/sister-moon struggle symbolized the day and night, the battle of light against the darkness, and good against evil.

One of the most spectacular finds in recent Mexican archaeology, discovered in 1978 at the Templo Mayor in Mexico City, was that of a huge circular carved stone portraying the dismembered body of Coyolxauhqui. Her head, which was decorated with bells on the cheeks, her torso, her arms and legs, and also a skull and other symbols of death are all depicted. Together they represent her destruction by Huitzilopochtli.

COZAANA

("the begetter"), or Cosana Nosana, or Noçana, or Pitao Cozaana, was the Valley and Southern *ZAPOTEC* creator god. He was the male counterpart of *HUECHAANA* and was associated especially with the city of Chichicapa and with children. As the creator god he was associated with animals and humans, and, in various aspects, with ancestors and with hunting and fishing. The Sierra Zapotec people knew him as Betahoxona.

COZCACUAUHTLI

("vulture") was the 16th of the 20 *AZTEC* day-names; it had a favourable augury and its patron deity was the "obsidian butterfly" *ITZPAPÁLOTL*. The *MAYA* and *ZAPOTEC* equivalent days were *CIB* and *LOO* or *Guiloo*. Because it was bald, the *cozcacuauhtli* was perceived to be the representative of old age.

COZICHA COZEE

was the principal deity of the Southern *ZAPOTEC* city of Ocelotepec. He was the god of war, and was portrayed as a fierce warrior clutching his bow and arrows. Native histories (*relaciones*) related to the Spanish chroniclers tell us that Ocelotepec was constantly at war with its neighbours, which made this special relationship between god and city appropriate. Cozicha Cozee was closely associated with *COPIJCHA*, the sun god.

THE CREATION MYTHS

of both the *AZTECS* and the *MAYA* were highly elaborate. Their essential elements were no doubt shared with the other peoples of Mesoamerica. A common component was the concept of a succession of worlds, in which one world was replaced by another after the first had been destroyed. Destruction was usually by natural forces sent by the gods, but sometimes also involved supernatural forces. The myths of each are explored in more detail on the following pages.

IN THE CREATION MYTHS, after the destruction of the Fourth Sun, the gods convened at Teotihuacán, "City of the Gods". The sun and moon of the Fifth World were created and set into motion through the sacrifice of the gods.

Aztec Creation Myth

The Aztec creation story was of five successive Suns. The First Sun (Night; glyph *Nahui Océlotl*; "Four Jaguar"), was ruled by TEZCAT-LIPOCA ("Smoking Mirror"). It was inhabited by giants, but ended when Tezcatlipoca's brother QUET-ZALCÓATL ("Plumed Serpent") caused the giants to be devoured by jaguars. The Second Sun (Air; glyph *Nahui Éhecatl*; "Four Wind"), was ruled by Quetzalcóatl. It was destroyed by winds, and its "people" were turned into monkeys. The Third Sun (Rain of Fire; glyph *Nahui Quiáhuitl*; "Four Rain") was ruled by the rain god TLÁLOC. It was destroyed by a rain of fire, and its inhabitants were transformed into birds. The Fourth Sun (Water; glyph *Nahui Atl;* "Four Water"), was ruled over by Tláloc's sister CHALCHIÚTLICUE. Floods destroyed this world, and surviving inhabitants were turned into fish. The Fifth Sun (glyph *Nahui Ollin*; "Four Movement/Earthquake"), that of the Aztecs, was ruled over by the sun god TONATIUH. It was predicted that it would end in cataclysmic earthquakes.

The Fifth Sun was created by the gods in an assembly at TEOTI-HUACÁN (literally "city of the gods") after the destruction of the Fourth Sun. A composite myth can be compiled from several sources, including details about the creation of the earth, sun and moon, the creation of humans, and the provision of essential elements in Aztec life, such as corn (maize) agriculture and the basis for the practice of human sacrifice.

Despite their earlier rivalry, Quetzalcóatl and Tezcatlipoca co-operated in the creation of the earth of the Fifth Sun. The great Earth Monster TLALTECUHTLI provided them with the raw materials. Quetzalcóatl and Tezcatlipoca descended from the sky to see Tlal-tecuhtli astride the world ocean. She greeted them ferociously and craved flesh to eat. Her jaws were

fanged, and her elbows, knees and other joints had gnashing mouths. Quetzalcóatl and Tezcatlipoca were appalled at the sight of her, and concluded that the world could not possibly exist while such a monster survived, so they plotted to destroy her. Transforming themselves into two great serpents, one seized Tlal-tecuhtli by the right hand and left foot while the other seized her by the left hand and right foot. In the ensuing struggle they succeeded in ripping her asunder – and Tez-catlipoca lost a foot. Her upper body became the earth and other portions were thrown into the sky to create the heavens. The other gods, however, were not pleased with these actions, and consoled the spirit of Tlaltecuhtli by decreeing that all plants essential to the wellbeing of humans must arise from parts of her body.

Eight gods divided this world into four quadrants by making four roads to the centre, and raised the heavens above it. To support the sky, Tezcatlipoca and Quetzalcóatl transformed themselves into two huge trees – the tree of Tezcatlipoca decorated with obsidian mirrors and that of Quetzalcóatl with emerald-coloured *quetzal* feathers. In appreciation, Tonacatecuhtli ("Lord of Sustenance") made them lords of the heavens and the stars.

THE PYRAMID OF Quetzalcóatl and Tláloc *at Teotihuacán symbolizes the importance of two of Mesoamerica's earliest deities. Masks of Tláloc and Quetzalcóatl alternate on the pyramid tiers.*

The Milky Way became their road and, in one variation, Tezcatlipoca was transformed into the Great Bear constellation.

The world was still dark, however, so the gods built a huge fire. The headstrong and haughty god TECUCIZTÉCATL boasted that he would sacrifice himself in this "funeral" pyre and rise again as the sun. But when faced with the flames he lost his nerve and it was his weak, humble and allegedly cowardly brother NANAHUATZIN who jumped first, thus persuading Tecuciztécatl to jump. Consequently Nanahuatzin rose as the sun while Tecuciztécatl emerged as the moon. Both shone equally brightly at first, until one of the gods obscured the light of the moon by throwing a rabbit (*tochtli*) into its "face" (see MEZTLI).

The sun and moon were set in motion by TLAHUIZCALPANTECUH-TLI – one of Quetzalcóatl's many guises. Nanahuatzin, who was now

the sun god TONATIUH, demanded blood sacrifice and fealty. Outraged at such arrogance Tlahuizcalpan-tecuhtli hurled a dart at the sun with his *atl-atl* (spear-thrower), but he missed. Tonatiuh retaliated, piercing Tlahuizcalpantecuhtli through the head and transforming him into stone – as the god of coldness, ITZTLACOLIUHQUI – an episode said to explain the dawn chill. So the gods and goddesses concluded that they must sacrifice themselves. Quetzalcóatl was called upon to cut out their hearts with a sacrificial obsidian blade – thus establishing the manner in which humans also had to be sacrificed to feed Tonatiuh, ironically perceived as "the life-giving sun", with the blood of life.

The Fifth Sun lacked inhabitants so the gods conferred again, and again called on Quetzalcóatl, this time in his guise as the wind god ÉHECATL. He was tasked to travel to the underworld, MICTLÁN, to retrieve the bones of the people of the former world. When he reached Mictlán, Quetzalcóatl announced his mission, but the suspicious MICTLANTECUHTLI, Lord of the Underworld, and his wife, MICTE-CACÍHUATL, asked him why the gods wanted the bones. Quetzalcóatl

explained that the gods felt compelled to people the newly created earth, but Mictlantecuhtli agreed to give up the bones only if Quetzalcóatl would perform an apparently easy task: travel around Mictlán four times while sounding a conch-shell trumpet continuously. In place of a conch-shell trumpet, however, the devious Mictlantecuhtli gave him a plain conch shell, with no finger holes. Quetzalcóatl saw through the ruse, and called upon worms to eat through the shell to make holes, and upon bees to fly into the shell and make it roar with their buzzing.

When he heard the blast of the conch Mictlantecuhtli reluctantly agreed to give up the bones, then changed his mind as Quetzalcóatl was taking them away. He ordered his servants to dig a huge pit to block Quetzalcóatl's escape. Quetzalcóatl fell into the pit when a quail burst into flight and startled him; he appeared to be dead, and the bones, scattered in the pit, were broken and pecked by the quail. But he eventually revived, collected up the broken bones and made good his escape to TAMOANCHÁN, the place of miraculous birth. (The different sizes of people were explained by the different sizes of the broken bones after they were used to fashion new humans.) Quetzalcóatl delivered the bones to the old goddess CIHUACÓATL, who ground them and mixed them with the blood of the gods (or in another version, with blood from Quetzalcóatl's penis) to mould into men and women.

In another version of this story, Quetzalcóatl was accompanied on his journey to the underworld by XÓLOTL ("dog animal"), who acted as his guide. In this variation it was Xólotl who brought back a bone to the gods, who then sprinkled it with blood and caused it to give birth to a boy and a girl. Xólotl then raised the children on thistle milk and thus peopled the world of the Fifth Sun.

Yet another variation describes how Tezcatlipoca attempted to preserve two people from the Fourth Sun. He told the man, Tata, and his wife Nene to hide in the hollow of a tree, where he cared for them. He told the couple to eat only one ear of corn (maize) each while they waited for the flood waters to abate. When it was safe to descend from the tree, however, they saw a fish, one of their transformed former brethren, and, unable to overcome their temptation they caught the fish, made a fire, and cooked and ate it. The smoke was noticed by the gods CITLALÍCUE and CITLA-TONA, who cried out in rage, whereupon Tezcatlipoca descended upon the hapless couple in fury. His plan undone, he cut off the couple's heads and placed them on their buttocks, thus creating the first dogs. Clearly this story, recorded after the Spanish conquest, has an element of Christian influence in its "first couple" and "first disobedience" themes.

The next task was to supply the new race with sustenance. The gods and goddesses set about searching for a suitable food for humans, and, once again, it was Quetzalcóatl who played a crucial role. His attention was drawn by a red ant, AZCATL, scurrying along the ground carrying a grain of corn. He asked the ant where such a wonderful food was to be found, but Azcatl refused to tell him. After much threatening, however, Azcatl agreed to reveal the source, and led Quetzalcóatl to Mount TONACA-TÉPETL (literally "mountain of sustenance"). There Quetzalcóatl changed himself into a black ant and made his way through a narrow entrance passage to follow Azcatl deep into the mountain,

THE FOUR QUADRANTS and directions of the universe, centred on the "Old Fire God"– the creator god Xiuhtecuhtli – are pictured on the first page of the early post-Spanish-conquest Codex Fejérváry-Mayer.

where there was a chamber filled not only with grains of corn, but also with many other types of seeds and grains. Quetzalcóatl took some of the corn kernels back to Tamoanchán, where the gods chewed it and fed some of the resulting mash (maza) to the infant humans, whereupon they gained strength and grew.

Then the gods asked, "What is to be done with Tonacatépetl?" Quetzalcóatl attempted to haul the entire mountain, by slinging a rope around it, to a more convenient place on earth, but it proved too heavy even for him to move. So, rather than try to bring the mountain and its grains and seeds to the humans, it was decided to scatter the grains and seeds from the mountain over the earth. The old diviners OXOMOCO and CIPACTONAL cast lots to determine how this was to be done, and the signs told them that it was the god Nanahuatzin who should do this, by splitting Tonacatépetl open. Nanahuatzin, in turn, called upon the help of the four gods of the directional winds, the rains, and lightning – the TLÁLOCS. Tonacatépetl was duly split asunder and the black, blue, red and white (or yellow) winds

blew the grains and seeds across the land, while the rains watered them so that they took root and grew where they fell. Humans were quick to take advantage of this renewable source of food.

Finally, the gods concluded that something further was needed to provide humans with pleasure and to cause them to sing and dance in their honour. The ever obliging Quetzalcóatl, in his manifestation as the wind god Éhecatl, persuaded the beautiful young virgin MAYÁ-HUEL to leave her abode in the sky and accompany him to the earth, where the two became lovers and embraced in the form of two entwined branches of a tree. Mayáhuel had been pursued by her guardian, the fierce "grandmother" goddess TZITZIMITL, but the latter was too late to stop the union. In her wrath she split the tree in two, destroying the branch representing Mayáhuel and feeding the shreds to her demon servants, the TZITZIM-IME. Éhecatl, however, remained unharmed and, after resuming his former shape, gathered Mayáhuel's bones and planted them in a field where they grew, and lived on, as the maguey that produces the white drink known as PULQUE.

Maya Creation Myth

Maya creation stories also describe a succession of worlds, created by HUNAB KU. The first world was inhabited by the SAIYAM UINICOB ("adjuster men"), a race of dwarfs who, so the Maya believed, had built the ruined cities of the past. This work had been done in darkness because the sun had not yet been created but, when the sun rose on the first dawn, the Saiyam Uinicob were turned to stone. This world was destroyed by the first great flood, haiyococab ("water over the earth"). The second world was inhabited by the Dzolob ("offenders"), a mysterious race. It, too, was destroyed by flood waters, which poured from the mouth of the great sky serpent. The third world, that of the Mazehualob (the ancient Maya), would also end in a flood, and a fourth world come about in which would live a mixture of all the inhabitants of the previous worlds. In due course the fourth world will also end in flood. The sacred book CHILAM BALAM of Chumayel explains that the third Maya world came about after the 13 Lords of the Heavens (the OXLAHUN TI KU) were defeated by the nine Lords of the Underworld (the BOLON TI KU) and the BACABS were set to support the four corners of the earth.

This cyclical universe of creation and destruction mirrored Maya daily life and reflected their concept of duality, in which the rain god CHAC brought forth new corn (maize) shoots and plants each year, while AH PUCH, god of death, attempted to nip off the buds and tender new leaves.

The creation myth of the Guatemalan Quiché Maya also survives in their sacred text, the POPUL VUH. In the beginning, "all was in suspense, all calm, in silence; all motionless, still, and the expanse of the sky was empty. . . There was nothing standing; only the calm water, the placid sea, alone and tranquil. . . Then came the word. TEPEU and GUCUMATZ conferred.

They talked then, discussing and deliberating; they agreed, they united their words and thoughts."

There was only water and darkness on this new earth. Then the gods created the animals, and Gucumatz and Tepeu attempted to fashion humans out of mud, but were disappointed because these humans could not speak or worship their creators. When the mud dried they crumbled to dust, so the world was destroyed by flood. Next the gods made men of wood and women of rushes. They were stiff and unable to move, although they could speak and multiply. But they lacked brains, and could not recognize their creators. They became wicked and had to be destroyed, as before, by flood. The survivors became monkeys.

Finally, the gods made beings from yellow and white corn dough. When the sun rose on the first day of this creation, the humans were flesh. They had brains, recognized their creators and worshipped them, but were too knowledgeable, so the gods clouded their eyes to keep them focused on day-to-day events. Unlike the other Maya sources, the Popul Vuh mentions no anticipated fate for this world.

CUAUHTLI ("eagle") was the 15th of 20 AZTEC day-names; it was unfavourable and its patron deity was XIPE TOTEC, the "flayed one". The MAYA and ZAPOTEC equivalents were MEN and NAA. The cuauhtli

CUAUHTLI, the eagle, was a powerful symbol in Mesoamerican cosmology and a symbol of the Aztec nation.

was the mascot of the Eagle Warriors (see WARRIOR CULTS).

CUAUHUITLEHUA
see ATLCAHUALO.

CUAUHXICALLI ("eagle house")
were carved stone receptacles in which the hearts and blood of sacrificial victims were placed after being torn from the victims' bodies. The earth lord TLALTECUHTLI was often carved on the underside of the box.

CUAXÓLOTL
was the AZTEC goddess of the hearth and an alternative name for CHANTICO. She was portrayed with two heads, to symbolize both the good and evil potentials of fire.

CUERAUÁPERI,
or Cueravápperi, "she who causes to be born", was the TARASCAN creator goddess (or the feminine creation principle), goddess of birth and agriculture and, curiously, patroness of sewing. Her consort was CURICAUERI, the sun god, in union with whom she produced the moon goddess XARATANGA. While Xaratanga was the new moon, Cuerauápperi represented the old moon.

As sworn enemies of the Méxica AZTECS, the Tarascans were almost constantly at war, and prisoners were a ready source of sacrificial victims for their gods. At the feast of SICUINDIRO, prisoners were sacrificed to Cuerauápperi, and priests dressed and danced in the victims' flayed skins (see also XIPE TOTEC). The hearts of the victims were thrown into the thermal springs of Araró, from which it was believed Cuerauápperi drew water to create clouds to water the crops.

CUETZPALLIN ("lizard")
was the fourth of 20 AZTEC day-names; with a favourable augury; its patron was HUEHUECÓYOTL, the trickster. The MAYA and ZAPOTEC equivalents were KAN and ACHE.

Cuetzpallin represented creative natural forces, dying and regeneration. In the codices it is depicted as a lizard, the front half painted blue (for night), and the rear half painted red (for day). Calendrical dates and deity associations included: 1 Cuetzpallin, as a calendrical name of the god ITZTLACOLIUHQUI; and 6 Cuetzpallin, for MICTLANTECUHTLI, the god of death.

CULHUACÁN
see under CE TÉCPATL MIXCÓATL.

CURICAUERI,
or Curicaveri, was the TARASCAN creator god (or masculine creation principle), sun god, fire god and god of corn (maize) as QUERENDA-ANGAPETI. He and his consort, the creator goddess CUERAUÁPERI, produced the moon goddess XARATANGA.

The centre of his cult was at the great fivefold temple complex of YÁCATAS at Tzintzuntzan. It was essential to honour him by keeping perpetual fires burning in the Yácatas and, for this purpose, there were five special priests called curihtsit-acha ("lord who is in charge of the fire"). Smoke was considered especially significant and believed to be a special form of contact between humans and gods. Tobacco was thrown into sacred fires to give fragrance, and only priests were allowed to smoke it. A group of women was also assigned to honour Curicaueri by weaving rich blankets and making corn bread to be burned on his fires.

War prisoners were sacrificed to Curicaueri and their blood offered to the sacred fires at the feast of SICUINDIRO. The priests dressed and danced in the flayed skins of the victims (see also XIPE TOTEC), and the victims' hearts were thrown into the thermal springs of Araró.

E

CURITA-CAHERI was the messenger of the *TARASCAN* gods.

DUBDO was another name for the *ZAPOTEC* god of corn (maize) and the Zapotec fifth *LORD OF THE NIGHT*. (See also *PITAO COZOBI*)

DZAHUI, or Tzahui, was the *MIXTEC* god of lightning and rain, equivalent to *AZTEC TLÁLOC*, *MAYA CHAC*, *TOTONAC TAJÍN* and *ZAPOTEC COCIJO*, and probably also to the *TARASCAN CHUPITHIRIPEME*.

DZOLOB, a mysterious race, were the "offenders", the inhabitants of the second world in Maya creation; see *HUNAB KU* and *CREATION MYTHS*.

EARTH MONSTER see *TLALTECUHTLI*.

EB ("bad rain") was the 12th of the 20 *MAYA* day-names; associated with the malignant rain god who sent mist, dew and dampness that caused mildew on the corn crop. The *AZTEC* and *ZAPOTEC* equivalent days were *MALINALLI* and *PIJA*.

ECOZTLI see *PACHTONTLI*.

DUBDO, *the Zapotec corn god, is depicted in this carving wearing a corn cob headdress.* (CLASSIC PERIOD.)

ÉHECATL, *NAHUATL* for "wind", was possibly of *HUASTEC* origin and became the god of winds throughout central Mesoamerica, and was associated with the cardinal points and colours. He was a manifestation of *QUETZALCÓATL*, the plumed serpent, and was often known as Quetzalcóatl-Éhecatl or Éhecatl-Quetzalcóatl. He was honoured, especially by the Huastecs, with round or round-ended temple-platforms in many cities – allegedly to offer less resistance to prevailing winds. In the codices and sculpture Éhecatl was shown wearing a bird-beak or duck-billed mask, most famously in the statue excavated at the Temple of Quetzalcóatl-Éhecatl in Calixtlahuaca, a city of the Matlazinca (in the Toluca Valley west of the Basin of Mexico). He ruled the second of the 20 Aztec days (*Éhecatl*; Maya *IK*; Zapotec *QUIJ* or *Laa*; all meaning wind).

Éhecatl was a rather enigmatic deity, with numerous guises and roles, many auguring unfavourable events. Calendrical references include: *1 Éhecatl Iztac Tezcatlipoca* – "white Tezcatlipoca", the equivalent of Quetzalcóatl; or *4 Éhecatl*

Xólotl – Quetzalcóatl's twin. As *6 Éhecatl* he was the sun. As *7 Éhecatl* he was associated with the day of the creation of humankind by Quetzalcóatl, and as *9 Éhecatl* he represented the winds from the four quarters. As Quetzalcóatl, he was instrumental in the creation of the Fifth Sun, and in the origin of humans (see *CREATION MYTHS*).

The gods decided that people were needed to populate the world and sent Quetzalcóatl, as Éhecatl, to *MICTLÁN* (the underworld) to retrieve the bones of the people of the former world. He arrived and announced his mission, at which the ruler *MICTLANTECHUHTLI* and his wife declared that Éhecatl-Quetzalcóatl could have the bones only if he would carry out an ostensibly easy task – travel around Mictlán four times while blowing on a conch-shell trumpet. In place of a trumpet, however, Mictlantecuhtli gave Éhecatl-Quetzalcóatl a conch shell with no finger holes. Spotting this deficiency, Éhecatl-Quetzalcóatl called upon worms to drill holes and upon bees to fly into the shell and make it roar with their buzzing. Mictlantecuhtli reluctantly gave up the bones, but attempted several times to get them back, each time being outwitted by Éhecatl-Quetzalcóatl. The bones were delivered to the old goddess *CIHUA-CÓATL*, who ground them and mixed them with the blood of the gods to mould men and women (or in a different version, mixed the ground bones with blood from Éhecatl's penis).

At their assembly at *TEOTI-HUACÁN*, the gods called upon Éhecatl-Quetzalcóatl again. The twin brothers *NANAHUATZIN* and

ÉHECATL, *Huastec-Aztec god of the wind, was one manifestation of Quetzalcóatl (the "plumed serpent"). He was most frequently portrayed with a buccal or duck-bill mask.*

TECUCIZTÉCATL leapt into the sacrificial fire and emerged as the sun and the moon. They remained motionless, however, until Éhecatl blew upon them, setting them on their journeys across the sky.

In yet another myth, Éhecatl brought physical love and the *maguey* or *agave* (*Agave americana*; from which the intoxicating drink *PULQUE* is made) into the world, by persuading the beautiful virgin *MAYÁHUEL* to leave her abode in the sky and descend to the earth with him. They became lovers by embracing each other as a tree of two entwined branches, but were pursued by *TZITZIMITL*, Mayáhuel's fearsome "grandmother" guardian. When she arrived too late to stop the union, in her wrath she split the tree in two, destroying the branch representing Mayáhuel and feeding the shreds to her demon servants. Éhecatl, however, remained unharmed and, resuming his former shape, gathered Mayáhuel's bones and planted them in a field where they grew into the *maguey* plant. (See also *COLOURS & THE CARDINAL DIRECTIONS*)

35

ORDERING THE WORLD

THE CONCEPT OF CYCLICITY permeated the entire fabric of Mesoamerican culture and society. From the daily journey of the sun across the sky, through the monthly cycles of the moon and the annual pattern of the seasons, to the super-annual countings of days and months according to the motions of the planets and stars, virtually every Mesoamerican act or task was believed to occur under the auspices of celestial movements. Cyclical time directed both men and the gods and goddesses, and regulated all thought, from people's everyday decisions to their world view to social evolution. Even the world itself had been created in a series of episodes and would ultimately end in a closing of the cycle by the destruction of the Fifth Sun.

Such belief in unremitting cyclicity was intimately connected to Aztec collapse in 1519–21, and helps to explain their complex and enigmatic reaction to the Spaniards. The Aztecs believed that Moctezuma II Xocoyotzin's reign, and the world of the Fifth Sun, would end upon the return of Quetzalcóatl the man-god, from the east, to claim his rightful rule and to create a new world order. The celestial movements ominously coincided with the arrival of Hernán Cortés, who cannily used the knowledge of this belief to his advantage.

THE INTRICATELY CARVED STONE (above) popularly known as the "calendar stone", found in Mexico City in 1790, represents the sun god Tonatiuh or his counterpart, the night sun Yohualtecuhtli. The sun and cosmic symbolism are manifest. A central image is surrounded by a series of ring-panels. In the centre is the sun, represented by a stylized human face with a sacrificial stone knife protruding from the mouth. The first ring contains, to right and left, two rounded claw-arms clutching human hearts, and four glyph panels representing each of the four previous suns – Jaguar, Wind, Rain (of Fire) and Water. The second ring contains the glyphs of the 20 Nahuatl day-names. A third (narrow) ring comprises repetitive, decorative designs, and is followed by a fourth ring with repeated symbols representing turquoise and jade, the colours for the heavens and symbols of the equinoxes and solstices. The outer border comprises two Xiuhcóatl (turquoise, or fire, snakes) symbolizing cosmic order, cyclicity and the present world.

THE TWENTY AZTEC *day-names (right, shown bottom right to top left) are crocodile, wind, house, lizard, serpent, death, deer, rabbit, water, dog, monkey, grass, reed, jaguar, eagle, vulture, movement, flint knife, rain, and flower. There were three chronological systems in Mesoamerican lives: the 365-day cycle, the 260-day cycle and a Venusian cycle of 584 days. The first two were combined by the Aztecs to form the Xiuhmolpilli, a 52-year cycle. The 365-day cycle was made up of 18 months of 20 days each, plus five extra, ill-omened days at the end of each year. Each month had special rites associated with it. The Aztecs also divided each day into 13 "hours" of daytime and 9 "hours" of nighttime. The sequence of days in each month was fixed, and therefore the day-name on which a new solar year began shifted by five days each year.* (ILLUSTRATION FROM RESEARCHES CONCERNING THE INSTITUTIONS AND MONUMENTS OF THE ANCIENT INHABITANTS OF AMERICA BY FRIEDRICH ALEXANDER BARON VON HUMBOLDT, 1814.)

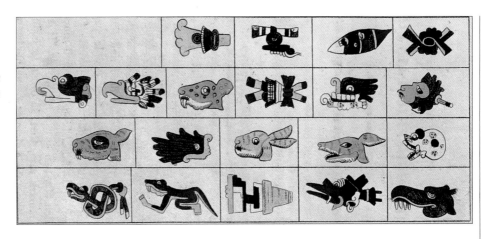

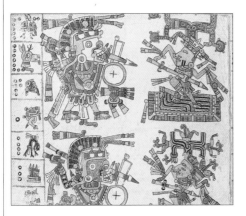

THE PYRAMID *of the Niches (right) at the Totonac site of El Tajín emphasizes the importance and widespread use of the 365-day calendar throughout Mesoamerica. The six tiers and temple of the pyramid-platform include 88 niches on the base tier, then successively 76, 64, 52, 40, 28 and 17 at the top.*

THE IMPORTANCE *of Venus (above), known as the god Tlahuizcalpantecuhtli – the morning and evening "stars", is demonstrated by his depiction in the codices and his influence over daily lives. During the periods of the Venusian synodical orbit he was believed to rule and attack the different social orders, his power over them being symbolized by the darts he hurls at them in these scenes.* (PRE-SPANISH CONQUEST CODEX COSPI.)

DAY-NAMES

	AZTEC (Cempolhualli)			MAYA (Uinal)	ZAPOTEC
	glyph	patron deity	augury	glyph	glyph
1	Cipactli (crocodile)	Tonacatecuhtli	good	Imix (earth-monster)	Chilla (crocodile)
2	Éhecatl (wind)	Quetzalcóatl;	evil	Ik (breath, wind)	Quij or Laa (wind)
3	Calli (house)	Tepeyolohtli	good	Akbal (darkness)	Guela (night)
4	Cuetzpallin (lizard)	Huehuecóyotl	good	Kan (ripe corn/maize)	Ache or Beydo (lizard)
5	Cóatl (serpent)	Chalchiúhtlicue	good	Chicchan (serpent)	Zee or Zij (serpent)
6	Miquiztli (death)	Tecciztécatl or Meztli	evil	Cimi (death)	Lana (blackness)
7	Mázatl (deer)	Tláloc	good	Manik (hand)	China (deer)
8	Tochtli (rabbit)	Mayáhuel	good	Lamat (Venus)	Lapa (rabbit)
9	Atl (water)	Xiuhtecuhtli	evil	Muluc (water)	Niza or Queza (water)
10	Itzcuintli (dog)	Mictlantecuhtli	good	Oc (dog)	Tella (dog)
11	Ozomatli (monkey)	Xochipilli	neutral	Chuen (monkey; craftsman)	Loo or Goloo (dog)
12	Malinalli (grass)	Patécatl	evil	Eb (bad or poor rain)	Pija (draught)
13	Ácatl (reed)	Tezcatlipoca or Itztlacoliuhqui	evil	Ben (growing corn)	Quij or Ij or Laa (reed)
14	Océlotl (jaguar)	Tlazoltéotl	evil	Ix (jaguar)	Gueche (jaguar)
15	Cuauhtli (eagle)	Xipe Totec	evil	Men (moon; wise one; eagle)	Naa (eagle)
16	Cozcacuauhtli (vulture)	Itzpapálotl	good	Cib (wax)	Loo or Guiloo (crow)
17	Ollin (movement, earthquake)	Xólotl	neutral	Caban (earth)	Xoo (earthquake)
18	Técpatl (flint knife)	Tezcatlipoca or Chalchiuhtotolin	good	Etz'nab (cutting edge)	Opa (cold)
19	Quiáhuitl (rain)	Tonatiuh or Chantico	evil	Cauac (rain; storm)	Ape (cloud)
20	Xóchitl (flower)	Xochiquetzal	neutral	Ahau (lord)	Lao (flower)

G

EIGHT DEER TIGER CLAW (AD 1011–63) was the legendary 11th-century ruler of the *MIXTEC* cities of Tilantongo (founded about AD 875) and Tututepec, whose exploits are recorded in the *Codex Nuttall*, the *Codex Colombino* and the *Codex Becker 1*.

He founded Tututepec in the early 11th century near the Pacific coast and co-ruled (AD 1030–63) Tilantongo with his half-brother, with whom he established that city's second dynasty. From Tututepec he conquered the surrounding Mixtec towns in Mixteca de la Costa and Mixteca Alta. The codices describe his five marriages, his murder of his half-brother and seizure of power in Tilantongo, and the end of his rule when he offered himself up for sacrifice. In the *Codex Nuttall* he is shown in *TOLTEC* dress, while his courtiers wear Mixtec costume, which has led some scholars to argue that he sought Toltec affirmation of his power. Some even argue that he visited the Toltec capital at Tollán (Tula) to receive his turquoise nose plug as a symbol of rank.

EK CHUAH, *MAYA* God M and known as "black war leader", was a Yucatecan god of war in his malevolent aspect, and simultaneously god of travellers, merchants and prosperity in his benevolent aspect (see also *THE OLD BLACK GOD*). As the latter he was usually portrayed as a merchant, with a bundle of merchandise on his back and staff in hand. In Yucatecan Maya "Ek" means both "black" and "star", and Ek Chuah was often associated with *XAMEN EK* ("north star"). At least one depiction shows him with the head of Xamen Ek, and thus the North Star and guide of merchants. As the "black scorpion", the god of merchants and as "black war leader" he was portrayed with a large, drooping lower lip, and was painted black, with black rings around his eyes. As war leader he was, of course, a special god of those who died in battle. (See also *BULUC CHABTÁN*.)

Ek Chuah was also the patron of *cacao* (*Theobroma cacao*; cocoa; chocolate), which, with honey (see *AH MUCEN CAB*), was one of the most important items of Maya trade. Mesoamericans also used *cacao* beans as a currency to purchase small household items; and in post-Spanish Conquest times *cacao* beans were even used to pay labourers' wages. Owners of *cacao* plantations held a ceremony in honour of Ek Chuah in the month of *Muan* (15th of the 18 months of the year). As god of merchants, his Aztec equivalent was *YACATECUHTLI*.

EK PAUAHTUN see *PAUAHTUN*.

EK CHUAH, Maya God M, was the "black scorpion" merchant god and "black war leader". He carries a merchant's staff and bundle on a tumpline, and has a typically drooping lower lip and ringed eye.

EK XIB CHAC see *THE CHACS*.

EL TAJÍN see *TAJÍN*.

ETZALCUALIZTLI ("meal of corn/maize and beans") was the seventh (or, in some sources, sixth) of the 18 months of the *AZTEC* year. As with *ATLCAHUALO*, the principal deities honoured were the god and goddess of water, *TLÁLOC* and *CHALCHIÚHTLICUE*.

ETZ'NAB, *MAYA* God Q, was god of evil, and probably of human sacrifice (see also *BULUC CHABTAN*). He was symbolized by the number two.

Etz'nab ("cutting edge") was also the 18th of the 20 *MAYA* daynames; it was associated with the number two and with God Q, who probably presided over the sacrifices. In the codices it is represented by a pressure-flaked obsidian knife, the sort used in performing human sacrifices. The *AZTEC* and *ZAPOTEC* equivalents were *TÉCPATL* and *OPA*.

THE EVIL GOD see *ETZ'NAB*.

THE FAT GOD, a pan-Mesoamerican deity of the Preclassic to Classic periods, was especially worshipped in the Classic Period city *TEOTIHUACÁN* and its "empire", and at Classic Period *TOTONAC* sites of the central Gulf Coast. His importance recedes towards the end of the Classic Period, corresponding to the waning of Teotihuacán. He is thought to have represented prosperity and sensuous pleasure, and his role appears to have been subsumed by the cults of *XOCHIPILLI* and *MACUILXÓCHITL* in the Postclassic Period.

FIRE CEREMONY see *TOXIUHMOLPILIA*.

THE FLOWERY WAR see *XOCHIYAÓYOTL*.

GOD I was the *OLMEC* god of the earth, sun, water and fertility. He is depicted as a "dragon" – a monster creature with flaming eyebrows, a prominent nose, L-shaped or trough-like eyes and a host of composite features, including a serpentine forked tongue, crocodilian limbs or eagle talons, jaguar fangs and human attributes. His prominence in the Olmec pantheon suggests a link to royal power and dynastic succession, political institutions that were nascent in Olmec civilization. His associations with earth, sun, water and fertility indicate that this was possibly a creator deity, ancestral to several later Mesoamerican gods and goddesses, in particular pan-Mesoamerican *HUEHUETÉOTL*, Maya *ITZAMNÁ* and Aztec *XIUHTECUHTLI*.

GOD II was the *OLMEC* corn (maize) god, identified as such by corn cob symbols sprouting from a cleft in his head, and the god of agriculture in general. Figures of God II depict a toothless infant – presumably a manifestation of youth and life – with a were-jaguar countenance of almond-shaped eyes, a wide, flat nose and a plump, flaring upper lip, and often a decorated band across his forehead. He was presumably antecedent to all Mesoamerican corn deities, in particular the Aztec god *CENTÉOTL*.

GOD III was the *OLMEC* deity associated with celestial matters, particularly with the sun, and agricultural fertility. For reasons not completely understood, God III is also connected with chinless dwarfs. He was a bird-monster, with combined avian and reptilian features: a raptor's beak with conspicuous cere (sometimes with a single, cleft upper fang), paw-like wings ending in talons and, in some figures, the head bears a harpy-eagle's crest. Like *GOD I*, he has L-shaped or trough-like eyes and flame eyebrows.

GOD IV was the *OLMEC* god of rain, and, by extension, of agricultural fertility. Like *GOD II*, he is depicted as an infant were-jaguar,

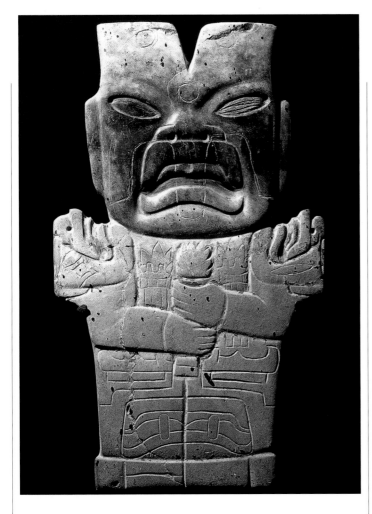

with almond-shaped eyes, a flattened, pug nose, flaring upper lip and an easily identifiable toothless mouth turned down at the corners. He is usually shown wearing a distinctive, sectioned headband, crenellated ear ornaments and a pectoral badge with crossed bands. Because of his special association with clouds, rain and fertility, he is thought to be ancestral to *MAYA CHAC* and *AZTEC TLÁLOC*.

GOD V is a designation no longer used by archaeologists.

GOD VI was a mysterious *OLMEC* deity thought to have represented spring and the concept of annual renewal or resurrection. He is portrayed as a disembodied cleft head with almond-shaped eyes, the open one of which has a distinct band or stripe across it. As with other Olmec gods, his toothless mouth has prominent gum ridges and is shaped in a hideous grin. Some of these attributes seem to suggest that God VI might have

GOD VI or X was the Olmec composite jaguar-monster god, with cleft head, almond-shaped eyes and a toothless, pouting mouth. The flame shoulders and "torch" are attributes of God I – earth, sun, water and fertility.

been antecedent to *XIPE TOTEC*, the *HUASTEC* and central Mesoamerican god of spring, whose priests dressed in the flayed skins of their human sacrificial victims.

GOD VII, sometimes referred to as the Olmec "dragon", was another less well-defined *OLMEC* deity, possibly an early "feathered serpent". Although he can be distinguished from them, his features are similar to those of *GOD I* and *GOD III* – a serpentine head and body with avian head crest and wings.

GOD VIII was the *OLMEC* fish-monster, associated with oceans, and with standing (as opposed to flowing) bodies of water in general. Appropriately, he has a fish body with a forked tail, crocodilian teeth

and shark-like features, but crescent-shaped eyes and a human nose. His decoration often consists of crossed bands or stripes along the body.

GOD IX is a designation no longer used by archaeologists.

GOD X was yet another *OLMEC* were-jaguar deity who had attributes similar to those of *GOD VI* – a cleft head, almond-shaped eyes and a toothless, prominent gummed mouth – but he is identifiable through the figure-of-eight motifs in his nostrils and the lack of eye bands or stripes. He was normally shown as a disembodied head and, in composite imagery, invariably occupied a position secondary to the other gods.

GOD A see *AH PUCH*.

GOD B see *CHAC*.

GOD C see *XAMEN EK*.

GOD D see *ITZAMNÁ*.

GOD E see *AH MUN*.

GOD F see *BULUC CHABTÁN*.

GOD G see *KINICH AHAU*.

GOD H see *CHICCHAN*.

GOD K see *BOLON DZ'ACAB*.

GOD L see *THE OLD BLACK GOD*.

GOD M see *EK CHUAH*.

GOD N see *PAUAHTUN*.

GOD Q see *ETZ'NAB*.

GODDESS I see *IX CHEL*.

GODDESS O see *IX CHEBEL YAX*.

GOLOO ("dog") see *LOO*.

GOZIO was the Sierra *ZAPOTEC* name for *COCIJO*.

GREAT GODDESS see *TEOTIHUACÁN SPIDER WOMAN*.

GUCUMATZ was the Quiché *MAYA* name for *KUKULKÁN*, the "feathered serpent". He is described in the Quiché sacred text of the *POPUL VUH*, in which the gods Gucumatz and *TEPEU* created the earth and all of the living things on it, although it took them many attempts before they were satisfied with their efforts to create humans (see *CREATION MYTHS*).

GUECHE ("jaguar") was 14th of the 20 *ZAPOTEC* day-names; *AZTEC* and *MAYA* equivalent days were *OCÉLOTL* and *IX*.

GOD VII, possibly the Olmec precursor to Quetzalcóatl the "plumed serpent", was depicted (above the serpent-masked human figure) on Monument 19 at the Gulf Coast site of La Venta.

H

GUELA ("night") was the third of the 20 *ZAPOTEC* day-names; the *AZTEC* and *MAYA* equivalent days were *CALLI* and *AKBAL*.

GUILOO ("crow") see *LOO*.

HISTORIA DE LOS REINOS DE CULHUACÁN see *ANALES DE CUAUHTITLÁN*.

HOBNIL see *THE BACABS*.

HOZANEK see *THE BACABS*.

HUAHUANTLI see *TEOYAOMIQUI*.

THE HUASTECS lived in northeast Mesoamerica, along the northern Gulf Coast. They spoke a *MAYA* or related language but, from about 1400 BC, had become split off from the more southerly Maya by the intervention of other groups into the central Gulf Coast. Indeed, Maya chronicles refer to their Huastec ancestry. Influences from *TEOTIHUACÁN*, especially architectural, and from the central Gulf Coast *TOTONAC* are evident at Classic Period Huastec sites. In the Postclassic Period the Huastecs were conquered by the México *AZTECS*.

Several Mesoamerican deities and religious concepts appear to be of Huastec origin. During the late Classic Period, the *TOLTEC* cult of *QUETZALCÓATL* might have originated among them, particularly the worship of him as *ÉHECATL*-Quetzalcoátl; a distinctive Huastec architectural form associated with this cult was round or round-ended temple platforms.

Another important central Mesoamerican god of Huastec, or earlier, origin was *XIPE TOTEC*, flayed god of spring (see also *GOD VI*). Other deities possibly of Huastec ancestry are the earth goddesses *TOCI*, *IXCUINAN* and *TLAZOLTÉOTL*, and the concept of *TAMOANCHÁN*, a terrestrial paradise.

HUAUHQUILTAMALCUALIZTLI see *IZCALLI*.

HUECHAANA, or Huichaana, also Cochana, *HUICHANATAO*, Nohuiçana, Nohuichana and Pitao Huichaana, was a Valley *ZAPOTEC* mother goddess associated, alongside her male counterpart *COZAANA*, with children. She was also associated with hunting and fishing – hunters and fishers offered her sacrifices for help in their endeavours. In addition, like *PICHANTO*, she was the intermediary for humankind with *PICHANA GOBECHE*.

HUEHUECÓYOTL, or Ueuecóyotl ("old coyote" – *cóyotl*), was the central Mesoamerican god of cleverness and trickery, the wily old coyote who wreaked spontaneous mischief, especially that associated with sex. He enjoyed a widespread cult among ancient Mesoamerican cultures, and might have been of pre-Nahuatl origin, possibly *OTOMÍ*. He was patron of the Aztec day *CUETZPALLIN*, and featherworkers (called *amantecas*) worshipped a god with a coyote companion (*cóyotl inahual*).

His unpredictability made the ordered and severe *AZTECS* especially suspicious and watchful of him. As the trickster coyote figured so prominently in southwest North American myth, it is tempting to speculate that this deity was an ancient accoutrement pre-dating Aztec migration from the northwest into the Basin of Mexico, and that the association continued to be reinforced by trading contacts between central Mesoamerica and northern peoples.

HUEHUETÉOTL, also called *XIUHTECUHTLI*, *OTONTECUHTLI* and Xócotl, was the name for an ancient Mesoamerican deity, literally the "Old One", the *OLD FIRE GOD*, possibly descended from the Olmec *GOD I*. He was usually portrayed as an old man, with wrinkled skin and toothless mouth, supporting an incense brazier on his head. He was first among the nine Aztec *LORDS OF THE NIGHT* and the 13 *LORDS OF*

HUEHUETÉOTL, or the Old Fire God, was represented as an old, bearded man, supporting a brazier for ritual fires and incense burning, as here in this late Classic Period terracotta from Veracruz.

THE DAY. The *AZTECS* called him Xiuhtecuhtli, as the god who presided over the New Fire Ceremony (see *TOXIUHMOLPILIA*).

HUEYMICCAILHUITL ("great feast of the dead") was the 11th (or, in some sources, the 10th) of the *AZTEC* 18 months, in which the fire god, *XIUHTECUHTLI*, and *YACATECUHTLI*, patron of merchants, were worshipped. Sacrificial victims were drugged, then roasted before their hearts were cut out. In the codices the month is represented by death symbols and mummy bundles. It is also called *Xocotlhuetzi* ("honouring of the fruit tree").

HUEYPACHTLI ("much hay") was the 14th (or, in some sources, 13th) of the *AZTEC* 18 months, in which the *TLÁLOCS* and *TEPICTOTON* were propitiated.

It is also called *Pillahuana* ("the children drink") and *Tepeílhuitl* ("feast of the mountains").

HUEYTECUILHUITL ("great feast of the lords") was the ninth (or, in some sources, eighth) of the *AZTEC* 18 months. It was a ritual feast day in which the corn (maize) god *XILONEN* and the "serpent woman" earth goddess *CIHUACÓATL* were honoured, and in which the Aztec lords feasted the commoners with food, song and dance, and sacrificed male and female impersonators of the two deities.

HUEYTOZOZTLI ("great watch") was the fifth (or, in some sources, fourth) of the *AZTEC* 18 months, a month in which sacrifices were held to propitiate the god and goddess of corn (maize) *CENTÉOTL* and *CHICOMECÓATL*, the purpose being to bring on the tender young corn plants (*toctli*). The ceremonial climax was a procession of virgins to the Temple of Chicomecóatl, where seeds were blessed and a corn-goddess impersonator was sacrificed. Children were offered to the rain god *TLÁLOC* for the success of crops.

HUICHAANA see *HUECHAANA*.

HUICHANATAO was a *ZAPOTEC* goddess of the city of Chichicapa who, like *HUECHAANA*, was associated with children; her male counterpart was *PITAO COZAANA*. She might have been the same as *PICHANTO*, who acted as the intermediary in appeals between people and *PICHANA GOBECHE*.

HUITZILOPOCHTLI ("Hummingbird of the South" or "Blue Hummingbird on the Left" – Mesoamericans regarded the west as "up", making the south the left) was an exclusively *AZTEC* deity who had no identifiable predecessors in earlier Mesoamerican cultures. His symbolic "brothers" in the Aztec pantheon were *QUETZALCÓATL*, *TEZCATLIPOCA* and *XIPE TOTEC*. In one legend he is the son of the creator couple *OMECÍHUATL* and *OMETECUHTLI*. In another he is the son of *COATLÍCUE*, whose life he saved by defeating his brothers and sisters *THE CENTZONHUITZNAHUAC* and *THE CENTZONMIMIZCOA*, who had plotted to kill her, although he first killed his sister *COYOLXAUHQUI* by mistake. (Coyolxauhqui was, in fact, attempting to warn Coatlícue of the plot but, as she approached ahead of them, her new brother Huitzilopochtli emerged fully armed from his mother's womb and did not realize this. He decapitated her in his haste and threw her head into the heavens to become the moon. In Aztec myth, this event recurs daily as the moon sets and the sun drives away the darkness – symbolic of the struggle between day and night, light and dark, good and evil.)

Huitzilopochtli was the sun god and the god of war (hummingbirds

were regarded as the souls of fallen warriors), the tribal god of the México Aztecs (the "people of the sun"), the last Aztec tribe to arrive in the Basin of Mexico and the one that created the empire, and the patron of the Aztec capital, *TENOCHTITLÁN*. As the sun, he was accompanied in his daily journey across the sky, from daybreak until noon, by the souls of warriors fallen in battle – the Aztecs regarded death in battle to be the most honourable way to die – then, from noon to sunset, by the *CIHUATETEO* in their descent into the west, symbolizing a falling eagle. Through the night he illuminated the underworld of the dead.

Huitzilopochtli was given equal status beside *TLÁLOC*, the life giver, and in Tenochtitlán their twin temples stood atop the Templo Mayor pyramid-platform, with a magnificent double stone staircase ascending to them. Huitzilopochtli's temple was plastered and painted blood red for war, while Tláloc's was painted in brilliant blue (representing water) and white, and the priests of both gods were afforded equal rank in Aztec society.

In legend, Huitzilopochtli led the México from a cave in *AZTLÁN*, in the deserts of the northwest, into central Mesoamerica. In their wanderings, the México were led by four priests, who carried a great idol of Huitzilopochtli before the people. Through the idol, Huitzilopochtli spoke secretly to the priests, telling them to call themselves the México, advising them on the best route to take, and

promising them that, if the México honoured him, they would overcome all their enemies and receive riches in tributes of precious stones, coral, gold and quetzal feathers. When they arrived in the Basin of Mexico he gave the México the sign of the eagle (which was his representative) alighting on a *nopal* (prickly pear) cactus, clutching a serpent in his claw, on an island (*MEZTLIAPÁN*) to show them the spot where they should build their capital.

As Huitzilopochtli's chosen people, the México felt compelled to supply their wilful god with the life-giving blood of sacrificial victims, and they fomented ritual wars to secure captives for these tributes (see *XOCHIYAÓYOTL*, "Flowery War"). The prisoners were handed over to the priests at the foot of the Templo Mayor, from where they were dragged up the steps, stretched out across the sacrificial stone, and their chests then sliced open with an obsidian knife. Then the heart of the sacrificial victim was wrenched out, the corpse was skinned, and the limbs dismembered. It is thought that pieces of the flesh were then sent down for

HUITZILOPOCHTLI, the Aztec war god, was frequently depicted in the codices dressed for war and carrying his favourite weapons – atl-atl (spear-thrower), clutch of feather-tipped arrows and shield.

the rulers and nobility to eat, while the heart was allegedly sometimes consumed by the priests. The priests also made offerings of flowers, incense and food to Huitzilopochtli, and they adorned his idol with wreaths and lavish garlands of flowers.

In the codices Huitzilopochtli is usually depicted brandishing his favourite weapon, an *atl-atl* (spear-thrower) made in the shape of *XIUHCÓATL*, the "fire serpent". He has blue-painted arms and legs, hummingbird feathers on his left leg, and arrows tipped with featherdown. His calendrical name was *Ce Técpatl* ("1 Flint"), and his messenger was called Paynal. His malevolent aspects were summed up in the alternative name *YÁOTL*, "the enemy".

HUITZILOPOCHTLI is depicted here in warlike mode, carrying his serpent-shaped atl-atl (spear-thrower), his shield and feathered arrows.

HUIXTOCÍHUATL, or Uixt-oxíhuatl, was the "inventor" and *AZTEC* patroness of salt. A young woman in the guise of Huixtocí-huatl was one of four who served a warrior-youth, himself in the role of *TEZCATLIPOCA*, destined to be sacrificed at the end of a year of honour and enjoyment. At the festival of *TÓXCATL* young girls and old women performed a dance wearing special flower-headdresses. The climax of the dance ceremony was the sacrifice of Huixtocíhuatl and of her "sister-wives" – *ATLATONAN*, *XILONEN* and *XOCHIQUETZAL*.

HUN AHAU see *AH PUCH*.

HUN BATZ and Hun Chouen, described in the *POPUL VUH*, were the sons of *HUN HUNAHPÚ*, and half-brothers of the hero twins *HUNAHPÚ* and *XBALANQUÉ*, of whom they were jealous. Trained by their father and uncle, *VUCUB HUNAHPÚ*, Hun Batz and Hun Chouen were skilled at the Meso-american ball game, and were expert acrobats, dancers and musicians, while the twins favoured hunting and exploring the forest. The spoiled older boys took all the twins' game, leaving them only scraps. One day, the twins returned from the day's hunt empty-handed but told their brothers that the birds they had shot were caught in a tree. Hun Batz and Hun Chouen followed them into the forest and agreed to fetch the birds down. As the two climbed, however, the tree trunk miraculously grew taller. The older boys panicked and called out for help. Hunahpú and Xbalanqué advised their brothers to untie their loincloths and wrap them around their hips, leaving the long ends dangling like tails, so as to be able to move more freely. By this trick the older twins were changed into monkeys, but they were not forgotten. To the *MAYA*, because of their former skills, they became the patrons of the arts and crafts, and of musicians and dancers.

THE BALL GAME, *a major Mesoamerican ritual, played an important part in the career of the hero twins. The stone ball court at Chichén Itzá, shown here, is the largest in Mesoamerica.* (POSTCLASSIC PERIOD)

HUN CAME ("one death") and Vucub Came ("seven death") were the leaders of the Lords of *XIBALBA* (underworld) in the *POPUL VUH*. Annoyed at the noise made by the brothers *HUN HUNAHPÚ* and *VUCUB HUNAHPÚ* when they played the ball game, they challenged the brothers to a game in Xibalba, in which they and the other Lords of Xibalba defeated and sacrificed them. Later, the hero twins *HUNAH-PÚ* and *XBALANQUÉ*, sons of Hun Hunahpú, avenged their father's and uncle's deaths by travelling to Xibalba and defeating Hun Came, Vucub Came and the rest of the Lords, and cutting up their bodies.

HUN CHOUEN see under *HUN BATZ*.

HUN HUNAHPÚ (literally "one Hunahpú") and *VUCUB HUNAHPÚ* ("seven Hunahpú") were *MAYA* deities and the first-born of the human race: the twin sons of the "grandfather" creator god *XPIYACOC* and the "grandmother" creator goddess *XMUCANÉ*. The twins and Hun Hunahpú's sons *HUN BATZ* and Hun Chouen were fond of the Mesoam-erican dice game and, especially, the ball game, but the noise they made when playing the latter on the hard stone ball court annoyed the Lords of *XIBALBA* (underworld). The Lords tricked the Hun Hunahpú and Vucub Hunahpú into travelling to Xibalba, where they were challenged to a ball game. There, they were tricked, defeated and sacrificed.

Hun Hunahpú's head was cut off and was hung among the fruits of a calabash tree as a trophy. The fruit of the tree, which was forbidden, tempted *XQUIC*, the maiden daughter of one of the underworld Lords. When she questioned aloud if she should pick some of the fruit the head overheard and spat into the hand of the unsuspecting girl. As a result she became pregnant and gave birth to the hero twins *HUNAHPÚ* and *XBALANQUÉ*, who later journeyed to Xibalba and avenged the deaths of their father and uncle.

HUNAB KU, an unusual *MAYA* deity, was a supreme, single, creator god of the Yucatecan Maya – an apparent attempt to focus on an over-arching concept of divinity. His name means "one" (*hun*) "state of being" (*ab*) "god" (*ku*). Hunab Ku was thought to be the father of *ITZAMNÁ* himself and, in one version of the *CREATION MYTH*, was believed to have made the world and set *THE BACABS* at its four corners to hold up the sky.

Unlike the other gods of the Maya pantheon, Hunab Ku was invisible, and therefore was not portrayed – or at least no representation in the codices has positively been identified as Hunab Ku. He was, rather, an abstract concept preached about by priests in the early Postclassic Period, perhaps an early attempt to view the universe under a monotheistic philosophy (see also *TLOQUE NAHUAQUE*).

HUNAHPÚ was one of the hero twins of the Quiché *MAYA*. The sacred *POPUL VUH* describes how Hunahpú and his brother *XBALAN-QUÉ* were conceived by the spittle of their father, *HUN HUNAHPÚ*, when his severed head spat into the hand of the unsuspecting *XQUIC*, maiden daughter of one of the Lords of *XIBALBA* (the underworld).

The twins went to Xibalba to avenge their father and uncle, *VUCUB HUNAHPÚ*, who had been defeated and slain by the Lords of Xibalba. In Xibalba they underwent several trials: they fought and destroyed the bird-monster *VUCUB-CAQUIZ* and his two giant sons, *CABRACÁN* and *ZIPACNÁ*; Hunahpú was beheaded with an obsidian knife by *CAMA ZOTZ* (the killer bat-god) in *ZOTZIHÁ* (the "House of Bats"); and they challenged the Lords of Xibalba to a ball game, in which Hunahpú participated by borrowing a turtle's head – or substituting a squash in another version – and fooling the Lords. When the Lords threw the ball at Hunahpú's head, which was suspended over the court, the ball bounced away, startling a rabbit and causing it to bolt from its hole; in this distraction, Xbalanqué snatched Hunahpú's head and stuck it back on.

The twins defeated the Lords by a ruse: they showed them that they (the twins) were able to cut themselves into pieces and reassemble themselves. The foolish Lords asked the twins to perform this feat on them too. So the twins dismembered the Lords, but left them that way. After this final victory they were reborn and ascended into the sky as the sun (Hunahpú) and the moon (Xbalanqué).

Hunahpú is also the name for the last day of the 20-day month of Quiché Maya calendar, corresponding to Yucatecan Maya *AHAU*. (See also *TWINS & CULTURE HEROES*)

IJ ("reed") see under *QUIJ*.

IK ("breath" or "wind") was the second of the 20 MAYA day-names; it was associated with the rain god and with the number six. The AZTEC and ZAPOTEC equivalent days were *ÉHECATL* and *QUIJ* or *Laa*.

ILAMATECUHTLI, an ancient central Mesoamerican earth and sky goddess, was associated with the earth and with the corn (maize) crop (see also *CENTÉOTL, XILONEN*), as the goddess of the old, dried-up corn ear. She was honoured at the feast *TÍTITL* ("shrunken", "withered", or "wrinkled"). She was also the last of the 13 *LORDS OF THE DAY*.

IMIX ("earth monster") was the first of the 20 MAYA day-names; it was associated with earth, water, water lilies, crocodiles, plenty, vegetation, the number five and "the beginning". AZTEC and ZAPOTEC equivalents were *CIPACTLI* and *CHILLA*.

ITZAMNÁ ("iguana house"), MAYA God D, was a supreme deity, second only to *HUNAB KU*, but less abstract (see also the *OLD FIRE GOD*). In one sense Itzamná and Hunab Ku were the same, and thus embodied another aspect of Maya monotheistic–polytheistic duality. The Maya universe was conceptualized as a reptilian configuration, or house (*na*), whose four sides (or walls), roof (or sky) and floor (or earth) were formed by the huge bodies of iguanas (*itzam*). Unlike Hunab Ku, whose son he was thought to be, Itzamná was frequently portrayed in the codices and in wall-paintings and sculpture, along with his wife *IX CHEBEL YAX*. He was the father of creation and of the gods, of the earth and the sky, and so had both terrestrial and celestial manifestations.

He was a benign deity, and was never accompanied by symbols of death or destruction. He invented writing and taught it to humankind, and was the patron of the arts

ITZAMNÁ, or "iguana house", was the Maya creator god. He is depicted here, carved onto a stone tablet, as an old man with a prominent nose. He is holding the writhing form of a double-headed "sky" or "vision" serpent. (EARLY CLASSIC PERIOD.)

and sciences. His sons were the four *BACABS*, whom Itzamná (or, in another myth, Hunab Ku), at the time of creation, set at the four corners of the earth to support the heavens above it.

Itzamná was ruler of the Maya days *MULUC* ("water") and *AHUA* ("king, monarch, prince, or great lord"; the last and most important day of the Maya 20-day month). He can be identified by the sun glyph, *Kin*, and, more especially, by a glyph whose main element is *ahau*. Itzamná was invoked in several ceremonies during the Maya year: as the sun god Itzamná-*KINICH AHAU* the sacred books were consulted in his name in the month *Uo* for auguries of the coming year; in the month *Zip* he was invoked as the god of medicine, along with *IX CHEL* (the moon

goddess); in the month *Mac* he was worshipped by old men in a ceremony in which the four aspects of the rain god *CHAC* played a role. In the important ceremonies at the Maya New Year, Itzamná was invoked especially to prevent calamities in the coming year.

He was portrayed either as a wise old man with a distinctive "Roman" nose, sunken cheeks and a mouth with only a single tooth, or as the creator god, a giant double-headed iguana/serpent in the sky. As the great fiery two-headed serpent he represented the Milky Way (see also *MIXCÓATL*). His right head, which faced east, symbolized the rising sun and the morning "star" (Venus), and thus life itself, while his left head, which faced the west, symbolized the setting sun and death.

As the supreme Maya deity, Itzamná was the principal patron of Maya rulers. The kings of the great Maya city-states identified themselves with Kinich Ahau, the sun god, himself a manifestation of Itzamná as Lord of the Day. For example, Itzamná-Kinich Ahau was a patron deity of the city of Palenque, where the Temple of the Cross, representing the creation of the world and of the gods, is partly dedicated to him.

ITZCUINTLI ("dog") was the tenth of the 20 AZTEC day-names; it had a favourable augury and its patron deity was *MICTLANTE-CUHTLI*, the god of death. The MAYA and ZAPOTEC equivalent days were *OC* and *TELLA*.

In Mesoamerican belief, dogs would guide the dead across the river to the underworld, and so were often buried along with them. The breed known as *itzcuintli* was also a domesticated dog, raised and eaten by the Aztecs. Calendrical dates and deity associations for *Itzcuintli* included: *1 Itzcuintli*, for the fire god *XIUHTECUHTLI*; *5 Itzcuintli*, for Mictlantecuhtli; *9 Itzcuintli*, for *CHANTICO*, patroness of metalworkers; and *13 Itzcuintli*, as the morning and evening "star" (Venus) *TLAHUIZCALPANTECUHTLI*.

ITZPAPÁLOTL ("obsidian butterfly") was a goddess of *CHICHIMEC* origin. She was the earth goddess and the mother of *MIXCÓATL* ("cloud serpent"), the principal god of the Chichimecs. She ruled the 16th of the 20 AZTEC days, known as *COZCACUAUHTLI* ("vulture"), and, when portrayed with jaguar claws, she represents one of the *TZITZIMIME*, who were the "demons of darkness".

ITZTLACOLIUHQUI was an alternate name for, or manifestation of, the *AZTEC* god *TEZCATLIPOCA*. In this guise he was the "Black Tezcatlipoca", the god of ice and cold, sin and human misery. Itztlacoliuhqui was patron of the day *ÁCATL* ("reed").

ITZTLI ("obsidian knife", the sort used in Aztec ceremonial human sacrifices) was the deputy of *TEZCATLIPOCA*. He was the second of the nine *LORDS OF THE NIGHT*.

IX ("jaguar") was the 14th of the 20 *MAYA* day-names and one of the year-bearing days – there were 13 *Ix* years in a 52-year cycle (see also *CAUAC*, *KAN* and *MULUC*). It was associated with the west cardinal direction and the colour black. Also associated with the *JAGUAR GOD*, it was represented by a glyph of circles (like jaguar-skin spots). The *AZTEC* and *ZAPOTEC* equivalent days were *OCÉLOTL* and *GUECHE*.

IX CHEBEL YAX, or Chebel Yax, *MAYA* Goddess O, was a creator goddess, a supreme deity by proxy, as the wife of *ITZAMNÁ*. She was the mother of all the gods and goddesses. She was patroness of weaving and associated domestic arts – in the codices she was portrayed as an old woman, painted red and holding a hank of cotton or woven cloth – and of painting. She corresponds to *COATLÍCUE* and *TOCI* in the México *AZTEC* pantheon.

IX CHEL, *MAYA* Goddess I, wife of the sun god *KINICH AHAU*, was

ITZTLACOLIUHQUI, one of the many manifestations of Aztec Tezcatlipoca, is depicted here as "Black Tezcatlipoca", the avenging god of justice. (CODEX VATICANUS B.)

moon goddess and had a number of manifestations. She was "she of the rainbow", the benevolent mother goddess, patroness of childbirth and procreation; also of medicine and healing; and, as a water goddess, she displayed benevolence as life-giving rain and malevolence through destructive floods.

Ix Chel was sometimes portrayed as a female warrior standing guard with spear and shield and surrounded by symbols of death and destruction. In other portrayals she was shown as "the angry old woman" emptying her vials of wrath as rainstorms and floods upon humankind, or, even more primevally, as a clawed goddess with a writhing serpent on her head and embroidered crossbones on her skirt. She ruled the day *CABAN* ("earth"). There was a special shrine and place of pilgrimage dedicated to the worship of her on the island of Cozumel, off the east coast of Yucatán.

AZTEC counterparts of her manifestations are in included both *COATLÍCUE* and *COYOLXAUHQUI*.

IXCUINAN, probably of *HUASTEC* origin, was an aspect of the earth goddess *TLAZOLTÉOTL*, representing the earth and fertility.

IXTAB ("goddess of the gallows"), was the *MAYA* goddess of suicide who is usually portrayed in the codices suspended from the sky by a rope noose, her eyes closed in death, and with a black ring – the symbol of decomposition – on her cheek. The Maya believed that those who took their own lives by hanging, warriors killed in battle, women who died giving birth, the victims of human sacrifice (and the priests who killed them) and rulers were all taken directly to paradise by Ixtab. There, in the shade of the cosmic *Yaxché* tree (see *WORLD TREE*), they were free from further work, suffering and want. Consequently, death in battle or in childbirth were considered to be honourable, and suicide by hanging was common amongst those who felt afflicted by sorrows, troubles or sickness. As a malevolent goddess, Ixtab may have been one aspect of *IX CHEL*.

IXTACCÍHUATL, a volcanic cone on the eastern rim of the Basin of Mexico, is sometimes identified in *AZTEC* myth with *TONACATÉPETL* ("sustenance mountain").

IXTLILTON was the *AZTEC* god of health and medical curing. He was the dark-hued brother of *MACUILXÓCHITL* and of *XOCHIPILLI*, the three together being different aspects of good health, pleasure and wellbeing. He was also associated with the dance, presumably because dancing formed a part of many medical cures.

IZCALLI ("resurrection") was the first (or, in some sources, the last) of the *AZTEC* 18 months in the solar year, in which the fire god *XIUHTECUHTLI* was honoured with

IX CHEL, Maya Goddess I, the moon goddess and wife of the sun god Kinich Ahau, is depicted here on a mural in the Temple of the Frescoes at Postclassic Period Tulum, Yucatán.

IXTLILTON, the Aztec god of health and medicine, taught the priests the use of herbal remedies to common ailments. Many such are still in use today, and the ingredients for them are widely sold in local markets.

the sacrifice, every four years, of his impersonators. Other names were *Huauhquiltamalcualiztli* ("eating of stuffed tamales"), *Xochitoca* ("plants, flowers"), *Xóchilhuitl* ("flower feast day") and *Pillahuanaliztli* ("intoxication of the children").

JAGUAR GODS appear widely in Mesoamerican mythology. The jaguar (*Felis onca*; *océlotl* in NAHU-ATL) figures prominently in art and iconography, along with its smaller cousin the ocelot (*Felis pardalis*; *tla-coocélotl* in Nahuatl). As symbols of the supernatural world, jaguar fangs, claws and other features are components of deities from OLMEC civilization onward: for example, as the were-jaguar of Olmec art, half-man, half-human, or in portrayals of Zapotec COCIJO or the Aztec TZITZIMIME. To the AZTECS, the *océlotl* was the NAHUAL (alter ego) of their god TEZCATLIPOCA.

The Jaguar god appears to have been a major deity in the ancient and powerful city of TEOTIHUACÁN from the first to the seventh centuries AD, and later became known by the Nahuatl name TLALCHITTO-NATIUH. It is depicted prominently

ONE OF a line of jaguars prowls along the top of a wall in the main precinct at Tollán (Tula), capital of the Toltecs. (EARLY POSTCLASSIC PERIOD.)

in the Palace of the Jaguars, one of several palaces – perhaps places of cult worship (see also QUETZAL-PAPÁLOTL) – around the Plaza of the Pyramid of the Moon.

From Teotihuacán, the cult of the Jaguar god spread south and east, probably as a by-product of Teotihuacán's extensive trade "empire" and perhaps through military conquest. It was disseminated to the highlands of Guatemala – where the architecture of the MAYA site of Kaminaljuyú also shows strong influence from Teotihuacán in the fourth to seventh centuries AD – and to other Yucatecan Maya cities.

Mythological texts dating from the Postclassic Period identify the jaguar as the night beast, signifying the earth, who devoured the sun each night. The Aztec god TEPEYOLOHTLI (literally "heart of the mountain") was the jaguar god who inhabited the interior of the earth, and possibly originated in the Olmec jaguar cult. Similarly, the Maya god KINICH AHAU was believed to turn into a jaguar at night for his journey through the underworld from sunset to sunrise. The name CHILAM BALAM (the Maya sacred texts) means "jaguar prophet", and the Maya Jaguar god ruled the day AKBAL ("darkness") and the number seven.

The 14th day of the Mesoamerican 20-day month was named after the jaguar/ocelot in the three great civilizations: those of the Maya (IX, "jaguar" or "jaguar skin"), Zapotec (GUECHE, "jaguar") and Aztec (OCÉLOTL, "jaguar"). Many

JAGUAR GODS and imagery featured in the iconography of every Mesoamerican culture, from the Olmecs to the Aztecs: this sculpted jaguar head decorates a wall at Classic Period Maya Copán, Honduras.

other jaguar calendrical references come from Aztec sources: XIPE TOTEC, the god of regeneration, was represented by the date *1 Océlotl*; *4 Océlotl* was the glyph for the First Sun in Aztec cosmology; *5 Océlotl* was patron god of the feather workers (*amentecas*); *8 Océlotl* was the birth date of Tepey-

olohtli; *9 Océlotl* represented the rain god, TLÁLOC; and *13 Océlotl* was a manifestation of the earth goddess, COATLÍCUE.

As a symbol of fierceness, courage and strength, the jaguar was highly revered by the cult or society of the "Jaguar Warriors". (See also CHACMOOL, TEZCATZONTÉCATL AND WARRIOR CULTS)

JONAJI BELACHINA was the Southern ZAPOTEC goddess of the underworld (see BENELABA).

KAN ("ripe corn/maize") was the fourth of the 20 MAYA day-names and one of the year-bearing days – there were 13 *Kan* years in a 52-year cycle (see also CAUAC, IX and MULUC). It was associated with the east cardinal direction, the colour red, and the number eight. The AZTEC and ZAPOTEC equivalent days were CUETZPALLIN and ACHE.

KAN PAUAHTUN
see THE PAUAHTUN.

DUALITY & OPPOSITION

DUALITY PERVADES DESCRIPTIONS OF the gods and goddesses, their world and the world of humans throughout Mesoamerica. Omeyocán, the 13th of the Aztec celestial levels, was literally "the place of the two". The concept of a "creator pair", male and female deities, and of a "first man" and a "first woman" was widespread. Most of the gods and goddesses had a counterpart, or male and female manifestations; for example, the name Ometeotl meant "twice god". More generally, duality – in terms of opposition – was a common feature in Mesoamerican cosmological and practical thought: such as celestial and under-world cosmic stratification, life and death, fertility and barrenness, good and evil, day and night (Day Sun and Night Sun), movement and stillness, sound and silence, order and chaos.

Many of the myths and legends illustrate such oppositions. For example, the Aztecs believed in the daily battle between the sun (Huitzilopochtli) and the moon (Coyolxauhqui) each dawn, and the Maya thought that the rain god Chac brought forth new shoots of corn (maize) and other plants each year, while the death god Ah Puch attempted to nip off the buds and tender new leaves. The opposition of conflict and peace, almost a daily affair, was expressed in the divine rivalry and occasional co-operation of Quetzalcóatl and Tezcatlipoca, and in the legendary history of the political struggles of Mixcóatl, Ce Ácatl Topiltzin Quetzalcóatl-Kukulkán, and Nezahualcóyotl.

THE COMPLEX DEITY Ometeotl (above), "twice god", was the ultimate Aztec expression of duality and opposition – here represented as Tonacatecuhtli, the old man of fate. With both male (Ometecuhtli) and female (Omecíhuatl) manifestations he/she was perceived as a remote creator deity, the source of all creation and power in the universe. He/she represented all aspects of opposition and transcended the concepts of time and space on earth. Such an enigmatic deity was both respected and feared, but was too abstract for normal daily worship.

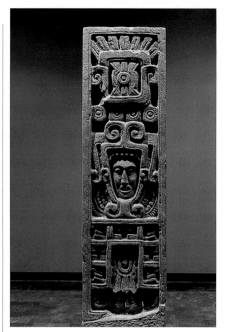

QUETZALCÓATL (left) and his twin Xólotl are divine representations of duality. One of Quetzalcóatl's principal roles was that of Venus as the morning "star", who rose from the jaws of the earth-monster, as depicted here in a stone stela from Azcapotzalco – a contemporary city on the mainland to the northwest of Aztec Tenochtitlán in the Basin of Mexico.

XÓLOTL (left) was in opposition to Quetzalcóatl. Hideous, distorted and burst-eyed, he was a disruptive god who, as Venus the evening "star", would force the sun down into the earth and darkness in the evening.

A TOTONAC STELA (left) from the Gulf Coast depicts Quetzalcóatl in his familiar conical cap. Here he is identifiable as Venus the morning "star" by his sun pendant.

A DIVINE DUALITY was incorporated in the god Tonatiuh (above), the ruler of the Fifth Sun. Like many of the other gods and goddesses, he was both a Lord of the Day and a Lord of the Night. As Tonatiuh, he ruled the day and was Cuauhtlehuánitl the "ascending eagle". His counterpart, Yohual-tecuhtli (or Yohualtonatiuh), was the Night Sun, who passed through the darkness of the underworld, and was Cuauhtémoc the "descending eagle". He is the central face in this Aztec "calendar stone", but scholars disagree about whether he represents Tonatiuh or Yohualtonatiuh on the stone.

L

KAN XIB CHAC
see *THE CHACS*.

KAPOK
see under *WORLD TREE*; see also feature spread *COLOURS & THE CARDINAL DIRECTIONS*.

KAWIL
, the name used in some Classic Period *MAYA* texts, was an alternative for *BOLON DZ'ACAB*, the god of lineage and descent.

KEDO
was the *ZAPOTEC* god of justice, possibly an ominous permutation of *COQUI BEZELAO*, god of death. His *AZTEC* equivalent was *MICTLANTECUHTLI*.

KINICH AHAU
, *MAYA* God G, also known as Ahau Kin and Ah Kinchil ("the sun-face one"), was the Maya sun god and husband of the moon goddess *IX CHEL*. He was closely associated with the supreme deity *ITZAMNÁ* and, in some ways, is regarded as a manifestation of the latter. Kinich Ahau was the day aspect of Itzamná and, as such, symbolized the life of the sun in its daily journey across the sky, a metaphor for life itself. After sunset, as he journeyed through the underworld overnight, he was believed to turn into a jaguar. He

KINICH AHAU, the Maya sun god/ God G, was a source of power and representative of the right to rule. Here, king "Stormy Sky" (upper left) cradles the sun god in his left arm (lower right).
(STELA 31, CLASSIC PERIOD TIKAL.)

was portrayed in Classic and Postclassic Period Maya art with a square eye and a stout nose. His head glyph was a personification of the number four.

Kinich Ahau was worshipped in particular by the rulers of the Maya city-states, who perceived themselves as his descendants, or even assumed his identity. For example, he was a patron deity of the city of Palenque, where the Temple of the Cross, representing the creation of the world and of the gods, is partly dedicated to him. The Maya date inscribed on the temple might refer to his mythical date of birth.

KUKULKÁN
(sometimes Kukulcán), or *GUCUMATZ*, was the *MAYA* translation of the central Mesoamerican "plumed-serpent" deity *QUETZALCÓATL*, and was introduced to Yucatán by the Putún Maya in the 10th century AD. Among the Quiché Maya of the Guatemalan highlands he was known as Gucumatz (see also *TAMOANCHÁN* and *TEPEU*). He was prominent in the Postclassic Period, in keeping with the increasing influence from central Mesoamerica into Mayaland.

Kukulkán was the god of the winds, and of hurricanes. In the *Dresden Codex* he is associated with Venus which, in turn, is Quetzalcóatl in the guise of morning "star"; and a birth date that is recorded on Palenque's Temple of the Cross, *9 Ik*, appears to correspond to an alternative name for Quetzalcóatl, *9 Wind* (Ik, which is the second day in the Maya 20-day month, means "life" or "breath").

In another interpretation Kukulkán is classified as one of the many manifestations of *ITZAMNÁ*, the supreme god. The two manifestations, Kukulkán on the one hand and Quetzalcóatl on the other, appear to represent yet another expression of Mesoamerican duality – one aspect associated with good omens and the other with evil omens – paralleled in the life and death manifestations symbolized by the two-headed celestial serpent spirit of Itzamná.

In legend, Kukulkán was a crypto-historical Maya or Maya-*TOLTEC* leader or culture hero – the "Feathered Serpent". He invaded the Yucatán Peninsula and brought Mexican (that is, Toltec) civilization to the region, in particular to the ancient Maya city-state of Chichén Itzá. There, a temple-pyramid (the Temple of Kukulkán or "El Castillo") was dedicated to him in the Postclassic Period section of the city, which has many structures almost identical to structures in the Toltec capital city of Tollán (modern Tula).

Kukulkán was said to have come by sea, from the west, traditionally in AD 987, having fled from an insurrection in his home city. About 30 years prior to this date, two factions in Tollán struggled for power, one faction lead by Kukulkán (Quetzalcóatl) and the other (victorious) one by *TEZCATLIPOCA* ("smoking mirror"). Intriguingly, Toltec-Aztec sources record that, at about the same time, the legendary king, *CE ÁCATL TOPILTZIN QUETZALCÓATL*, was expelled from Tollán, also having been defeated by Tez-

KUKULKÁN, the "plumed serpent" (the Maya name for Quetzalcóatl), was especially important at Postclassic Period Chichén Itzá, where the Temple of Kukulkán was dedicated to him.

catlipoca. A further clue is provided by the legend of the Itzá, a Chontal Maya people in the Gulf Coast region of Tabasco, which records that they were led by Kukulkán to resettle the more ancient city of Uucil Abnal ("Seven Bushy Place"), which they renamed Chichén Itzá – "[The place] at the rim (edge, mouth) of the well of the Itzás". Kukulkán might, therefore, be more a generic term for a leader than a personal name, and the two figures might have been one and the same.

(The association of Kukulkán the god and the man provides an interesting parallel in ancient American mythology. In the central Andes, the legendary eighth Inca ruler of Cuzco, Viracocha Inca, was similarly identified with their creator god Viracocha.)

LAA
("wind" and "reed") see under *QUIJ*.

LAMAT
(Venus) was the eighth of the 20 *MAYA* day-names; it was associated with the number 12 and was the day of the planet Venus. The *AZTEC* and *ZAPOTEC* equivalent days were *TOCHTLI* and *LAPA*.

LANA
("blackness") was the sixth of the 20 *ZAPOTEC* day-names; the *AZTEC* and *MAYA* equivalent days were *MIQUIZTLI* and *CIMI*.

LAO
("flower") was the last of the 20 *ZAPOTEC* day-names; the *AZTEC* and *MAYA* equivalent days were *XÓCHITL* and *AHAU*.

LAPA
("rabbit") was the eighth of the 20 *ZAPOTEC* day-names; the *AZTEC* and *MAYA* equivalent days were *TOCHTLI* and *LAMAT*.

LAXEE, LAXOO
see *PITAO XOO*.

THE LONG COUNT of the Maya recorded the dates of significant events depicted on stone monuments: here, Shield Jaguar of Yaxchilán is shown preparing for battle in 9.14.12.6.12 (the glyphs above the figures) or 12 February AD 724.

LERA ACUECA (OR ACUECE)

was the Southern ZAPOTEC god of sickness and healing.

LETA AHUILA was the Southern ZAPOTEC name for COQUI BEZELAO.

LETA AQUICHINO, or Lira-aquitzino, was the Southern ZAPOTEC name for COQUI XEE.

LOCIYO was the Southern ZAPOTEC name for COCIJO.

LOCUCUY was the Southern ZAPOTEC name for the corn (maize) god PITAO COZOBI.

THE LONG COUNT, or Initial

Series, was the Maya calendrical system that enabled them to reckon from a date "0", and thus to calculate the exact number of days since time, as they knew it, began. (The zero was invented independently by the Maya; the only two other inventors were the ancient Babylonians and Hindus.) To do this they used a number of cumulative numerical positions or place values: 1 *kin* = 1 day, 1 *uinal* = 20 days (20 *kins*), 1 *tun* = 360 days (18 *uinals*), 1 *katun* = 7,200 days (20 *tuns*), 1 *baktun* = 144,000 days (20 *katuns*) and 1 *piktun* = 2,880,000 days (20 *baktuns*). This system closely resembles a vigesi-

mal counting system, except that the *tun* was only 18 *uinals*, not 20 because, as 360 days, it was closer to the solar year. The Maya zero date was *13.0.0.0.0. 4 Ahau 8 Cumkú* – that is, 13 *baktuns* on the day *4 Ahau* of the month *8 Cumkú*, the day- and month-names being the beginning of the next *baktun*.

Although there are several systems for converting Maya dates to Christian dates, the most accepted system is the Goodman-Martínez-Thompson Correlation (GMT), which renders the Maya date "1" as 13 August 3114 BC.

The Short Count, related to the Long Count, was a shorter date reckoning system that had come into use in the Postclassic Period, long before the Spaniards arrived in Mesoamerica. Instead of counting from a year "1" of 13 *baktuns*, the Short Count began at the end of *katun 13 Ahau* and used only *tuns*, numbered consecutively, and *katuns*, which were named. The *katun* cycles thus established always finished on a day in *Ahau* in the sequence *katun 13 Ahau*, *katun 11 Ahau*, *katun 9 Ahau*, then 7, 5, 3, 1, 12, 10, 8, 6, 2 *Ahau*, and, after 256.43 years, back to *katun 13 Ahau*. The cyclical nature was important, and certain events were expected to be repeated.

THE LONG-NOSED GOD

see BOLON DZ'ACAB.

LOO ("dog"), or *Goloo*, was the 11th of the 20 ZAPOTEC day-names; the AZTEC and MAYA equivalent days were OZOMATLI and CHUEN. At the same time *Loo*, or *Guiloo* ("crow") was also the 16th of the 20 ZAPOTEC day-names; the AZTEC and MAYA equivalent days of this were COZCACUAUHTLI and CIB.

THE LORDS OF THE DAY

(NAHUATL, Tonalteuctin; MAYA, OXLAHUN TI KU) were the 13 deities especially associated with particular day signs, identities and "birds" (*volátiles*, or "flyers") in the Mesoamerican calendar, and with the 13 day-time "hours" of the Aztec day. In the Aztec TONALAMATL (translated as the "Book of the Days") each deity accompanies a day sign

SOME AZTEC SCULPTURES, such as this turquoise and shell inlaid mask, remain as enigmatic as the gods themselves. This might be Quetzalcóatl, ninth Lord of the Day, or Tonatiuh, fourth Lord of the Day.

and a number. The concept of 13 lords might also be related to the 13 heavens of the CREATION MYTH. Some of the gods were simultaneously Lords of the Day and LORDS OF THE NIGHT. Five of the lords presided over the five Aztec cosmic suns, in order of succession: TEZCATLIPOCA, QUETZALCÓATL, TLÁLOC, CHALCHIÚTLICUE and TONATIUH.

The Maya equivalent names of the Oxlahun ti Ku are unknown. However, the Nahuatl names and associated identities and "birds" were as follows:

Nahuatl name	Associated identity	Associated "bird"
1st Lord:	Xiuhtecuhtli/Huehuetéotl as god of fire	the blue hummingbird
2nd Lord:	Tlaltecuhtli as earth god	the green hummingbird
3rd Lord:	Chalchiútlicue as water goddess	the hawk
4th Lord:	Tonatiuh as sun god	the quail
5th Lord:	Tlazoltéotl as goddess of love	the eagle
6th Lord:	Teoyaomiqui/Mictlantecuhtli as god of fallen warriors	the screech owl
7th Lord:	Xochipilli-Centéotl as god of pleasure/of corn (maize)	the butterfly
8th Lord:	Tláloc as god of the rains	the eagle
9th Lord:	Quetzalcóatl as god of the winds	the turkey
10th Lord:	Tezcatlipoca as god of sustenance	the horned owl
11th Lord:	Mictlantecuhtli/Chalmecatecuhtli as god of the underworld	the macaw
12th Lord:	Tlahuizcalpantecuhtli as god of the dawn	the quetzal
13th Lord:	Ilamatecuhtli as goddess of the sky	the parrot

M

THE LORDS OF THE NIGHT

(NAHUATL, Yohualteuctin; MAYA, BOLON TI KU) were the nine gods and goddesses who were especially associated with particular day signs, identities and auguries as good or evil in the Mesoamerican calendar, and with the nine night-time "hours" of the Aztec day. In the Aztec TONALAMATL ("Book of the Days") each deity accompanies a day sign and a number. The concept of nine lords might also be related to the nine layers in the underworld in the CREATION MYTH. Some of the gods were simultaneously LORDS OF THE DAY and Lords of the Night.

The Maya equivalent names of ti Ku are unknown, but the Nahuatl names and associated identities and auguries were:

the sacred ball game (NAHUATL tlachtli; MAYA pok-ta-pok). Macuilxóchitl was identified with the calendrical day-name "5 flower" through his relation to XOCHIPILLI, but was also called Ahuíatl and AHUIATÉOTL, one of the five genies of the south (see AHUIATETEO). In general, the brothers Macuilxóchitl, IXTLILTON and Xochipilli together comprise three aspects of good health, pleasure and well-being,

The MAYA and ZAPOTEC equivalent days were EB and PIJA. Calendrical dates and deities associated with it included: 1 Malinalli, for TLAZOL-TÉOTL as the earth goddess and goddess of love; and 8 Malinalli, for the earth goddess COATLÍCUE.

MANIK

("hand") was the seventh of the 20 MAYA day-names; it was associated with the number 11. The AZTEC and ZAPOTEC equivalent days were MÁZATL and CHINA.

MATLALCUEITL

("lady of the green skirts"), or Matlalcueye, was the second wife of TLÁLOC, the AZTEC god of rain, after TEZCATLIPOCA had abducted his first wife XOCHIQUETZAL. She was the goddess of rain, Matlalcueye, and, in her honour, this name was given to an extinct volcano located between Puebla and Tlaxcala, to the east of the Basin of Mexico; the same volcano was renamed La Malinche during the Spanish colonial period.

Nahuatl name	Associated identity	Augury
1st Lord:	Xiuhtecuhtli/Huehuetéotl as god of fire	unfavourable
2nd Lord:	Itztli as god of obsidian/flint	unfavourable
3rd Lord:	Piltzintecuhtli-Tonatiuh/ as the youthful sun god	
	Piltzintecuhtli-Xochipilli	excellent
4th Lord:	Centéotl as god of corn (maize)	excellent
5th Lord:	Mictlantecuhtli as god of the underworld	favourable
6th Lord:	Chalchiútlicue as water goddess	favourable
7th Lord:	Tlazoltéotl as goddess of love	unfavourable
8th Lord:	Tepeyolohtli-Tezcatlipoca as the heart of the mountain	favourable
9th Lord:	Tláloc as god of the rains	favourable

MACUILXÓCHITL

was one of several AZTEC gods devoted to pleasure. He was patron of games in general, for example the ancient board game of patolli (somewhat like modern pachisi), and of all the celebrations associated with them, but was especially associated with

Macuilxóchitl being the aspect given over more to excess or over-indulgence in pleasure. In this last capacity he was particularly associated with the name Ahuiatéotl.

MALINALLI

("grass") was the 12th of the 20 AZTEC day-names; it had an unfavourable augury and its patron deity was PATÉCATL, god of PULQUE drinking.

MACUILXÓCHITL, an Aztec god of pleasure and patron of games, watches over a patolli game. (EARLY POST-SPANISH-CONQUEST CODEX MAGLIABECCHIANO.)

THE MAYA

inhabited the eastern and southern regions of Mesoamerica, east of the Isthmus of Tehuantepec, including the Yucatán Peninsula (modern Campeche, Yucatán and Quintana Roo states), parts of modern Tabasco and Chiapas states, all of Guatemala and Belize, and western Honduras and El Salvador. They were part of a Macro-Mayan language group that migrated from North America to the Guatemalan highlands by about 2500 BC. During the next 1,000 years, various groups split off and migrated north

into the lowlands of Yucatán and northwest into the Gulf Coast region. More than 30 Maya languages are recognized, including, Quiché, Chontal/ Putún, Itzá and HUASTEC. The Huastecs of the central and northern Gulf Coast eventually became cut off.

Archaeologists traditionally recognize three main geographical and cultural Maya areas, with subdivisions based on architectural and other culturally distinctive styles. These divisions and their areas are: the Highland Maya, who occupied the Guatemalan and western Honduran and El Salvadoran highlands; the Southern Lowland Maya, who occupied the lowlands of central and northern Guatemala, and the adjacent regions of Belize and northwest Honduras and the southern Yucatán Peninsula from the Caribbean to the Atlantic; and the Northern Lowland Maya, who occupied the northern two-thirds of the Yucatán Peninsula. Major cultural subdivisions include the Quiché Maya of the Guatemalan highlands; the Classic Period Petén style of the Southern Lowland Maya in central and northern Guatemala; and the Classic Period Río Bec, Chenes and Puuc styles of the Northern Lowland Maya.

Distinctive Maya cultural traditions in architecture, sculpture, ceramics, wall-painting and other arts developed from the Preclassic Period, especially in the Highland area, into the great Classic Period city-state civilization of the Southern Lowland area and the southern part of the Northern Lowland area. Central Mesoamerican influence, especially on the architectural style of TEOTIHUACÁN, was also of great importance. During the Postclassic Period, the emphasis of Maya civilization shifted into the Northern Lowland area, where numerous city-states dominated the northern Yucatán Peninsula by the time the Spaniards arrived.

In addition to their distinctive urban, political, architectural,

THE MAYA SITE *of Tikal in central Guatemala was one of the longest occupied, and had trade and diplomatic contacts throughout Mesoamerica, including with Teotihuacán in the Basin of Mexico.*

artistic, and religious developments, other important Maya achievements include the development of a sophisticated calendrical system, a hieroglyphic writing system, vigesimal mathematics and the independent invention of the zero and place values in counting.

THE MAYA GODS were numerous.

Among the various Maya groups at least 166 named gods and goddesses are known. Some were universally worshipped, while others were special to particular regions or patrons of specific cities or city-states. In 1904, before linguists had begun to make progress in the decipherment of Maya writing, an alphabetical letter list of some of the principal Maya deities was proposed by P. Schellhaus: A = AH PUCH or Yum Cimil, B = CHAC, C = XAMAN EK, D = ITZAMNÁ, E = AH MUN or Yum Kaax, F = BULUC CHABTÁN, G = KINICH AHAU, H = CHICCAN god, I = IX CHEL, (J was not used), K = BOLON DZ'ACAB, L = OLD BLACK GOD, M = EK CHUAH, N = PAUAHTUN, O = IX CHEBEL YAX, (P was not used), Q = ETZ'NAB, R = formerly used for Buluc Chabtán. (See GOD A to GODDESS O).

A thematic classification of the Maya gods and goddesses is proposed by Linda Schele and Mary Ellen Miller, in which they all fall into one of four categories: worldly phenomena, anthropomorphs, zoomorphs and animals. A deity can be manifested in more than one form and, while the imagery of some deities appear to have remained fixed, others clearly changed, developed, or even "aged" through time.

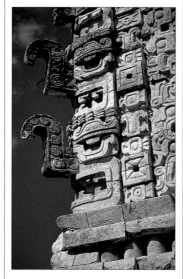

CHAC, *the god of rain, was of crucial importance to Maya daily life and agriculture; he was frequently featured in repetitive, stacks of masks, as at Classic Period Uxmal, on the corners of buildings.*

MAYÁHUEL, the AZTEC goddess

of the *maguey* or *agave* plant (*Agave americana*), was "mother" of the CENTZÓNTOTOCHTIN (the numberless gods of drunkenness), and, by association, of the alcoholic drink, PULQUE, made from it. She was thought to have "400 breasts" to feed them – the NAHUATL root word *centzontli* means, literally, "without number". With her consort PATÉCATL she presided over drunken excess. She ruled the day TOCHTLI ("rabbit"), the eighth of the 20-day Aztec month, and was represented by the glyph *Ce Tochtli* ("one rabbit").

The origin of *pulque* is explained in the story of Mayahuél's abduction by the wind god ÉHECATL, which also relates the introduction of physical love to the world. Having helped to bring corn (maize) and other edible plants to the notice of humankind, the gods concluded that something further was needed to provide humans with pleasure and to cause them to sing and dance in honour of the gods. QUETZALCÓATL, in the guise of Éhecatl, persuaded the beautiful young virgin Mayáhuel to leave her abode in the sky, where she was guarded by the fierce "grandmother" goddess TZITZIMITL, and to descend to the earth with him. The two became lovers, embracing each other in the form of a tree with two entwined branches.

Tzitzimitl pursued the couple but arrived too late to prevent the union so, in her wrath, she split the tree in two, destroying the branch representing Mayáhuel and feeding the shreds to her demon servants, the TZITZIMIME. Éhecatl, however, remained unharmed; resuming his former shape, he gathered together Mayáhuel's bones and planted them in a field where they grew, and lived on, as the *maguey* used to produce the white "wine" known as *pulque*.

MÁZATL ("deer") was the sev-

enth of the 20 AZTEC day-names; it had a favourable augury and its patron deity was the rain god TLÁLOC. The MAYA and ZAPOTEC equivalent days were MANIK and CHINA. The deer was a symbol of fire and drought. Calendrical dates and deities associated with it included: *1 Mázatl*, for the creator deities; *4 Mázatl*, for ITZTLACOLI-UHQUI; and *5 Mázatl*, for XÓLOTL.

THE MAZEHUALOB were the

MAYA peoples themselves, the inhabitants of the Third World in Maya creation (see HUNAB KU and CREATION MYTHS).

MBAZ was a ZAPOTEC earth

god/goddess and the Zapotec seventh or eighth LORD OF THE NIGHT. He/she was the equivalent of the Aztec deities TEPEYOLOHTLI and TLAZOLTÉOTL.

MDI was a ZAPOTEC rain god and

the Zapotec ninth LORD OF THE NIGHT, with aspects similar in nature to those of the Teotihuacano and AZTEC deity known as TLÁLOC (see also COCIJO).

MEN ("moon", "wise one", or

"eagle") was the 15th of the 20 MAYA day-names; it was associated with the aged moon goddess, patroness of weaving. The AZTEC and ZAPOTEC equivalent days were CUAUHTLI and NAA.

MAYÁHUEL, *goddess of the maguey or agave plant is seen here beside an octecomatl (pulque vessel). Note the serpent coiled around its base, and the stake piercing a human heart). The brew is being tasted by the figure on the left.*

MÉXICA see *AZTEC*.

MEZTLI was the *NAHUATL* name for the "moon". In the *AZTEC CREATION MYTH*, the moon and the Fifth Sun were created in an assembly of the gods at *TEOTIHUACÁN*. The moon was the ascendant god *TECUCIZTÉCATL*, who leapt into the ceremonial fire after his brother *NANAHUATZIN*, who became the sun. The moon shone as bright as the sun until one of the gods threw a rabbit (*tochtli*) into its "face" – rather than a "man in the moon", Mesoamerican peoples perceived the outlines of a rabbit in the shadows and craters of the moon, crouching on its back legs with its ears prominent to the right.

The word is also an element in the Aztec names *Meztlipohualli* ("counting of the lunar months") and *MEZTLIAPÁN* ("Lake of the Moon"), and was the term applied to the Aztec god *TEZCATLIPOCA* in his nocturnal manifestation.

MEZTLIAPÁN ("Lake of the Moon") was Lake Texcoco, the central lake in the Basin of Mexico. Near its western shore lay the island where *HUITZILOPOCHTLI* gave the México *AZTECS* the sign of his representative, the eagle alighting on a nopal cactus (prickly pear), clutching a serpent in its claw, to show them where to build their capital, *TENOCHTITLÁN*.

MICCAILHUITONTLI ("small feast of the dead") was the tenth (or, in some sources, ninth) of the 18 months in the *AZTEC* solar year, in which the gods and goddesses in general were propitiated, but especially the war god *HUITZILO-POCHTLI*, whose image was covered in flowers, and the "smoking mirror" *TEZCATLIPOCA*. It was also called *Tlaxochimaco* ("the surrendering of flowers").

MICTECACÍHUATL was the wife of *MICTLANTECUHTLI*, god of the underworld.

MEZTLI was the Aztec name for the moon. The rabbit, thrown into its face to dull its brightness after creation, can be seen, with some imagination, in the light and dark features of the surface.

MICTLÁN ("that which is below us"), ruled by *MICTLANTECUHTLI* and *MICTECACÍHUATL*, was one of the *AZTEC* underworlds and part of the three-part Aztec universe, comprising Mictlán, *TLALTÍCPAC* and *TOPÁN*. As opposed to other abodes of the dead – for example the underworld of warriors who died in battle (east) or of women who died while giving birth (west) – Mictlán was the specific destination of the souls of those who died a natural death. It was believed that the spirits of the deceased passed through nine magical trials before finding repose. After four years, however, the soul was believed to disappear forever. The *MAYA* equivalents were *MITNAL* and *XIBALBA*.

MICTLANTECUHTLI, one of the most popular of the *AZTEC* pantheon, was honoured throughout central Mesoamerica. He was the god of death and, together with his wife Mictecacíhuatl, ruled the underworld, *MICTLÁN*, the place of silence and rest from the toils of the world. As the god of death, he was appropriately portrayed covered in bones, or as a skeleton, and wearing a skull mask with ear plugs of human bones. He had black, curly hair (unusual in a land of straight-haired people), star-like eyes that enabled him to see in the dark, and was sometimes depicted wearing a conical bark-paper hat and clothes made of bark-paper. Animals accompany him in the codices – owls (symbols of war and death), bats and spiders.

He was instrumental in the origin of humans in the account of the Fifth Sun of the Aztec *CREATION MYTH*, in which, being reluctant to relinquish the bones of the people of the previous world, he tried to delay *QUET-ZALCÓATL* by setting him several tasks to perform.

Mictlantecuhtli was the ruler of the day *ITZCUINTLI* ("dog"), the tenth day in the 20-day month, the fifth *LORD OF THE NIGHT*, and variously the sixth or 11th *LORD OF THE DAY*. Both in form and domain he was the equivalent to Maya god *YUM CIMIL* (see also *AH PUCH*).

When Hernán Cortés landed in Mexico, the Aztec ruler Moctezuma II Xocoyotzin was told by his priests that the news of inextinguishable fires, odd flights of birds and the appearance of comets in the night sky portended impending disaster, so

MICTLANTECUHTLI, the god of death, was one of the most popular Mesoamerican deities. In this example he wears a bark-paper hat and sits with staring eyes, contemplating the futures of souls. (CLASSIC PERIOD TOTONAC.)

he ordered human sacrifices and offered the flayed skins of the victims to Mictlantecuhtli. It was thought that, in his fear and uncertainty, he was seeking the peace of Mictlán, for the Spaniards' arrival appeared to be the return of Quetzalcóatl from the east, and the beginning of the end of the world of the Fifth Sun, as foretold in Aztec myth and legend. (See also *COLOURS & THE CARDINAL DIRECTIONS*)

MIQUIZTLI ("death") was the sixth of the 20 *AZTEC* day-names; it had an unfavourable augury and its patron deity was the moon god *TECCIZTÉCATL*. The *MAYA* and *ZAPO-TEC* equivalents were *CIMI* and *LANA*.

In the codices, *Miquiztli* is shown as a skeleton or as a hollow-eyed skull with a hole in the side where the pole for the *TZOMPANTLI* rack would have been inserted. Calendrical dates and deity associations

N

included: *1 Miquiztli*, for *TEZCAT-LIPOCA* as the god of sustenance; *5 Miquiztli*, for the sun god *TONATIUH* or "flower prince" *XOCHIPILLI*; and *13 Miquiztli*, for the god of death.

MITNAL, the lowest of the nine Lowland *MAYA* underworlds, was ruled by *AH PUCH*. The word might be derived from the *AZTEC NAHU-ATL* word *MICTLÁN*, the northern Mesoamerican underworld. It was also the equivalent of the Quiché Maya underworld, *XIBALBA*.

MIXCÓATL ("cloud serpent") was the legendary leader of the *TOLTEC-CHICHIMEC* peoples – his full name was *CE TÉCPATL MIXCÓATL* – and the father of *CE ÁCATL TOP-ILTZIN QUETZALCÓATL*. After his murder by a rival faction he was deified as the god of the hunt, and in his deified state acquired several divine wives. The Chichimec goddess *ITZPAPÁLOTL* ("obsidian butterfly"), an earth goddess, was his mother, and, perhaps in the same guise as the earth goddess, *COATLÍCUE* ("serpent lady") was also said to be his wife. He was patron deity of the *TLAXCALTECANS*.

In Toltec legendary history, as interpreted by the Aztecs, the hero Ce Técpatl Mixcóatl led his people into the Basin of Mexico, where they established the city of Cul-huacán and founded the Toltec dynasty. In this account he took to wife a local Nahua woman named *CHIMALMAN*, whom he symboli-cally impregnated with an arrow from his bow. After his death she gave birth to Ce Ácatl Topiltzin Quetzalcóatl, the legendary foun-der and ruler of Tollán (Tula), a new Toltec capital to the northwest of the Basin of Mexico.

As the "cloud serpent" Mixcó-atl's name was also applied to the Milky Way (see also *ITZAMNÁ*).

(The leadership and the later deification of Mixcóatl provide an interesting parallel in ancient Amer-ican mythology. The association of Viracocha, the creator god, and

Viracocha Inca, the eighth ruler of Cuzco, assumed deification of a sort after an encounter with the cre-ator god in a time of tribulation.)

THE MIXTECS were the peo-ples who settled in the southern highlands and adjacent coast of central Mesoamerica, in and around the Valley of Oaxaca (in the present Mexican state of that name). The region is subdivided into the Mixteca Baja (western and northwestern Oaxaca), the Mixteca Alta (eastern and southern Oaxaca) and the Mixteca de la Costa (the Pacific coastal lowlands). They spoke one of the languages of the Oto-Zapotecan group in the region.

By about AD 1000, in the early Postclassic Period, they had estab-lished a highly developed urban civilization based on a loose con-federation of city-states. Some of their most famous cities were Coix-tlahuaca, Teozacoalco, Tilantongo, Tlaxiaco, Tututepec, Yanhuitlán, Mitla and Yagul, only the last two of which survive as well-preserved ruins. Having thus established themselves in the former territory of the Classic Period *ZAPOTEC* state, they made use of the ancient tombs in the Zapotec capital, Monte Albán, to bury their own rulers with rich trappings (the most famous of these is Tomb 7). They also built new cruciform tombs with polychrome murals at Mitla, which later became known as the "city of the dead". Their dynastic history can be traced back to AD 692 and includes the legendary ruler *EIGHT DEER TIGER CLAW* (AD 1011–63) of Tilantongo.

Although conquered and sub-jugated by the *AZTECS* in the 15th century, their culture had a strong influence on the latter, in particu-lar the exquisite craftsmanship of their polychrome pottery, the mas-tery of Mixtec metalsmiths in gold-working and their skill and artistry in compiling painted codices (seven of the surviving pre-Spanish-conquest codices are

Mixtec). Mixtec deities were, for the most part, those of the central Mesoamerican pantheon, although they called their rain god *DZAHUI*.

THE MONKEY-FACED GOD was probably the *MAYA* god *XAMEN EK*, who was god of the North Star. As such he ruled the Maya day *CHUEN* ("monkey").

The two Maya brothers, *HUN BATZ* and Hun Chouen were also "monkey-faced gods", having been turned into monkeys in the forest by the trickery of their younger, twin brothers *HUNAHPÚ* and *XBAL-ANQUE*. The skills of Hun Batz and Hun Chouen were honoured by the Maya in the codices by depict-ing them as the patrons of the arts and crafts, and of artists, musicians and dancers.

MSE was a *ZAPOTEC* earth god-dess and the Zapotec seventh *LORD OF THE NIGHT*; she resembled *MBAZ* and Aztec *TLAZOLTÉOTL*.

MULUC ("water") was the ninth of the 20 *MAYA* day-names and one of the year-bearing days – there were 13 *Muluc* years in a 52-year cycle (see also *CAUAC*, *IX* and *KAN*). It was associated with the north cardinal direction and the colour white. It was a favourable day, rep-resented by the glyph of a fish head. The *AZTEC* and *ZAPOTEC* equi-valents were *ATL* and *NIZA* or *Queza*.

MIXCÓATL, the legendary Toltec-Chichimec leader and god of the hunt, is shown here with raised atl-atl *(spear-thrower) and a clutch of hunting darts, and is associated with the jaguar, whose hunting prowess was greatly admired.* (CODEX VATICANUS B.)

NAA ("eagle") was the 15th of the 20 *ZAPOTEC* day-names; the *AZTEC* and *MAYA* equivalent days were *CUAUHTLI* and *MEN*.

NAHUAL was the *NAHUATL* word for "alter ego", used to describe the dual nature of many Mesoamerican deities and for alternative aspects or manifestations of the deities. Nahual or Nahualli was the soul companion of a person, that usu-ally took the form of an animal (for example, the nahual of *ITZPA-PÁLOTL* was a deer). The term is still used among the present-day Maya.

NAHUATL, or Nauatl, a dialect of the Nahua language group (which also includes Nahual and Nahuat), is one of the Uto-Aztecan languages of ancient Mesoamerica and is still spoken by nearly 1.5 million people in central and western Mexico. "Classical" Nahu-atl was the language of the *TOLTECS* and *AZTECS* of central Mesoamerica and became the *lingua franca* of ancient Mesoamerica, spread by Toltec and, later, Aztec conquest and trade.

NANAHUATZIN, the weak and syphilitic god, was the special deity of twins and physically deformed people. He played a key role in the story of the creation of the Fifth Sun in the Aztec *CREATION MYTH*.

The creation of the (present) Fifth Sun and of the moon was the result of the self-sacrificial deaths by cremation of the gods Nanahuatzin – the poor and syphilitic one, weak, humble and allegedly cowardly – and *TECUCIZTÉCATL*, his rich, healthy, haughty and headstrong twin brother. The gods had assembled at the ancient city of *TEOTIHUACÁN* after the destruction of the Fourth Sun and built a huge sacrificial fire. The proud and noble Tecuciztécatl boasted that he would sacrifice himself in the fire and rise again as the sun. When faced with the flames, however, he lost his nerve and only jumped after he was inspired by Nanahuatzin, who leaped into the fire first. Consequently, it was Nanahuatzin who rose as the sun, while Tecuciztécatl emerged as the moon. Nevertheless, both were equally bright until one of the gods threw a rabbit (*tochtli*) into the moon's face, dulling its shine (see also *MEZTLI*). Still motionless, the sun and moon were stirred, in one version of the story, by *ÉHECATL* (who blew on them) and, in another version by *TLAHUIZCAL-PANTECUHTLI* (who threw a dart at the sun in outrage at the latter's demand for human blood sacrifice).

Nanahuatzin also played a crucial role in bringing corn (maize) and other edible plants to humankind, when he was selected by the old diviners *OXOMOCO* and *CIPAC-TONAL* to split open *TONACATÉPETL* (literally "sustenance mountain"), which he accomplished with the help of the four *TLÁLOCS*.

NAPPATECUHTLI ("four times lord"), or Nappateuctli, was one of the four directional *TLÁLOCS* and the patron deity of Chalco, and of the artisans who wove reed matting.

He was particularly prone to produce draughts.

NAUAL see *NAHUAL*.

NAUATL see *NAHUATL*.

NDAN, the *ZAPOTEC* deity of oceans and one of the nine *LORDS OF THE NIGHT*, was depicted both as god and a goddess, or even as a bisexual being. His/her messenger was *NDOZIN*.

NDO'YET was a *ZAPOTEC* god of death and one of the nine Zapotec day names for sacred objects or natural forces.

NDOZIN, a *ZAPOTEC* god of death and justice, was one of the nine *LORDS OF THE NIGHT* and the messenger of *NDAN*.

NEMONTEMI, or Nentli ("worthless"), was the *NAHUATL* term for the five ill-omened days at the end of the *AZTEC* solar calendar year. With 18 months of 20 days each (that is, 360 days, the *XÍHUTL*), there were five days left over to complete the sun–earth cycle. These were considered a time to be wary and to avoid the chance of misfortune. The *MAYA* equivalent was the *UAYEB*.

NENE, first woman (see under *CREATION MYTHS*).

NENTLI see *NEMONTEMI*.

NEW FIRE CEREMONY see *TOXIUHMOLPILIA*.

NEZAHUALCÓYOTL ("Fasting Coyote") was a mid-15th-century king of *TEXCOCO* and advocate of the abstract concept of the deity *TLOQUE NAHUAQUE*. Nevertheless, in deference to his people, he was careful not to neglect the conventional gods and goddesses of the *AZTEC* pantheon. A ruler given to recondite, metaphysical thought on the nature of things, the pursuit

THE OCÉLOTL (Nahuatl for "jaguar") was an important figure in Mesoamerican religion and art. The océlotl was the mascot of the jaguar warriors and is frequently depicted on temple walls.

(EARLY POSTCLASSIC PERIOD, TOLLÁN [TULA])

of peace and the rule of order, Nezahualcóyotl was wary of the increasing belligerence of the Méxica and tried to stem their aggression, condemning especially the *XOCHIYAÓYOTL* ("Flowery War"). He was a gifted poet, and sponsored and fostered the arts and crafts, music, poetry and history. He was the first to codify and set down the ancient laws of Texcoco and established what was probably Mesoamerica's first library. In partnership with the rulers of neighbouring city-states, he also carried out public works, including building a dyke across Lake Texcoco and an aqueduct to bring fresh water from Chapultepec (west of *TENOCHTITLÁN*) to the Aztec capital. In and around Texcoco he built a magnificent ten-level temple-pyramid to represent the heavens, a special temple dedicated to Tloque Nahuaque, and a summer palace at Texcotzingo (in the foothills east of Texcoco) that included numerous temples, fountains, aqueducts from mountain springs, and baths.

NIZA, or Queza, ("water") was ninth of the 20 *ZAPOTEC* day-names; the *AZTEC* and *MAYA* equivalent days were *ATL* and *MULUC*.

NOÇANA see *COZAANA*.

NOHUIÇANA see *NOHUICHANA*.

NOHUICHANA, an alternative name for *HUECHAANA*, especially in relation to childbirth and creation.

OC ("dog") was the tenth of the 20 *MAYA* day-names; it was associated with Venus as the evening "star". The *AZTEC* and *ZAPOTEC* equivalent days to *Oc* were *ITZCUINTLI* and *TELLA*.

OCÉLOTL ("jaguar") was the 14th of 20 *AZTEC* day-names; it had an unfavourable augury and its patron was the earth goddess *TLAZ-OLTÉOTL*. The *MAYA* and *ZAPOTEC* equivalents were *IX* and *GUECHE*.

In Mesoamerican myth it was the *océlotl* (as the earth) that devoured the sun at the end of the day, and therefore represented the night (see also *JAGUAR GODS*). It was also the mascot of the Jaguar *WARRIOR CULT* (see also *THE RITUAL BALL GAME*). Calendrical dates and deity associations included: *1 Océlotl*, for *XIPE TOTEC*, the "flayed god"; *4 Océlotl*, for the First Sun of the Aztec *CREATION MYTH*; *5 Océlotl*, as patron of featherworkers (*amantecas*); *8 Océlotl*, the mythical birth date of *TEPEYOLOHTLI*; *9 Océlotl*, for the rain god *TLÁLOC*; and *13 Océlotl*, for the earth goddess *COATLÍCUE*.

OCHPANITZTLI ("road sweeping") was the 12th (or, in some sources, the 11th) of the 18 months in the *AZTEC* solar year, in which a harvest festival was held to worship the old earth goddess and mother of the gods *TETEOINNAN-TOCI* and her corn- (maize-) goddess manifestation as *CHICOMECÓATL*. Rituals included the slaying of honoured war captives in the *TLACALILIZTLI* arrow sacrifice.

Ochpanitztli was also called *Tenahuatiliztli* ("clearing up and putting in order").

THE OLD BLACK GOD, *MAYA* God L, a rather enigmatic deity, was a lord of the Maya underworld, *XIBALBA*, a god of death and ruler of the day *AKBAL* ("darkness"),

THE OLMEC civilization of the Gulf Coast was the first in Mesoamerica to build ceremonial precincts. Olmec rulers were portrayed by colossal stone heads, each with distinctive facial features and head gear, such as at San Lorenzo Tenochtitlán (left); and La Venta (far left).

third day of the 20-day Maya month. He is usually associated with *AH PUCH*, possibly as his predecessor or as one of his companions. The codices show him smoking a rolled-leaf cigar and wearing a *Muan*-bird (or *Moan*-) headdress, but also sometimes with a merchant's bundle, which associates him with *EK CHUAH* and *XAMEN EK*.

THE OLD FIRE GOD was a

primitive deity whose worship began early in Mesoamerica with the *OLMECS*. Their *GOD I* is thought to have been his prototype. He was later included in the Maya pantheon as *ITZAMNÁ* and in the Aztec pantheon as *HUEHUETÉOTL* and *XIUHTECUHTLI* (his weapon and sign of office was the *XIUHATLATL* spear-thrower). At TEOTIHUACÁN, he might have been the consort of the *TEOTIHUACÁN SPIDER WOMAN*.

OLLIN ("movement" or "earth-

quake") was 17th of the 20 *AZTEC* day-names; it had a neutral augury and its patron was *XÓLOTL*, Venus the evening "star". The *MAYA* and *ZAPOTEC* equivalents were *CABAN* and *XOO*.

Calendrical dates and deity associations for this day included *1 Ollin*, for Xólotl and *4 Ollin*, for the Fifth Sun of the Aztec *CREATION MYTH*, which was destined to end in catastrophic earthquakes.

THE OLMEC civilization of the

Mexican Gulf Coast region, known as the Olmec Heartland, was the first to arise in Mesoamerica and to build monumental temple mounds and ceremonial precincts. Their antecedents are unknown, nor do we know what they called themselves – the word Olmec means "rubber people" in *NAHUATL*, the language of the *AZTECS*.

Olmec civilization flourished in the Preclassic Period, their most famous Gulf Coast sites being occupied in an overlapping sequence: first at San Lorenzo Tenochtitlán (occupied *c.* 1450–400 BC; flourished *c.* 1150–900 BC) and at La Venta (occupied *c.* 2250–500 BC; flourished *c.* 900–500 BC), then at Tres Zapotes (occupied *c.* 1000–50 BC; flourished *c.* 600–50 BC).

At these sites, in addition to monumental precincts, they carved and erected 17 colossal stone heads (including one found at the site of Cobata), often using stone that had been brought from considerable distances away, and each one so distinct in its facial features and its head-gear that they are thought to be the portraits of actual Olmec rulers. Other distinguishing monuments that have survived include carved stone altars and stelae and turquoise mosaic floor masks, as well as a wealth of stone and ceramic figurines.

The Olmec art style and architectural organization of ceremonial spaces were exported in the early stages of long-distance trading networks and, possibly, empire-building. Their influence spread north along the Gulf Coast and inland to the Basin of Mexico and the present states of Morelos, Guerrero and Oaxaca south of it.

That they exercised a certain amount of power in these areas is indicated by the existence of "gateway" ceremonial communities, such as Chalcatzingo, which was sited at a pass giving access into the Valley of Morelos and where they carved the faces of numerous boulders with feline beings and figures of power and rulership, and Teopantecuanitlán, 300 miles (480 km) west of La Venta, where four huge Olmec feline faces were carved on stone blocks. In Guerrero they painted mythological beings onto the walls of the caves of Oxtotitlán and Juxtlahuaca. (See also *COLOURS & THE CARDINAL DIRECTIONS, THE RITUAL BALL GAME*)

THE OLMECS were the first to adopt the Mesoamerican reverence for jade and turquoise as the most precious stones. Long-distance trade routes were established to obtain them, and control of their sources became an important feature of the politico-economic structure. (PRECLASSIC PERIOD CEREMONIAL JADE MASK.)

THE OLMEC civilization of the Gulf Coast was the first in Mesoamerica to build ceremonial precincts. Olmec rulers were portrayed by colossal stone heads, each with distinctive facial features and head gear, such as at San Lorenzo Tenochtitlán (left); and La Venta (far left).

THE OLMEC GODS have no

names that have come down to us, so anthropologists have designated them by numbers (see *GOD I* to *GOD X*). No Olmec deities can be categorically defined as male or female, but many of their attributes and much of their imagery can be seen in the gods and goddesses of later Mesoamerican civilizations, and they are therefore regarded as the sources of many aspects of pan-Mesoamerican mythology and religion, and as prototypes of later gods and goddesses.

OMÁCATL, a manifestation of

the *AZTEC TEZCATLIPOCA*, presided over banquets and feasting. His name *Two ÁCATL* means "Two Reed".

OMECÍHUATL, or *CITLALÍCUE*,

Citlalinícue or Tonacacíhuatl, was the female counterpart of *OMETE-CUHTLI*, and therefore the female aspect of the androgynous duality *OMETEOTL*. She was a primitive central Mesoamerican creator deity.

COLOURS & THE CARDINAL DIRECTIONS

THE MESOAMERICAN WORLD, all living things, and the gods and goddesses were grouped according to the four cardinal directions on earth, and personified by special colours that were assigned to these directions. The Mesoamerican fifth (or fifth/sixth) cardinal direction was the centre, and went up to the heavens or celestial layers of the universe, and down into the earth and the underworld layers. The numbers four (representing the four horizontal directions) and five (for the fifth direction) were thus especially important in Mesoamerican cosmology. The Maya centre was a *Ceibe* tree (*Bombax pentandra*), called either *Yaxché* or *Kapok*, whose roots penetrated the underworlds, and whose branches spread into the celestial levels. The Aztec centre was ruled by the god and goddess Ometecuhtli and Omecíhuatl, unified as Ometeotl, literally "twice god".

The colour–direction combinations varied from one region to another. In addition to colours, the Aztecs also associated particular trees, birds or animals, day and year signs, deities, and favourable or unfavourable auguries with each direction. For the Maya, death ruled from the south; for the Aztecs, death ruled from the north.

MAYA DIRECTIONS AND COLOURS

	North	South	East	West
Name	*Xamen*	*Nohol*	*Likin*	*Chikin*
Colour	*zac* (white)	*kan* (yellow)	*chac* (red)	*ek* (black)
Year-bearing day-name	*Muluc*	*Cauac*	*Kan*	*Ix*

AZTEC DIRECTIONS, COLOURS AND ASSOCIATIONS

	North	South	East	West
Name	*Mictlampa*	*Huitzlampa*	*Tlapcopa*	*Cihuatlampa*
Colours	black (or red, or white)	blue (or red, or white)	red (or yellow, or blue-green)	white (or yellow, or blue-green)
Sky-bearing deity	a fire god	Mictlantecuhtli	Tlahuizcalpantecuhtli	Éhecatl-Quetzalcóatl
Trees	*ceibe* or *mesquite*	willow or palm	*ceibe* or *mesquite*	cypress or *maguey* (*agave*)
Birds/animals	eagle or jaguar	parrot or rabbit	quetzal or eagle	hummingbird or serpent
Days	*Océlotl, Miquiztli, Técpatl, Itzcuintli, Éhecatl*	*Xóchitl, Malinalli, Cuetzpalin, Cozcacuauhtli, Tochtli*	*Cipactli, Ácatl, Cóatl, Ollin, Atl*	*Mázatl, Quiáhuitl, Ozomatli, Calli, Cuauhtli*
Year	*Técpatl*	*Tochtli*	*Ácatl*	*Calli*
Augury	unfavourable	indifferent	favourable	"too humid"

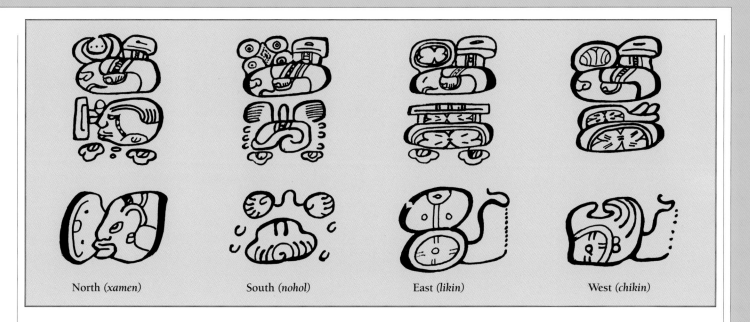

North (*xamen*)   South (*nohol*)   East (*likin*)   West (*chikin*)

THE FOUR CARDINAL DIRECTIONS *(above) were recognized by the Maya, who had established colour associations for them by the early Classic Period. Their fascination with them possibly originated with the Olmecs, to whom the directions clearly formed an important part of their ideas regarding the cosmos – for example, at La Venta they laid out jade and serpentine celts in crosses oriented to the four directions. At early Classic Period Maya Río Azul, Guatemala, directional glyphs painted on the walls of Tomb 12 (top row) were confirmed by well-known Postclassic Period glyphs from, among other sources, the Dresden Codex (bottom row).*

THE AZTECS *and other central Mesoamericans were equally convinced of the importance of the directions, but were less uniform and consistent in their colour associations. The Aztecs, however, assigned four sky-bearing gods to the four quadrants of the earth: the Old Fire God (above left) supporting the north (here represented in the* Codex Borbonicus*), Mictlantecuhtli (left) supporting the south (in the* Codex Magliabecchiano*), Tlahuizcalpantecuhtli (above) supporting the east (in the* Codex Cospi*) and Éhecatl (far left) supporting the west (in a buccal-masked and conical-capped stone figurine).*

P

OMETECUHTLI, also called Citlatona and Tonacatecuhtli, was the male counterpart of *OMECÍHUATL*, therefore the male aspect of the androgynous duality *OMETEOTL*. He was a primitive central Mesoamerican creator god, perceived as a remote power. With his consort Omecíhuatl he lived in the 13th level of the *AZTEC* heaven, *OMEYOCÁN* and was patron of the day *Cipactli* ("crocodile"), representative of the earth and the first day of the Aztec 20-day month.

The sons of Ometecuhtli and Omecíhuatl were the four corners of the earth, the cardinal directions, and their associated colours: north=Black *TEZCATLIPOCA*; south =Blue Tezcatlipoca (or *HUITZILOPOCHTLI*); east=Red Tezcatlipoca (or *XIPE TOTEC* or *CAMAXTLI*); and west=White Tezcatlipoca (alternatively *QUETZALCÓATL*).

As Tonacatecuhtli ("Lord of Sustenance"), he rewarded the gods Quetzalcóatl and Tezcatlipoca for helping to create the Fifth Sun (see *CREATION MYTHS*), making them lords of the heavens and the stars.

OMETEOTL, literally "twice god" or "dual lord" in *NAHUATL*, was a primordial central Mesoamerican "notional" deity, two gods in one, but indivisible, a bisexual divinity expressive of androgynous duality.

The source of all existence and the creative energy from which all the other gods and goddesses descended, he/she was above the events of the world, beyond the heavens and the stars, and outside of space and time. His/her realm was *OMEYOCÁN*, the "place of the two". Ometeotl was the supreme being, the unity of opposites: male (*OMETECUHTLI*) and female (*OMECÍHUATL*), light and dark, action and inaction, movement and stillness, sound and silence, order and chaos. Such a concept of "first principle" was too abstract for daily, active cult worship, and was used only by *AZTEC* (and presumably earlier) priests in their cosmic defi-

nition and divinations. (See also *DUALITY & OPPOSITION* and *TLOQUE NAHUAQUE*)

OMETOCHTLI ("two rabbit") was a generic calendrical term for *THE CENTZÓNTOTOCHTIN* ("400 rabbits") or for *TEPOZTÉCATL* (a *PULQUE* god of the city of Tepoztlán).

OMEYOCÁN (literally "place of the two") was the supreme, 13th, heaven in the *AZTEC* (central Mesoamerican) cosmos and the realm of *OMETEOTL*, the supreme expression of androgynous duality. It was the abode of *OMETECUHTLI* (maleness) and *OMECÍHUATL* (femaleness), and of light/dark, action/inaction, movement/stillness, sound/silence, order/chaos and all other dualities and oppositions.

In the Aztec world of the Fifth Sun (their present) the two great opposed spirits of world – represented by *TEZCATLIPOCA* and *QUETZALCÓATL* – were in temporary exile from Omeyocán. They were associated with the four corners of the earth as the cardinal directions and their associated colours: north=Black Tezcatlipoca; south=Blue Tezcatlipoca; east= Red Tezcatlipoca; and west=White Tezcatlipoca. Alternatively, they were Quetzalcóatl, who would return from the east to inaugurate a new religion and world order.

OPA ("cold") was the 18th of the 20 *ZAPOTEC* day-names; the *AZTEC* and *MAYA* equivalent days were *TÉCPATL* and *ETZ'NAB*.

OPOCHTLI ("left-handed one") one of the *Tlálocs*, was a manifestation of the rain god *TLÁLOC*. He was identified with the south, and the particular deity of those who lived on or near water. He invented and

PACHTONTLI, or Ecoztli, and Panquetzaliztli were two Aztec months during which their patron god Huitzilopochtli was offered sacrifices.
(CODEX MAGLIABECCHIANO)

gave to such people the tools of their trade: fishing net, bird net or snare, three-pronged fisherman's harpoon, spear-thrower (*atl-atl*) and the boatman's pole.

THE OTOMÍ, called in one legend the Otontlaca, were a group of people of *CHICHIMEC* origin who settled the region to the north and west of the Basin of Mexico. Following the late 13th- or 14th-century Chichimec invasion of central Mesoamerica under the legendary leader Xólotl, they moved into the Basin itself, and their own leader married one of Xólotl's daughters. They established the kingdom of Xaltocán and were later incorporated into the Tepanec Empire, contemporary with the México *AZTECS*. The Tepanecs-Otomí were Aztec allies at first, but were subjugated by them in the 15th century.

OTONTECUHTLI, also called Xócotl, was the primitive fire god and patron god of the *OTOMÍ* and their neighbours the Tepananeca and Mazahua (see also *HUEHUETÉOTL* and *XIUHTECUHTLI*).

THE OXLAHUN TI KU were the 13 *MAYA* Lords of the Heavens/ upper world, identified as glyphs but whose names are otherwise unknown. They were the arch rivals of, and overcame, the nine

Lords of the Underworld (*THE BOLON TI KU*) at the creation (see *CREATION MYTHS*). Their *AZTEC* equivalent were the Tonalteuctin (see *LORDS OF THE DAY*).

OXOMOCO was the "first woman" in the *TOLTEC* and *AZTEC CREATION MYTH* and the wife of *CIPACTONAL*. Together they were regarded as the first sorceress and sorcerer, and the inventors of astrology and of the calendar. Her *MAYA* equivalent was *XMUCANÉ*.

OZOMATLI ("monkey") was the 11th of the 20 *AZTEC* day-names; it had a neutral augury and its patron deity was *XOCHIPILLI*, the "flower prince". The *MAYA* and *ZAPOTEC* equivalent days were *CHUEN* and *LOO* or *Goloo*.

In Mesoamerica, the monkey was a frolicsome animal, representing pleasure, and associated with lust. Calendrical dates included: *1 Ozomatli*, as one of the *CIHUAPIPILTIN*; *2 Ozomatli*, for the feast day of merchants; *6 Ozomatli*, for the moon god *TECCIZTÉCATL*; *8 Ozomatli*, also for the moon; *9 Ozomatli*, for *ITZPAPÁLOTL*, the "obsidian butterfly"; and *12 Ozomatli*, for *HUEHUECÓYOTL* as god of music and dance.

PACHTONTLI ("a bit of hay") was the 13th (or, in some sources, the 12th) of the 18 *AZTEC* months,

a month of general deity worship, but especially of the war god HUIT-ZILOPOCHTLI, the "smoking mirror" TEZCATLIPOCA and the patron of merchants YACATECUHTLI.

It was also called *Ecoztli* ("letting of blood") and *Teotleco* ("the coming of the gods").

PANQUETZALIZTLI ("raising of banners") was the 16th (or, in some sources, 15th) of the 18 AZTEC months, in which honours and sacrifices were made to the war god HUITZILOPOCHTLI.

PATÉCATL, one of THE CENT-ZÓNTOTOCHTIN, was chief AZTEC god of drinking and of drunkenness. His consort, MAYÁHUEL, was goddess of the *maguey* or AGAVE plant (*Agave americana*), and it was Patécatl who cured the fermenting juice of the plant to turn it into PULQUE. *Pulque* was consumed in quantity at many ceremonies and festivals to worship the gods, and was believed to possess magical powers. (See also COQUIHUANI, QUIABELAGAYO, TEPOZTÉCATL and TEZCATZONTÉCATL)

Patécatl was ruler of MALINALLI ("grass"), the 12th day of the 20 AZTEC day-names, and god of medicine and curing. In the latter capacity he was associated with herbs and narcotic plants, including *peyote* and various mushrooms.

THE PAUAHTUN, MAYA God N, were the four winds of the cardinal points. As THE BACABS or CHACS they were also associated with rain. Each was associated with a colour and a direction, thus: *Zac* Pauahtun (white and north), *Kan* Pauahtun (yellow and south), *Chac* Pauahtun (red and east) and *Ek* Pauahtun (black and west).

PAYNAL was the messenger of HUITZILOPOCHTLI, the AZTEC god of war.

PECALA, or Pixee Pecala, was the Valley ZAPOTEC god of love.

PETELA was the name applied to the deified ruler of the Southern ZAPOTEC city of Ocelotepec. Curiously, the element *tela* in the name is thought to mean "dog".

PEZALAO see COQUI BEZELAO.

PICHANA GOBECHE was the principal deity of Valley ZAPOTEC Chichicapa. He was the god of healing, but nevertheless had to be constantly appeased and appealed to through a female intermediary called Pichanto.

PICHANTO see under HUE-CHAANA and PICHANA GOBECHE.

PIJA ("draught") was the 12th of the 20 ZAPOTEC day-names and one of the year-bearing days – there were 13 *Pija* years in a 52-year cycle (see also CHINA, QUIJ and XOO). The AZTEC and MAYA equivalent days were known as MALINALLI and EB.

PIJE XOO, ("the source of time"), was an alternative name for Zapotec COQUI XEE.

PIJETAO ("great time") was an alternative name for the Zapotec COQUI XEE.

PILALAPA CAACHE see BENELABA.

PILLAHUANA see HUEYPACHTLI.

PILLAHUANALIZTLI see IZCALLI.

PILTZINTECUHTLI was the youthful manifestation of TONA-TIUH – appropriately referred to as "the young (sun) god" – and a manifestation of the XOCHIPILLI. He was the third of the nine Aztec LORDS OF THE NIGHT.

PITAO COCHANA was an alternative name for HUECHAANA.

PITAO COCIJO see COCIJO.

PITAO COPIJCHA see COPIJCHA.

PITAO COZAANA see COZAANA.

PITAO COZOBI ("abundant sustenance"), or Betao Yozobi, or Locucuy, was the Valley ZAPOTEC god of corn (maize). His Southern and Sierra Zapotec names were Locucuy and Betao Yozobi. He was sometimes represented as a BAT-GOD. On collecting the first ears of corn at harvest time, special ceremonies were held in which native

fowl were sacrificed and the blood sprinkled on 13 pieces of *copal* incense (in honour of the principal deities), and on the house patio. The *copal* was then burned while incantations for a good harvest were recited. He was equivalent to Aztec CENTÉOTL.

PITAO HUICHAANA see HUECHAANA.

PITAO PEZALAO see COQUI BEZELAO.

PITAO XICALA (OR ZICA-LA) was the Valley ZAPOTEC god of dreams.

PITAO XOO, or Laxee, or Laxoo, was the Valley ZAPOTEC god of earthquakes, which were a frequent occurrence in their homeland. He was known as Laxoo among the Sierra Zapotec and Laxee among the Southern Zapotec.

PIXEE PECALA see PECALA.

POCHTECA see under YACATE-CUHTLI.

Q

THE POPUL VUH was one of the most sacred books of the Quiché *MAYA* of highland Guatemala, written between 1554 and 1558. Its tells the stories of the creation by the "grandfather" god *XPIYACOC* and the "grandmother" goddess **XMUCANÉ**, and the adventures in *XIBALBA* (the underworld) of the hero twin brothers, and gives the chronology of the Quiché rulers down to 1550. The first set of twins were *HUN HUNAHPÚ* and *VUCUB HUNAHPÚ*, the sons of Xpiyacoc and Xmucané, and the second were *HUNAHPÚ* and *XBALANQUÉ*, the sons of Hun Hunahpú and *XQUIC*.

The manuscript was discovered by Fray Francisco Jiménez in the early 18th century, but is now lost. However, he both copied and translated it into Spanish, now in the Newberry Library, Chicago, US. (See also *CREATION & THE UNIVERSE, TWINS & CULTURE HEROES*)

PULQUE, the *AZTEC* (and Mexican) alcoholic drink made from the *maguey* or *agave* plant (*Agave americana*), was consumed in large quantities at ceremonies and festivals (see *CENTZÓNTOTOCHTIN*) and was believed to possess magical powers. It was drunk to excess, for example, at ceremonies devoted to Aztec *XOCHIPILLI* and *MACUILXÓCHITL* and to Zapotec *QUIA BELAGAYO*, god of pleasure, and *COQUIHUANI*, god of light. In ancient Tepoztlán, Morelos, the patron deity was *TEPOZTÉCATL*, a moon god and god of *pulque*. Another god of *pulque*, possibly the *CHACMOOL* figure, was *TEZCATZONTÉCATL*. (For the mythical origins of *maguey* and *pulque* see *MAYÁHUEL* and *PATÉCATL*.)

QUAXOLOTL ("split at the top") was a goddess related to the earth goddess *CHANTICO*. Her image parted into two heads, and represented twins. She signified flame bifurcated into tongues and, by extension, was concerned with duality. (See also *OMETEOTL*)

PULQUE was made from the juice of the maguey *cactus (Agave americana).*

QUECHOLLI ("valuable feather") was 15th of the 18 *AZTEC* months, in which the hunting gods *MIXCÓATL* and *CAMAXTLI* and their female consorts were honoured.

It was also called *Tlacoquecholli* ("half-*Quecholli*") and *Tlamiquecholli* ("end-*Quecholli*").

QUERENDA-ANGAPETI, literally "the stone that is in the temple", was the *TARASCAN* god of corn (maize), a manifestation of the sun god *CURICAUERI*. His cult was at Zacapu, where Tarascan lords offered the first fruits of the harvest to his idol. His *AZTEC* equivalent was *CENTÉOTL*.

THE QUETZAL (*Pharomachrus mocinno*) is the brilliant green bird of the humid mountain forests of Chiapas and Guatemala. Mesoamerican rulers and nobility coveted its tail feathers and obtained them through long-distance trade. (Strong *TEOTIHUACANO* influences at *MAYA* Kaminaljuyú and Tikal demonstrate this contact.) Its rarity made it a symbol of value and preciousness, along with jade, and the element *quetzal* in numerous *NAHUATL* words means "plumed" or "feathered".

QUETZALCÓATL was a deity venerated throughout Mesoamerica and one of the most ancient and fundamental gods; he might have been descended ultimately from *OLMEC GOD VII*. His *NAHUATL* name means "plumed serpent", but he was known by other names in different parts of Mesoamerica:

QUETZALCÓATL is pictured enthroned and holding a plumed serpent opposite the goddess Chantico. (CODEX BORBONICUS.)

Quetzalcóatl to central Mesoamericans; *KUKULKÁN* to the *MAYA*; *GUCUMATZ* to the Guatemalan Quiché; and *ÉHECATL* to the Gulf Coast *HUASTECS*. Like his brother *TEZCATLIPOCA*, he was a child of *OMETEOTL* and played a vital role in the *CREATION MYTHS*. His *AZTEC* brothers were Tezcatlipoca, *HUIZILOPOCHTLI* and *XIPE TOTEC*, and he was frequently associated with the rain god *TLÁLOC*. He was ninth of the 13 *LORDS OF THE DAY*.

The mystery and duality of Quetzalcóatl was manifest in his many guises and roles, both divine and human. He was a creator god and a father of the gods, the god of learning, science, arts and crafts. He was a god of agriculture, who gave humankind corn (maize), the inventor of the calendar and god of the winds and cardinal directions. He was patron of priests, who often assumed his name.

In contrast to the destructive gods *XIUHCÓATL* and Tezcatlipoca, Quetzalcóatl was benevolent, and brought knowledge and prosperity to humankind. He was Éhecatl the wind god (represented by the four colours: black=north, blue=south, red=east, and white=west); *TLAHUIZCALPANTECUHTLI*, the morning "star", and his twin *XÓLOTL*, the

THE PYRAMID OF THE SERPENT, *at Xochicalco, depicts Quetzalcóatl face-on, alternating with images of the rain god Tláloc. Quetzalcóatl, the "plumed serpent", was portrayed on architecture, sculpture, portable objects and in the codices. He is also depicted, more famously, on the Pyramid of Quetzalcóatl at Teotihuacán*

evening "star"; *CE ÁCATL TOPILTZIN QUETZALCÓATL*, the legendary *TOLTEC* leader and founder of Tollán (Tula); and *KUKULKÁN*, the Maya-Toltec founder of Chichén Itzá.

As one of the five world rulers (Tezcatlipoca, Quetzalcóatl, Tláloc, Chalchiútlicue and Tonatiuh) he played a key role in the *CREATION MYTH* of the five suns – he ruled the Second Sun, having overthrown his brother Tezcatlipoca. He featured prominently in the Classic Period *TEOTIHUACÁN*, where a six-tiered pyramid was dedicated jointly to him and to Tláloc, and it was here that Mesoamericans believed that the gods assembled and created the world of the Fifth Sun.

QUETZALCÓATL was often sculpted by the Aztecs as free-standing stone pieces and as architectural embellishment.

In the Postclassic Period, Quetzalcóatl was portrayed with many attributes in numerous combinations: wearing a conical hat (*copilli*), divided vertically and painted half dark, half light; with a hat-band holding the tools of autosacrifice (*ómitl* and *huitzli*); with a flower to symbolize blood; with a fan of black crow and yellow macaw feathers at his neck; wearing a bird-beak mask and beard; with a black body and with his face divided vertically, and painted black on the front and yellow on the back, with a dark, vertical band through the eye; wearing jade-disc or spiral-shell ear ornaments (*epcololli*); wearing a breast plate cut from a conch shell (*ehecailacacózcatl*); or holding a spear-thrower (*atl-atl*), the symbol of the fire god.

Quetzalcóatl played several roles in the creation of the Fifth Sun. *NANAHUATZIN* and *TECUCIZTÉCATL*, having sacrificed themselves in the fire and risen as the sun and moon, remained motionless. Nanahuatzin, now *TONATIUH*, demanded blood sacrifice. Outraged at such arrogance, Quetzalcóatl-Tlahuizcalpantecuhtli hurled a dart at him but missed. Tonatiuh retaliated, and his dart pierced Tlahuizcalpantecuhtli through the head and transformed him into stone (the god of coldness *ITZTLACOLIUHQUI*). To get the sun and moon into motion, therefore, the gods were forced to sacrifice themselves, calling upon Quetzalcóatl to cut out their hearts with an obsidian blade, establishing the manner in which humans were to sacrifice and be sacrificed to feed Tonatiuh with blood.

Quetzalcóatl also played a vital role in peopling the world and providing them with sustenance. As Éhecatl-Quetzalcóatl, they sent him to *MICTLÁN* (the underworld) to bring back the bones of the people of the Fourth Sun. After overcoming challenges from *MICTLANTECUHTLI* and *MICTECACÍHUATL* (Lord and Lady of Mictlán), he escaped and brought the bones back to the old goddess *CIHUACÓATL*, who ground them up and mixed them with divine blood to mould men and women. In the search for food for these humans, Quetzalcóatl noticed the red ant *AZCATL* and persuaded it to lead him to *TONACATÉPETL* ("sustenance mountain"), where it kept its store of grain. He brought corn (maize) and other seeds back to the gods, who chewed them and fed them to the infant humans. Quetzalcóatl also attempted to drag Tonacatépetl to a more convenient place but, failing, the gods called upon Nanahuatzin, who enlisted the help of the four *TLÁLOCS* to split the mountain open and scatter the grains and seeds where the rain could water them and the sun cause them to grow.

Finally, Éhecatl-Quetzalcóatl created the *maguey* (*Agave americana*) and alcoholic *PULQUE* to cause humans to sing and dance in honour of their creators. He abducted the virgin sky goddess *MAYÁHUEL*, and on earth they embraced as the intertwining branches of a tree. Mayáhuel's guardian *TZITZIMITL* pursued them but, when she saw that she had arrived too late to prevent their union, she splintered the branches apart and fed Mayáhuel's shreds to her demon servants. Éhecatl, who remained unharmed, collected Mayáhuel's bones and planted them in a field, where they grew into the *maguey*.

Quetzalcóatl the man was the legendary ruler of the Toltecs, Ce Ácatl Topiltzin Quetzalcóatl, whose memory was perpetuated by the Aztecs in reverence for all things Toltec. The quasi-historical leader was the son of *CE TÉCPATL MIXCÓATL*, born after his father's murder by a rival faction, raised in exile and brought up to avenge his father. This relatively straightforward legend was mystified by the Aztecs, however, in variations on the tale and its characters. Ce Ácatl Topiltzin's father was deified as the god of the hunt, *MIXCÓATL*, and his mother elevated in some versions to the goddess *CHIMALMAN*. His mother's impregnation became symbolic (accomplished with an arrow from Mixcóatl's bow), and his upbringing was consigned to the goddess *QUILAZTLI*, herself a manifestation of the goddess Cihuacóatl, the "serpent woman".

In a further permutation, again interweaving divine and human affairs, the young Ce Ácatl Topiltzin led the Toltecs out of the Basin of Mexico (where his father had established their dynasty) and founded Tollán (Tula) to the northwest (in AD 968, according to Aztec tradition). Later, like his father, he got caught up in political rivalry: as Quetzalcóatl, he required only peaceful sacrifices involving offerings of jade, birds, snakes and butterflies. His political rivals, however, were resolved on expansion by conquest – symbolized by Tezcatlipoca ("smoking mirror", patron of warriors and Quetzalcóatl's perpetual rival) – and demanded human sacrifice to appease the gods. The contest ended with Quetzalcóatl being expelled from Tollán and leading his followers east, to the Gulf of Mexico, where he immolated himself on a pyre and was reborn as the "star" Venus. In a formal, divine version, Tezcatlipoca plied Quetzalcóatl with drink and, inebriated, he slept with his own sister. His subsequent anguish and shame led him to burn his palace, bury his treasures and sacrifice himself on a funeral pyre, from which his ashes rose as rare birds. In another variation, he left on a raft of serpents and disappeared over the eastern horizon, vowing to return one day for revenge and to build a new, peaceful world order.

In the Maya version, Kukulkán invaded Yucatán by sea to found the Maya-Toltec dynasty at Chichén Itzá (traditionally in AD 987, which coincides roughly with the Aztec dates for the departure of Quetzalcóatl from Tollán). See also *TEPEU*.

The significance of these legends was grasped, and taken advantage of, by Hernán Cortés in 1519, and recognized by the 16th-century Spanish historian Bernadino de Sahagún, who wrote: "In the city of Tollán reigned many years a king called Quetzalcóatl. . . He was exceptional in moral virtues. . . [and] the place of this king among the natives is like [that of] King Arthur among the English."

QUETZALCÓATL the ruler and hero in the post-Spanish conquest Codex Florentine, *holding an atl-atl (spear-thrower), and wearing a feathered cloak and conical feathered hat.*

T

QUETZALPAPÁLOTL ("quetzal butterfly", "plumed butterfly" or – because of the Mesoamerican value of *quetzal* feathers – "precious butterfly") was a mythical creature revered in the ancient city of *TEOTI-HUACÁN*. A palace at the southwest corner of the Plaza of the Pyramid of the Moon appears to have been dedicated to her and has decorations that undoubtedly represent religious symbolism; but, apart from obvious water symbols and the mythical Quetzalpapálotl, neither the significance nor the role of this creature is known.

QUEZA ("water") see *NIZA*.

QUEZELAO was "provider of the seasons" (probably a permutation of *COCIJO*), a Sierra *ZAPOTEC* god of agriculture and principal deity of the city of Atepec.

QUIABELAGAYO ("five flower"), or Quiepelagayo, was Valley *ZAPOTEC* god of pleasure, music and flowers, the equivalent of Aztec *MACUILXÓCHITL* and *XOCHIPILLI*. Curiously, in the worship of Quiabelagayo there were periods of fasting lasting from 40 to 80 days, during which the devotee was only allowed to use a certain tobacco every four days to stem hunger. He also pierced his tongue and ears to let blood as an offering. Other, luckier, devotees consumed much *PULQUE*, and feasted and danced.

QUIÁHUITL ("rain") was the 19th of the 20 *AZTEC* day-names; it had an unfavourable augury and its patron deity was the sun god *TONATIUH* or *CHANTICO*, goddess of the hearth. *MAYA* and *ZAPOTEC* equivalents were *CAUAC* and *APE*.

Calendrical dates included: *4 Quiáhuitl*, for the Third Sun of the Aztec *CREATION MYTH*; and *9 Quiáhuitl*, for the rain god *TLÁLOC*.

QUIJ, or *Laa*, ("wind") was the second of the 20 *ZAPOTEC* day-names and a year-bearing day –

QUETZALPAPÁLOTL was a mythical creature, portrayed in bas-relief on the square stone pillars of the Palace of Quetzalpapálotl at Teotihuacán. The eyes and other shallow circles, perhaps representing coloured spots on its wings, were filled with obsidian and other polished stones.

there were 13 *Quij* years in a 52-year cycle (see also *CHINA, PIJA* and *XOO*). The *AZTEC* and *MAYA* equivalents were *ÉHECATL* and *IK. Quij*, or *Ij*, or *Laa*, ("reed") was also the 13th of the 20 *ZAPOTEC* day-names; the *AZTEC* and *MAYA* equivalent days of this were *ÁCATL* and *BEN*.

QUILAZTLI, an aspect of the goddess *CIHUACÓATL*, was the goddess of pregnancy and childbirth, and patroness of the sweat bath (*NAHUAL temescal*). She raised the legendary ruler *CE ÁCATL TOPILTZIN QUETZALCÓATL*, founder of the Toltec capital at Tollán (Tula), after

his mother, *CHIMALMAN*, died when giving birth to him. Thus, through her association with Cihuacóatl, she was patroness of the *CIHUATETEO* (spirits of women who died in childbirth).

THE QUINAMETZIN were the giants who inhabited the *AZTEC* world of the First Sun (see *CREATION MYTHS*), and the servants of *TEZCATLIPOCA*. This world ended when Tezcatlipoca's brother, *QUETZALCÓATL*, caused them to be eaten by jaguars.

THE RITUAL OF THE BA-CABS is a Yucatecan *MAYA* codex of medicinal incantations, rich in symbolism and with frequent mythological allusions to stories about plants, birds and insects. However, without the text of these stories, the meanings cannot be fully understood.

SACRED FIRE CEREMONY see *TOXIUHMOLPILIA*.

SAIYAM UINICOB ("adjuster men") were the dwarf inhabitants of the first world in the *MAYA CRE-ATION MYTH*. They were believed to have built the great ruined Maya cities, working in darkness because the sun had not yet been created. When the sun rose on the first dawn, they were turned to stone, and their world was destroyed in the first great flood called *haiyoco-cab* ("water over the earth").

SERPENTS see *CÓATL*.

THE SHORT COUNT see under *LONG COUNT*.

SICUINDIRO was a *TARASCAN* ceremony honouring the deities *CURICAUERI* and *CUERAUÁPERI*, the masculine and feminine aspects of creation, in which Tarascan priests dressed and danced in the flayed skins of human sacrificial victims (see also *XIPE TOTEC*). The hearts of the victims were thrown into the thermal springs of Araró, while the body parts were reserved for ritual cannibalism. From the springs, Cuerauáperi created the clouds to water the crops.

SKY-BEARER see under *WORLD TREE*, and see also *COLOURS & THE CARDINAL DIRECTIONS*.

SPIDER WOMAN see *TEOTI-HUACÁN SPIDER WOMAN*.

TAJÍN was the *TOTONAC* god of rain and associated elements, including thunder, lightning and coastal hurricanes. He was equivalent to Aztec *TLÁLOC*, Maya *CHAC*, Zapotec *COCIJO* and Mixtec *DZA-HUI*, and probably also to Tarascan *CHUPITHIRIPEME*.

Tajín is also the name of a Classic Period ceremonial centre in the central Gulf Coast (Veracruz state), believed to have been the Totonac capital. It was occupied from the

first century BC to the 13th century AD and had several building phases in which pyramid-platforms and ball courts were built around numerous plazas. Its architecture and iconography show a combination of OLMEC, HUASTEC, TEOTIHUACANO and Maya influences but it also has its own characteristic style of stone slab niches, flying cornices and other elements. It was the most powerful Gulf Coast city after the demise of Teotihuacán.

Its two most famous monuments are a 12th-century ball court (one of seven) with six panels carved with ball-game scenes and associated ritual sacrifice, and the Pyramid of the Niches (begun in the fifth century AD), which has 365 stone-panelled niches in its six tiers and temple (88 on the base, 76 on the second tier, 64 on the third, 52 on the fourth, 40 on the fifth, 28 on the sixth and 17 on the temple). These probably correspond to the days of the solar year.

TAMOANCHÁN, a terrestrial paradise, was where, in one account of the CREATION MYTH, the gods convened and decided to repopulate the world of the Fifth Sun. They sent QUETZALCÓATL (the "plumed serpent") to MICTLÁN (the underworld) to fetch the bones of the beings who had inhabited the world of the Fourth Sun. After a struggle with MICTLANTECUHTLI and MICTECACÍHUATL (the rulers of Mictlán), he brought the bones to the old goddess CIHUACÓATL, who ground them to powder and mixed them with the blood of the gods to mould men and women.

Tamoanchán was a pan-Mesoamerican concept, spread by the TOLTECS/México AZTECS, and probably of HUASTEC origin. The word itself derives from a MAYA toponym meaning "land of the plumed serpent" (ta=prefix for "of", moan=a tropical bird, chán=an older form of can, "serpent"), that is, Quetzalcóatl himself. This interpretation associates Tamoanchán with the

TAJÍN, the Totonac rain god, is thought to be represented by a double, angular scroll motif set into the niches of Structure C and other buildings at El Tajín.

legend of CE ÁCATL TOPILTZIN QUETZALCÓATL, the fabled Toltec hero and founder of Tollán (Tula) who, after he was ousted by his political rivals, travelled east from Tollán to the Gulf Coast – through the southern territory of the Huastecs – and, in one version, put out to sea on a raft of serpents. In Maya legend, the founder/hero of the later Maya-Toltec city of Chichén Itzá was KUKULKÁN, the Maya name for Quetzalcóatl. He arrived in Yucatán by sea from the west, presumably having crossed the Gulf of Mexico.

THE TARASCANS lived in a state in western Mesoamerica, north and west of the Basin of Mexico, which was focused around ceremonial centres – Pátzcuaro, Ihuatzio and Tzintzuntzan – on the shores of Lake Pátzcuaro in present-day Michoacán. Their capital was shifted to Tzintzuntzan in the 15th century, where a five-fold complex of temples known as YÁCATAS was built.

Sworn enemies of the México AZTECS, the Tarasacans vigorously resisted Aztec attempts to conquer them in the 15th and early 16th

centuries. Although not as extensively as the Aztecs, they practised both human and autosacrifice, particularly blood-letting from the ears, to their gods CURICAUERI, CUERAUÁPERI and others. Since the two states were almost constantly at war, captives were a ready source of sacrificial victims. Blood sacrifice was accompanied by ritual cannibalism at special feasts. Having drugged or intoxicated them, the king and higher nobles cut open victims' chests before the temple fires; the heads were severed and put aside in a special place, and the hearts were extracted and offered to the gods. The remainder of the body provided the feast.

Whether war captives or honoured Tarascan citizens, the victims were believed to take on the personality of Curita-caheri, the messenger of the gods, and such a death was considered to be as glorious as death in battle. In one ceremony, the feast of SICUINDIRO, Tarascan priests dressed and danced in the flayed skins of the victims (see also XIPE TOTEC), and threw the hearts into the thermal springs of Araró, from which the rain god Cuerauáperi caused the clouds to form to water the crops.

The principal Tarascan gods were the creator and sun god Curicaueri, his creator consort Cuerauáperi and the moon

goddess XARATANGA, CHUPITHIRIPEME the god of rain, TIHUIME the god of death, QUERENDA-ANGAPETI the god of corn (maize), and XIPE TOTEC the flayed god of sacrifice and springtime. TARIÁCURI, the Tarascan king and founder of the dynasty, was deified as a wind god. Associated with the gods were the messenger Curita-caheri and the reclining deity CHACMOOL, the alleged receptacle of sacrificial hearts and blood.

TARIÁCURI was the culture hero who founded the TARASCAN state. According to legend he consolidated the Tarascan peoples into a kingdom in the late 14th century, and established a capital city at Pátzcuaro; his successors later moved the capital to Tzintzuntzan. He was deified after his death as god of the winds and the patron of learning and wealth.

TATA was the first man (see under CREATION MYTHS).

TECCIZTÉCATL was the central Mesoamerican "old moon god", in both masculine (see also TECUCIZTÉCATL) and feminine forms. He was also a deity of fertility. In male form he was portrayed as an old man carrying a huge white seashell on his back as a representation of the moon.

63

TÉCPATL ("flint knife") was the 18th of the 20 AZTEC day-names and a year-bearing day – there were 13 Técpatl years in a 52-year cycle (see also ÁCATL, CALLI and TOCHTLI). It had a favourable augury and its patron was CHALCHIUHTOTOLIN-TEZCATLIPOCA; its orientation was north. MAYA and ZAPOTEC equivalent days were ETZ'NAB and OPA.

Calendrical dates and deity associations included: 1 Técpatl, for HUITZILOPOCHTLI-CAMAXTLI; 4 Técpatl, for the moon god TECCIZTÉCATL; 7 Técpatl, for CHICOMECÓATL; 8 Técpatl, for the maguey plant (see PULQUE); and 12 Técpatl, for the earth or death god.

TECUCIZTÉCATL, the AZTEC moon god of the world of the Fifth Sun, was the haughty, healthy and headstrong twin brother of the weak, humble and allegedly cowardly NANAHUATZIN, whom he followed in leaping into the ceremonial fire lit by the gods at TEOTIHUACÁN (see also CREATION MYTHS). The brightness of his radiance was diminished when one of the gods threw a rabbit (tochtli) into his face, which explains the Aztec belief in the "rabbit in the moon." He was ruler of MIQUIZTLI ("death"), sixth of the 20 Aztec days-names.

TECUILHUITONTLI ("small feast of the lords") was the eighth of the 18 AZTEC months, in which HUIXTOCÍHUATL, goddess of salt, was honoured.

TELLA ("dog") was the tenth of the 20 ZAPOTEC day-names; the AZTEC and MAYA equivalent days were ITZCUINTLI and OC.

TENAHUATILIZTLI see OCHPANITZTLI.

TENOCH, TENOCHCA see under TENOCHTITLÁN.

TENOCHTITLÁN was the México AZTEC capital, built on an island near the west shore of the central

THE MÉXICA Aztecs built a magnificent city on an island just off shore from the western edge of Lake Texcoco. They carved out first a kingdom within the Basin of Mexico and then beyond, eventually to conquer and exact tribute from a vast empire. (WOODCUT FROM LETTERS OF HERNÁN CORTÉS TO EMPEROR CHARLES V, 1524.)

lake in the Basin of Mexico. The México also called themselves the Tenochca, after the semi-legendary priest and leader Tenoch associated with the founding of the city.

According to legend, the sun and war god HUITZILOPOCHTLI led the México from a cave in AZTLÁN, a land in the deserts of the northwest, into central Mesoamerica. In their wanderings the México were led by four priests, who carried a great idol of Huitzilopochtli before the people. The god spoke secretly to them through the idol, telling them to call themselves the México, advising them on the best route to take and promising them victory and riches if they honoured him. In the Basin of Mexico, he gave the México the sign of the eagle (his representative) alighting on a nopal cactus (prickly pear), clutching a serpent in its claw, on an island in the "Lake of the Moon" (MEZTLIAPÁN), to show them where to establish their capital.

The Great Temple-Pyramid that dominated the ceremonial precinct supported the twin temples of Huitzilopochtli and the rain god TLÁLOC. From these temples, the priests could survey the entire city and see far across the lakes of the basin in all directions.

THE TEOMAMAQUE (singular "Teomama") were the chosen bearers of the tribal idols during the early

AZTEC migrations from AZTLÁN into the Basin of Mexico, one of whom was CHIMALMAN. After the Aztecs had settled in the Basin, the title continued to be used for those chosen to carry out this honour symbolically by carrying the idols on their shoulders at state festivals.

TEOTIHUACÁN ("city of the gods") was the largest and most powerful state in central Mesoamerica during the Classic Period, and flourished from the first to the eighth century AD in the Teotihuacán Valley off the northeast of the Basin of Mexico. Later, its dilapidated and overgrown pyramid-platforms were believed by the Aztecs to be the burial mounds of giants and of the gods (see CREATION MYTHS). At its apogee it covered more than 20 sq kilometres (8 sq miles) and supported a population of as many as 200,000.

The core of the city was a huge ceremonial precinct, divided into hundreds of smaller compounds and precincts along a ritual avenue more than 2 km (1 mile) long. Aligned north–south, this so-called Avenue of the Dead ran from the Ciudadela compound at the south end to the Pyramid of the Moon at the north. Roughly halfway along, on the east side, stood the Pyramid of the Sun, the largest pyramid-platform in the city, buried beneath which was a sacred cave and spring. Around this religious core, the residential and industrial suburbs stretched in all directions, and beyond these, were the irrigated fields of the farmlands that were needed to support the city's dense population.

The influence of Teotihuacán was spread throughout Mesoamerica, as far south as the MAYA cities of Tikal and Kaminaljuyú and as far north as the northern deserts. Its influence was manifestly artistic and architectural, in particular the spread of the talud–tablero profile of an upright plate (tablero) cantilevered on a sloping plate

THE VAST CITY of Teotihuacán dominated much of Mesoamerica economically, and perhaps politically as well, throughout much of the Classic Period. Its ceremonial core alone included an avenue, more than 2 km (1 mile) long, lined with pyramids, temples and palaces.

(talud), used to clad the rubble cores of the pyramid-platforms.

Diplomatic relations were apparently long-standing with the kingdom of the ZAPOTECS at Monte Albán in the Valley of Oaxaca. Each maintained an enclave of its own citizens in the other's city. However, scholars continue to debate the exact nature of their political or military control over the rest of Mesoamerica. What is certain is that the city and its ruler commanded a vast network of trade in manufactured goods and raw materials, for example, jade and other precious stones, obsidian (black volcanic glass), ceramics and quetzal feathers.

The reasons for Teotihuacán's collapse are uncertain. There is clear evidence for worsening climatic conditions and for invasions or migrations coming in from the north in the seventh and eighth centuries. Simultaneously, several central Mesoamerican city-states – Cholula, Teotenango, Xochicalco and El Tajín – reasserted regional control. Another factor may have been a decline in relations with the Zapotecs. There was widespread economic implosion, vast population migrations and a rise in city-state rivalry in the ensuing century of the early Postclassic Period.

THE PYRAMID OF THE SUN at Teotihuacán mimics the bulk of the surrounding mountains.

TEOTIHUACANO GODS are

well-documented. A principal temple-pyramid of *TEOTICHUACÁN*, on the west side of the great sunken plaza of the Ciudadela, comprised six diminishing tiers (of which only four now survive) with alternating sculptured images of *QUETZALCÓATL* and *TLÁLOC* around the upright faces (*tablero*) of the tiers. Each outward-facing serpent head – in high relief – is surrounded by a feathered collar, and a scaly serpent body in low relief writhes to the left of each head and ends in a vertebrae-like section representing a rattle. In ancient times the sculptures would have been smoothly plastered, and remnants still retain traces of the brilliant colours with which they were originally painted, with red jaws, white serpent fangs, green *quetzal* plumes on their collars, red, yellow and blue shells around the bodies, and blue side ramps to the central, ceremonial staircase.

Palatial structures in the city testify to the other major deities that were worshipped at Teotihuacán. In the Tepantitla palace murals, a mythical world is depicted, once thought to represent *TLALOCÁN* (the Paradise of Tláloc). It has more recently been interpreted as the world of the *TEOTIHUACÁN SPIDER WOMAN* or Great Goddess, who was the supreme Teotihuacano deity and creator goddess. Other palace murals depict various birds, especially owls, and jaguars and other feline creatures. Stone statuary attests to the worship of *CHALCHIÚTLICUE* ("she of the jade skirt"), and the wealth of incense burners representing the *OLD FIRE GOD* confirms his importance, possibly as the consort of the Spider Woman/Great Goddess. A Sun God and a Moon Goddess, who were otherwise nameless, were also important at Teotihuacán, and the flayed god of springtime, *XIPE*

TOTEC represented the renewal of vegetation during the all-important rainy season.

TLALCHITONATIUH ("land of *TONATIUH*"), the later *NAHUATL* name for the Jaguar or Falling sun, was a major god from the first to the seventh centuries AD, and his cult was disseminated to Kaminaljuyú, Tikal and other Maya cities in the fourth to seventh centuries. At Teotihuacán, near the Plaza of the Pyramid of the Moon, the Jaguar Palace complex might have been the temple of *JAGUAR GOD* worship. The complex is comprised of three chambers on the north, south and west sides of a courtyard and an open platform on the east. A central staircase is flanked by ramps decorated with bas-relief serpents, their rattles at the bases of the ramps. The main chamber contains a mural depicting two "plumed jaguars" wearing fancy feather headdresses and with a row of shells running down each of their backs to the tips of their tails; each is blowing a plumed *Strombus*-shell trumpet (the sound is symbolized by small scrolls) from which fall drops of blood or water. Above the figures is a row of masks representing Tláloc, that alternate with year-sign glyphs. A narrow passage leads from the northwest corner of the courtyard to several more rooms decorated with murals

THE PYRAMID-TEMPLE of Quetzalcóatl and Tláloc at Teotihuacán is decorated with alternating near full-relief sculptures of the plumed serpent and the rain god, both of whom were vital to the wellbeing of the city and its inhabitants.

depicting pairs of human hands clutching feline-like animals caught in a net; scrolls representing their roars issue from their mouths. These murals undoubtedly represent religious symbolism that attached importance to water and/or blood, but we have no idea of the significance, or of the role played by the creatures, or of what ceremonies might have been performed in the rooms.

Another palace complex (also near the Plaza of the Pyramid of the Moon), aptly named the Palace of *QUETZALPAPÁLOTL* ("quetzal butterfly" or "plumed butterfly"), might also have been a place of worship and/or priestly quarters for a cult of that being. The rooms sit beyond a wide staircase entrance, flanked by carved serpent heads. Within a portico, the entrance hall walls are decorated with abstract "half-eyes" and symbols representing rippling water. In an inner patio beyond the hall, stout stone pillars around the open court have bas-reliefs of the mythical "plumed butterfly" and other symbols. Obsidian discs are

still set in some of the symbols, and other semi-precious stones might also have been set into the eyes of the creatures and other symbols. The walls of the patio have the remains of what were once brilliantly painted murals, the most complete of which (the north wall) depicts various geometric designs and what appears to be the cross-section of a huge seashell. Small circles remain around the walls where discs of polished mica were once set into the plaster. Around the roof of this gallery are crenellations carved with the Teotihuacano year-signs. As with the Jaguar Palace, the symbolism in these rooms was important, but its meaning is now lost.

That these palaces had long histories as places of religious importance is indicated by an earlier palace beneath the base platform of the Palace of the Quetzalpapálotl. Called the Palace of the Caracoles Emplumados ("plumed shells"), it was also approached by a staircase, which, in this case, is decorated with green parrots out of whose yellow beaks flow streams of blue water. The façades of this building had bas-reliefs of "plumed seashells", painted various colours, and what appear to be the mouthpieces of musical instruments. Two pilasters are decorated with bas-reliefs of four-petalled flowers, also painted. A narrow tunnel from the west side leads to a small chamber containing an "altar" painted with red circles on a white background.

DEATH & SACRIFICE

MESOAMERICANS LEARNED TO control their environment to some extent through agriculture and city living. Nevertheless, death was ever-present. To the Aztecs and other central Mesoamericans, death in battle (for men), in childbirth (for women) and in human sacrifice were considered particularly honourable. The Maya, in contrast, feared death greatly, even though warfare and conquest were frequent, and the bereaved expressed extreme mourning, weeping silently by day and giving out shrieks of grief during the night. The Aztec underworld was called Mictlán; the Maya equivalent was Mitnal or Xibalba.

Sacrifice – in terms of time given to participating in special ceremonies, as autosacrifice, and as offerings of flowers, animals and humans – was congenital in Mesoamerican culture. Human sacrifice began in the Preclassic Period, but its institutionalization was a Toltec and, in particular, an Aztec speciality. As in the case of death, the Maya and Aztec views on sacrifice differed. For the Maya, the victim's blood was needed to replenish and ensure the smooth progress of cyclical events, and sacrifice demonstrated obeisance to the deities. To the Aztecs, the sacrifice of humans was necessary on an ever-increasing scale, in order to hold the universe together, and to strengthen the sun for its nightly journey and battle against the forces of darkness. In practice, Aztec human sacrifice also became a means of political coercion and social control.

AUTOSACRIFICE – as penance and as an offering of blood to the deities – was an important method of appeasing the gods and goddesses, and of ensuring the smooth progress of the world. Bloodletting from the ears was common and, for Maya men, a favoured organ was the penis, while for women it was the tongue (above): a worshipper kneels before her lord and ruler, Shield Jaguar, and draws a spiked cord through her tongue. (LINTEL 24, LATE CLASSIC PERIOD YAXCHILÁN.)

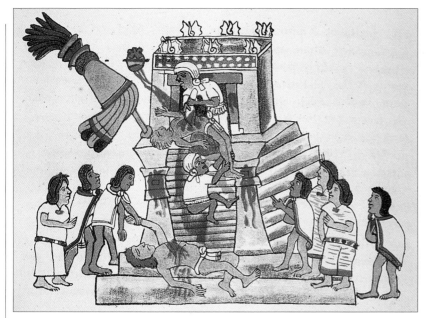

HUMAN SACRIFICE (far left) was a necessity of life to the Aztecs – the victim's life blood fed and sustained the sun god Tonatiuh and thus ensured that their world survived. Such sacrifices were frequently depicted in the codices, as here, in the early post-Spanish conquest Codex Magliabecchiano. At major festivals, the sacrifices were allegedly in the thousands, according to Spanish chroniclers. Here there seems to be something of an assembly line operating, the victims being thrown down the steps of the pyramid after being dispatched. Parts of the victims might also have been eaten by priests in ritual feasts, and their skulls displayed on the municipal tzompantli (skull rack) (left), here represented as a stone sculpture.

FIRE (right) played an important part in sacrifice, as the ultimate fate of the human hearts torn from victims' bodies – possibly placed and burnt on the abdomens of Chacmools – and as a medium in its own right and for burning incense and tobacco in ritual ceremonies.

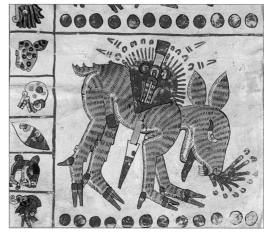

A DEER (above) is sacrificed by killing it with an atl-atl (spear-thrower) dart, depicted in the pre-Spanish conquest Codex Vaticanus B. As well as humans, all manner of animals and plants – and even objects – were sacrificed and/or offered to the gods and goddesses. Quetzalcóatl, as the ruler/hero of Tollán (Tula), went so far as to advocate that sacrifices should be limited to offerings of jade, birds, serpents and butterflies. This policy led to his undoing when his political rivals – supporters of Tezcatlipoca and human sacrifice – defeated and banished him from the city.

THE SHROUD-ENCASED body (above) of a young man, perhaps one who died in battle, has been prepared for cremation and is accompanied by beans and tamales for his journey. Death was not feared by the Aztecs, but was recognized as inevitable, ever-present and often sudden. One's fate after death was unrelated to conduct on earth, although warriors who died in battle and women who died giving birth went straight to eastern and western paradises, respectively. (ILLUSTRATION FROM THE CODEX MAGLIABECCHIANO.)

AUTOSACRIFICE (above) was also used to induce sacred visions. Lady Wak Tun, one of the wives of Prince Yaxun Balam, experiences a serpent vision, rising from an incense burner, presumably after a ritual auto-sacrificial bloodletting. (LINTEL 15, LATE CLASSIC PERIOD, YAXCHILÁN.)

THE TEOTIHUACÁN SPIDER WOMAN, or Great Goddess of the Classic Period, whose ancient name we do not know, is thought to have been the supreme Teotihuacano deity, and to have been the creator of the present universe.

She is depicted in the murals of the palatial residence of Tepantitla, 500 m (545 yds) to the east of the Pyramid of the Sun and its ceremonial precinct. The most famous of the murals of Tepantitla was long thought to depict Tlalocán, the "Paradise of the rain god" TLÁLOC, and to include the dominating figure of Tláloc himself. More recently, however, careful examination of the figure's details has revealed that it is almost certainly female, and that its mouth has the fangs and palps of a spider; hence its revised attribution.

The place depicted in the murals appears, therefore, to be the setting of the Teotihuacano origin myth. It includes a sacred mountain with springs gushing forth at its base, and might well have been inspired by the looming presence of Cerro Gordo, which dominates the horizon to the north of the ancient city. Around the figure of the Spider Woman, human figures – who are tiny in comparison to the

THE TEOTIHUACÁN SPIDER WOMAN, or Great Goddess, was the city's supreme deity and creator goddess, depicted both on palatial murals and in stone, as carved blocks that fit together to make up her image. (DRAWING AFTER KARL TAUBE)

goddess – engage in a happy, frolicsome scene: they dance, sing (speech scrolls come from their mouths) and play games amid the butterflies and flowering trees.

Spider Woman dominated the Teotihuacano pantheon and ruled in her own world; she might well have been the precursor to Aztec TOCI, "our grandmother", and her consort was probably the OLD FIRE GOD, also evident at TEOTIHUACÁN.

TEOTLECO see PACHTONTLI.

TEOYAOMIQUI, or Huahuantli, was a god specific to the AZTECS, honoured by warriors as the patron and protector of those who died in the XOCHIYAÓYOTL ("Flowery War"), initiated specifically to capture victims for sacrifice to the war god HUITZILOPOCHTLI. In some calendar representations Teoyaomiqui replaced MICTLANTECUHTLI as the sixth of the 13 LORDS OF THE DAY.

TEPEÍLHUITL see HUEYPACHTLI.

TEPEU ("conqueror"), despite his central Mesoamerican name, was a creator god of the Quiché MAYA of the highlands of Guatemala. The Quiché sacred text, the POPUL VUH, describes how Tepeu and GUCUMATZ created the earth and all living things on it, but were only able to create satisfactory humans after many failed attempts (see CREATION MYTHS).

Interestingly, the Tepeu were also one of the tribes of TOLTEC origin from northwest of Mesoamerica. In the Postclassic Period they emigrated across north-central Mesoamerica and then down the Gulf Coast. From there they moved into the Guatemalan highlands, where they are known as the Yaqui-Tepeu – who were the ancestors of the Quiché Maya. This accumulation of connections in the word "Tepeu" – a creator god with a NAHUATL name meaning "conqueror" as companion to Maya Gucumatz (himself the equivalent of the "feathered serpent" KUKULKÁN), and a Toltec tribe as the ancestor of the Quiché Maya – gives further tantalizing clues to the legendary events in ancient Tollán (Tula) and the journeys of the Toltec hero CE ÁCATL TOPILTZIN QUETZALCÓATL (or Yucatecan Maya

Kukulkán). (For further information, see MIXCÓATL, QUETZALCÓATL and TAMOANCHÁN.)

TEPEYOLOHTLI ("heart of the mountain") was a fundamental and primitive central Mesoamerican earth deity: the JAGUAR GOD who inhabited the interior of the earth. He might have been the successor to the OLMEC jaguar cult. He was one of the many manifestations of TEZCATLIPOCA and was eighth of the nine LORDS OF THE NIGHT. His calendrical glyph was 8 OCÉLOTL (the jaguar) and he was patron of CALLI ("house"), the third day of the Aztec 20-day month.

THE TEPICTOTON, the little TLÁLOCS, were the gods of the mountain rains. They dwelt in recesses in the mountain and were perceived as dwarfs by the AZTECS.

TEPOPOCHTLI see TÓXCATL.

TEPOZTÉCATL was the patron deity of ancient Tepoztlán, a TLALHUICA and later AZTEC town in the present-day Mexican state of Morelos. He is identified as a moon god through his calendrical name, OMETOCHTLI ("2 rabbit"; ancient central Mesoamericans saw a rabbit in the moon, rather than a man), and as a PULQUE god and god of drunkenness through association with PATÉCATL.

His shrine – Tepozteco – stood on a clifftop overlooking the town. Begun by the TLALHUICA in about 1250, a small pyramid-platform and other structures were built on an artificially levelled space on the summit. After the Aztec ruler Ahuitzotl had conquered the town in the late 15th century, the shrine was rebuilt as a three-tiered pyramid-platform that supported a two-chambered temple, the back and side walls of which were lined with carved stone benches. The carvings include a glyph to Ahuitzotl, "ten rabbit", and it was probably at this time that the

TEPOZTÉCATL was the patron deity and culture hero who relieved the city of Tepoztlán from the burden of sacrificial tribute to Xochicalco. (ILLUSTRATION FROM THE CODEX MAGLIABECCHIANO.)

shrine was dedicated (or perhaps rededicated) to the honour of Ometochtli-Tepoztécatl.

As the moon god, and god of darkness, Tepoztécatl was often portrayed with a crescent-moon nose, and with half his face painted red and the other half painted black. It was believed that he helped to bring the earth out of its winter hibernation and assisted in the spring rebirth, and for this reason he was worshipped, with much revelry and consumption of *pulque*, in an autumn festival in which the seeds of his work were planted symbolically.

Tepoztécatl was also a Tlalhuica culture hero. In legend he delivered them from the onus of providing the ancient city of Xochicalco – west of Tepoztlán – with an annual sacrificial victim. The victim had to be an old man, who was to be eaten by a dragon – the Pyramid of the Plumed Serpents at Xochicalco, one of the principal pyramid-platforms, has a main panel around which are carved eight writhing feathered serpents. The young Tepoztécatl, disguising himself as an old woodcutter, volunteered himself as that year's sacrificial offering and, when the dragon appeared, he slew it, thus ending the dreadful tribute. (Rivalry between the various city-states was a common feature of Mesoamerican history, especially in the Postclassic Period, and it is conceivable that this tale contains a kernel of truth relating to a war or battle in which Tepoztlán defeated Xochicalco and threw off its domination.) (See also *TWINS & CULTURE HEROES*)

TETEOINNAN ("mother of the gods") was a central Mesoamerican earth-mother concept, more primitive than, but certainly related to, *CIHUACÓATL, COATLÍCUE, TLAZOL-TÉOTL* and *TOCI*. The earth-mother cult was particularly strong in the late Postclassic Period, especially in the Gulf Coast cultures and among the *CHINAMPA*-dwellers who lived on the "floating islands" (really artificially-created rectangular fields built out from the shores of lakes) in the Basin of Mexico. Teteoinnan was worshipped at the feast of *OCHPANITZTLI*.

TEXCOCO, which was a city on the eastern shore of Lake Texcoco in the central Basin of Mexico, was a joint foundation of the *CHICHIMECS* of Tenayuca and the Acolhua *AZTECS*. Its mid-15th-century king, called *NEZAHUALCÓYOTL*, joined with the México Aztec king, Moctezuma I Ilhuicamena, to form the Triple Alliance with the cities of *TENOCHTITLÁN* and Tlacopán against the states of Tlaxcala and Huexotzingo east and southeast of the Basin. Although the México were soon feeling less in need of the alliance, Texcoco remained powerful and autonomous, and the rulers of the city co-operated with the Aztec emperors in major construction projects, such as building bridges to link the island of Tenochtitlán with the mainland, an aqueduct to bring fresh water to the island and the extension of the *CHINAMPA* style of agriculture from the lake shores.

TETEOINNAN, "mother of the gods" and primeval earth-mother, was especially honoured by rural people and the chinampa-*dwellers around the lakes of the Basin of Mexico.*

TEYOLLOCUALOYÁN was the name used by the *AZTECS* for their own universe. (See *CREATION & THE UNIVERSE*)

69

TEZCATLIPOCA ("smoking mirror") was one of the major deities of the Postclassic Period. His worship was prominent among the *TOLTECS* from the 10th century AD onwards, and the México *AZTECS*, in their reverence for everything Toltec, adopted him and gave him his Nahuatl name. He was a special god in the city of *TEXCOCO*, in the Basin of Mexico across the lake from the Aztec island capital *TENOCHTITLÁN*, and was probably also important to the México for that reason. He was the tenth of the 13 *LORDS OF THE DAY*, and central Mesoamericans honoured him, especially the México, in the month *TÓXCATL*, the sixth of the 18 months of the solar year.

His brothers in the Aztec pantheon were *HUITZILOPOCHTLI*, *QUETZALCÓATL* and *XIPE TOTEC*. Like Quetzalcóatl, Tezcatlipoca was a child of *OMETEOTL* and played a prominent role in the *CREATION MYTHS*: he ruled the world of the First Sun until he was defeated by Quetzalcóatl, who caused the giants who inhabited that world to be eaten by jaguars. Later, however, the two brothers co-operated in the creation of the Fifth Sun when, as serpents, they defeated and dismembered the great Earth Monster *TLALTECUHTLI* and used the body parts to create the earth and the heavens. The perpetual tension between Tezcatlipoca and Quetzalcóatl is also reflected in the quasi-historical legend of *CE ÁCATL TOPILTZIN QUETZALCÓATL*, for it was the followers of Tezcatlipoca who defeated Ce Ácatl Topiltzin and the followers of Quetzalcóatl, and exiled them from the Toltec capital Tollán (Tula).

Tezcatlipoca was portrayed with a polished black obsidian mirror in place of his left foot, which had been ripped off in his mythological battle with the Earth Monster. Another accoutrement was often a turquoise serpent. His alter ego (or *NAHUAL*) was the *OCÉLOTL* (see *JAGUAR GODS*), the night beast who

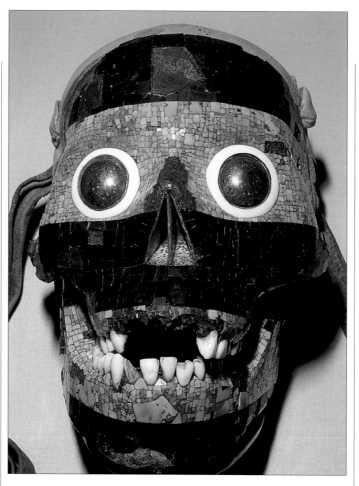

TEZCATLIPOCA, the "smoking mirror" creator god. This mosaic-decorated skull, which possibly represents him, is covered with tiny chips of polished black lignite and bright blue turquoise. The eye sockets are filled with large, shining orbs of impenetrable black iron pyrite ringed in brilliant white shell – staring, all-seeing, all-knowing. (SKULL FROM THE BRITISH MUSEUM.)

fought a daily battle against the sun. He was also associated with the cardinal points and colours – for each direction his colours and affiliations changed: for the north he was Black Tezcatlipoca, the "smoking mirror", god of Texcoco and of the day *ÁCATL* ("reed"); as the south he was Blue Tezcatlipoca, who was the "hummingbird sorcerer", god of Tenochtitlán and associated with the sun and war god Huitzilopochtli; as the east he was blood Red Tezcatlipoca, the "flayed one" as the god *XIPE TOTEC*, god of the *TLAXCALTECANS*, and associated also with *CAMAXTLI* and with *MIXCÓATL*, and ruler of the day *CUAUHTLI* ("eagle"); and finally, as

the west he was White Tezcatlipoca, or the "plumed serpent" Quetzalcóatl, who was the god of Cholula, as well as of education and the priesthood.

Tezcatlipoca was thus a creator god of many forms and aspects. Some authorities regard all other creator gods and goddesses in the Aztec creation myths as manifestations of his omniscience and omnipotence, and the Aztecs certainly called him by more names and gave him more manifestations than any other deity. He was conceived of as invisible, ever-present and lord of the shadows, wielding his magic mirror to see into, and manipulate, the lives of humans. He was capricious in nature, and was capable of dispensing evil and misery or valour and good fortune with equal unpredictability.

He was the god of conflict and, because of this association, he was – along with Huitzilopochtli – a special god to warriors. One of his many names was *YÁOTL* ("enemy" in Nahuatl) and he was patron of

the *telpochcalli* ("houses of war", that is, military training colleges). As *Yáotl-ÉHECATL* ("night wind") he was associated with warfare, death and the realm of darkness, and it was believed that he could appear at crossroads during the night to challenge warriors – surely an evil omen. He was sometimes also referred to as *MEZTLI* ("moon") and, in jaguar imagery, he was *TEPEYOLOHTLI*, the jaguar at the heart of the mountain of the earth.

His Nahuatl name represented simultaneously the penetration of the mirror and the cloud-like haze of smoke. He was seen as "black" Tezcatlipoca – *CHALCHIUHTECÓLOTL* ("precious owl") or *CHALCHIUHTOTOLIN* ("precious turkey") – the god of night and mystery, the representative of evil, destruction and death, but he could just as easily wreak revenge on one's behalf as bring personal misery. He was also *ITZTLACOLIUHQUI* – the god of ice and cold, sin and misery. He was the patron of the Toltec and Aztec nobility – as *OMÁCATL* he presided over banquets and feasting – but, at the same time, was the patron of sorcerers, thieves and those generally up to no good. In keeping with his malevolent nature, Tezcatlipoca is credited with the corruption of his virtuous brother Quetzalcóatl – by intoxicating him and inducing him to seduce his own sister – and with abducting *XOCHIQUETZAL*, the first wife of *TLÁLOC*. These malevolent aspects were summed up best in one of his many alternative names: Yáotl. He was the "adversary", and his "justice" was inescapable; an epithet applied to his worshippers – *titlacauan* ("we are his slaves") – was not unjustified. (See also *CREATION & THE UNIVERSE, DEATH & SACRIFICE*)

TEZCATZONTÉCATL was one of the many Mesoamerican *PULQUE* gods and one of the *CENTZÓNTOTOCHTIN*. His image might have been represented by the numerous *CHACMOOL* figures found both in

TEZCATZONTÉCATL was one of the Centzóntotochtin – the pulque gods of drinking and drunkenness. (ILLUSTRATION FROM THE CODEX VATICANUS B.)

central Mesoamerican and MAYA cities. For related deities, see MAYÁHUEL and PATÉCATL.

TEZCOCO see TEXCOCO.

TIANQUIZTLI (the Pleiades) see under TOXIUHMOLPILIA.

TIHUIME was the TARASCAN god of death and of the underworld. His AZTEC counterpart was called MICTLANTECUHTLI.

TÍTITL ("shrunken" or "wrinkled") was the last of the 18 months in the AZTEC solar year. It occurred during the winter solstice (by this time of the year, any stored corn/maize ears would indeed be dry), and the principal ritual was in honour of the ancient moon goddess ILAMATECUHTLI.

TITLACAUAN ("we are his slaves"); see TEZCALIPOCA.

TLACALILIZTLI, a special sacrifice of war captives to ensure a good harvest, was a widespread Mesoamerican practice, and was the highlight of the AZTEC ceremonies of OCHPANITZTLI honouring the corn (maize) goddess CHICOMECÓATL and the old earth mother

TETEOINNAN. The victims were bound, spread-eagled, on an upright wooden frame as a target, and shot with arrows. The custom was also practised by the MAYA, as depicted in graffiti on Temple II at the Guatemalan site of Tikal. For a related ritual, see TLAHUAHUANALIZTLI.

TLACATZINACANTLI see BAT-GOD.

TLACAXIPEHUALIZTLI ("flaying of men") was the third (or, in some sources, second) of the 18 months in the AZTEC solar year, occurring in spring. Ancient fertility rites were observed, possibly of HUASTEC origin, in which the spring god XIPE TOTEC was propitiated with sacrificial victims who were slain and then flayed. Priests donned the bloody skins and performed frenzied dances wearing them. (These ceremonies were completed in the next month – see TOZOZTONTLI.) The bravest of the prisoner victims was honoured with death by the TLAHUAHUANALIZTLI. It was also known as Coaílhuitl ("snake festival"), presumably in recognition of the snake's shedding of its skin.

TLACOQUECHOLLI see QUECHOLLI.

TLAELQUANI ("eater of excrement") was the manifestation of the goddess TLAZOLTÉOTL as the

source of, and force behind, all manner of "unclean" behaviour; she was also associated with witchcraft and the purging of sin. The literal meaning of her NAHUATL name expresses her association with confession and purification, and she acted as a delegate for the penitent to the god TEZCATLIPOCA. She was often portrayed with a blackened mouth to symbolize this unpleasant but unavoidable duty.

She was especially associated with the darker side of sex and, in this capacity, was the patroness of a special corps of military prostitutes: young girls recruited, as an obligation, from among the ordinary citizenry of the AZTEC capital TENOCHTITLÁN, whose purpose was allegedly to sustain the fanaticism of Aztec warriors. They were maintained in special quarters where they worshipped Tlaelquani, and groups of them were periodically brought to the military barracks for a "festival" of licentiousness, at the culmination of which they were ceremonially sacrificed.

TLAHUAHUANALIZTLI was the height of the ceremonies at the feast of TLACAXIPEHUALIZTLI in honour of the god of springtime, XIPE TOTEC. In addition to other human sacrifices, those war captives judged to have been the most valorous in avoiding capture were sacrificed in a special "gladiatorial"

contest. However, since the object was to honour the god by offering him human blood as a symbol and supplication for a good future harvest, the outcome of the combat was hardly in doubt. The captive, bound in order to restrict his movements, stood atop a large circular stone platform known as a *temalacatl* (for example, the "Stone of Tizoc" in the Museo Nacional de Antropología, Mexico City might have been one such platform, used in TENOCHTITLÁN.) Upon this, he was forced to defend himself against the onslaughts of successive Eagle and Jaguar "knights" of the Aztec warrior cult, armed with the dreaded *macuauhuitl*, a flat-sided hardwood war sword that had edges of long, razor-sharp blades made of obsidian (volcanic glass). The victim's *macuauhuitl*, however, had had its obsidian blades removed and replaced by somewhat less effective cotton tufts or feathers. The contest appears to have been of ZAPOTEC origin, from the Oaxaca or Guerrero region. (For details of a related ritual, see TLACALILIZTLI; see WARRIOR CULTS for more information about the Jaguar and Eagle "knights".)

TÍTITL was the month during which a feast was celebrated at the winter solstice, at which the dead and the moon goddess Ilamatecuhtli were honoured. (ILLUSTRATION FROM THE CODEX MAGLIABECCHIANO.)

TWINS & CULTURE HEROES

MANY CITIES IN ANCIENT Mesoamerica had special patron deities and, for some, it is difficult to separate the god from a legendary hero of the same name who benefited the city in some way. The stories in the highland Quiché Maya sacred book *Popul Vuh* of the twins Hun Hunahpú and Vucub Hunahpú, and of the hero twins Hunahpú and Xbalanqué, and of their journeys and conflicts with the underworld lords and involvement with creation, are just two examples of culture heroes who provided an exemplar to Maya rulers in their relations with the gods. Other heroes, who provided inspiration or who embodied tribal and legendary history and claims to lineage, might have been the end product of conflated histories that originally included several rulers or heroes.

Such might have been the case with Mixcóatl, the Toltec founder of Culhúa, and with his son Ce Ácatl Topiltzin and the man-god Quetzalcóatl/Kukulkán, founder of Tollán (Tula) and of Chichén Itzá. The México Aztecs deliberately sought marriage alliance with the Culhúa, accepted rule by a Culhúa prince in order to secure their claim to Toltec ancestry and lineage, and subsequently rewrote Toltec history to suit and support their claim. In another example, to the Tlalhuica Aztecs of the Valley of Morelos, south of the Basin of Mexico, the god/hero Tepoztécatl delivered the people of Tepoztlán from the dominance of the city of Xochicalco.

THE HERO TWINS *Hunahpú (above) and Xbalanqué of the Quiché Maya sacred text, the* Popul Vuh, *who played the ball game for their lives, were perhaps the most well-known heroes of ancient Maya Mesoamerica. Maya vases and other ceramic vessels depicted a wealth of such figures. (CLASSIC PERIOD POLYCHROME VASE FROM HIGHLAND GUATEMALA, POSSIBLY SHOWING HUNAHPÚ.)*

THE MOST CELEBRATED hero of both central and southern Mesoamerica, and of both Toltec-Aztec and Maya civilizations, was the legendary leader and god Quetzalcóatl/Kukulkán. His politically and religiously charged peregrinations led him to found two cities, and the prophesy of his triumphant return, seized upon by Hernán Cortés, made inevitable the downfall of the Aztec Empire. At the two cities that he allegedly established – Tollán (ancient Tula) (top left and top right) and Chichén Itzá (above and right) – there are pyramid-temples dedicated to his honour, and nearly identical palatial structures.

A PRINCIPAL structure at Xochicalco is the Pyramid of the Plumed Serpents (left), whose bodies coil around the base of the pyramid-platform. According to local legend, the town of Tepoztlán was obliged to offer an annual sacrificial victim – an old man – to its rival Xochicalco, to be devoured by the latter's dragon. Tepoztécatl disguised himself as an old woodcutter and, presenting himself as the sacrificial victim, slew the dragon, thus ending the tribute. The story is possibly a long folk memory and metaphor for a time when Xochicalco dominated Tepoztlán but was eventually defeated and its domination overthrown.

TLAHUIZCALPANTECUHTLI,

a manifestation of *QUETZALCÓATL* and of *XÓLOTL*, was the twin deity of the planet Venus, as both morning and evening "star": as the former, he was Quetzalcóatl; as the latter, he was Xólotl, the twin brother. As the morning star he was Lord of the Dawn, 12th of the 13 *LORDS OF THE DAY*. The dual nature of the Venus "star" was represented in the codices as a living man (the morning) and as a skull (the evening).

The movements of Venus were of considerable importance in the Mesoamerican calendar and religion. Not only were its movements calculated and monitored with great accuracy in day-to-day life through the seasons of the year, but the grand coincidence of the Venusian and other celestial cycles was also of supreme importance in the "Calendar Round" (that is, the commencement, on exactly the same named day and month, of several calendrical cycles: the Venusian orbit of 584 days, the solar year of 365.25 days, the shorter day-and-month cycle of 260 days, and two 52-year ritual cycles). The eve of the day of this coincidence was felt to be a time of apprehension, fear and foreboding by the Aztecs; it was a period of evil and of immense potential for menace and destruction. Consequently great sacrifices, offerings and strict adherence to ritual were required at these times (see *TOXIUHMOLPILIA*).

In the Aztec *CREATION MYTH* Tlahuizcalpantecuhtli was ultimately responsible for setting the sun and the moon into motion. The two bodies had ascended into the sky as the spirits of *NANAHU-ATZIN* and *TECUCIZTÉCATL*, but they remained motionless. Nanahuatzin (the sun) demanded blood sacrifice (see also *TONATIUH*) and, for such arrogance, Tlahuizcalpantecuhtli hurled a dart at him with his *atl-atl*. It missed its mark, and he received in return a dart through the head, transforming him into stone – the god of coldness, *ITZTLACOLIUHQUI*. The gods and goddesses concluded that only their own sacrifice would persuade the sun and moon to move, so Tlahuizcalpantecuhtli (as Quetzalcóatl) cut out their hearts one by one with an obsidian knife. (See also *ORDERING THE WORLD, COLOURS & THE CARDINAL DIRECTIONS*)

TLALCHITONATIUH

("land, or place, of *TONATIUH* – the sun") was a later *NAHUATL* name for an early Mesoamerican deity worshipped at the ancient city of *TEOTIHUACÁN*. He was the Jaguar sun or Falling sun and, as such, became the special deity to the later *TOLTEC*, *MAYA*-Toltec and *AZTEC* Jaguar and Eagle *WARRIORS CULTS*.

A major god at Teotihuacán during the first to the seventh centuries AD, his cult was disseminated into the highlands of Guatemala – where the art and architecture of the Maya highland site of Kaminaljuyú shows strong Teotihuacano influence in the fourth to seventh centuries AD – and into other Maya cities in the Yucatán.

At Teotihuacán itself, the Jaguar god might have been worshipped in the Palace of the Jaguars, one of several palaces around the Plaza of the Pyramid of the Moon.

The Jaguar Palace complex comprises three chambers on the north, south and west around a central courtyard, and an open platform on the east. The central staircase has flanking ramps decorated with bas-relief serpents, their rattles at the bases of the ramps. The main chamber is decorated with a mural depicting two "plumed jaguars" – they wear fancy feather headdresses – with rows of shells running down their backs to the tips of their tails. Each is shown blowing on a plumed *Strombus*-shell trumpet – the sound of which is symbolized by small scrolls that issue from the shells. Drops of blood or water also fall from the shells. Above the figures is a row of masks representing *TLÁLOC*, alternating with year-sign glyphs. A narrow passage, leading from the northwest corner of the courtyard, enters several more rooms, in which there are further murals. These depict pairs of human hands, clutching feline-like animals caught in a net, with scrolls representing their roars issuing from the animals' mouths.

These murals undoubtedly represent religious symbolism. Apart from the obvious importance of water and/or blood, however, and of the surreal beasts, we have no idea of their significance, of the role played by the creatures, or of what ceremonies might have been performed in the rooms.

THE TLALHUICA

were one of the original seven *AZTEC* tribes from the legendary caves of *CHICOMOZTOC*. These people migrated from northwestern Mesoamerica, in the 12th century AD, into the Valley of Morelos south of the Basin of Mexico. There, they established a loose confederation of city-states based around Cuernavaca. They were eventually conquered by the México Aztecs in the latter's 15th-century expansions, and the ceremonial centre of Teopanzolco was built in Cuernavaca. The city became a favourite vacation retreat for Aztec rulers.

TLÁLOC (*tlalli* "earth", *oc* "something on the surface") was the *AZTEC* name for one of the most ancient and fundamental of Mesoamerican gods, a giver of life and a source of destruction, but, first and foremost, the god of rain. Images of him were made from at least the second or third century AD at *TEOTIHUACÁN*, and he is probably descended from the more "primitive" Olmec *GOD IV.* He is directly equivalent to Maya *CHAC*, Mixtec *DZAHUI*, Totonac *TAJÍN* and Zapotec *COCIJO*, and possibly also to Tarascan *CHUPITHIRIPEME*.

In the Aztec capital of *TENOCH-TITLÁN*, Tláloc was given equal status with the exclusively Aztec god *HUITZILOPOCHTLI*. Their twin temples stood atop the Templo Mayor pyramid-platform, with a magnificent double staircase leading up to them – Tláloc's plastered and painted in brilliant blue (representing water) and white, and Huitzilopochtli's plastered and painted blood red, for war. The priests of both gods were afforded equal rank in Aztec society.

Associations with other deities include his sister-consort *CHALCHI-ÚHTLICUE* – alongside whom he governed Tlaloque (literally, the Tlálocs), his two wives *XOCHIQUET-ZAL* (abducted by *TEZCATLIPOCA*) and *MATLALCUEITL*, as well as the plumed serpent *QUETZALCÓATL*. Tláloc was the ruler of the seventh day, *MÁZATL* ("deer"), and his calendrical name was *9 OCÉLOTL* ("9 jaguar") in the 365-day calendar cycle; he was eighth of the 13 *LORDS OF THE DAY* and ninth of the nine *LORDS OF THE NIGHT*. He ruled over the Third Sun of the Aztec *CREATION MYTH*.

Tláloc was associated with all forms of precipitation and their related events and conditions: rain, hail, ice, snow, clouds, floods, drought, thunder and lightning. Presumably on account of these attributes, he was also associated with mountains (for example, on the appropriately named volcanic

TLÁLOC, god of rain and agriculture, was an ancient and fundamental Mesoamerican deity (his carved head alternates with that of Quetzalcóatl on the Pyramid of Quetzal-cóatl at Teotihuacán) and he appears frequently in the codices, as here, with bespectacled eye. (ILLUSTRATION FROM THE CODEX MAGLIABECCHIANO.)

peak of Tláloc, southeast of Mexico City, the ruins of a long pair of walls mark a processional way approaching the artificially flattened summit, where there are two quadrangular structures, a courtyard and various other mounds). He was also frequently depicted with serpents, as at Teotihuacán, where his sculpted images alternate with those of Quetzalcóatl on the tiers of the Pyramid or Temple of Quetzalcóatl.

He was most spectacularly portrayed with rings or "spectacles" around his eyes, and with fangs, and often also with a volute across his mouth; at Teotihuacán and other sites, his importance to agriculture is shown by a symbolic corn- (maize-) cob-shaped mouth. Elsewhere he was represented in free-standing sculptures, and he was also depicted in pre-Spanish-

conquest and post-conquest codices. His Maya counterpart, Chac, was depicted singly and repeatedly in stacks of heads at Copán and Chichén Itzá and elsewhere in the Petén and Puuc regions of Yucatán.

In ritual, Tláloc presided over numerous other fertility gods and goddesses, and was celebrated in regular rites. Frequent human sacrifices were offered to him and to these associated deities, symbolically bringing together the blood and the water of human existence. Less violently, corn ears and stalks were kept and venerated in households and were used as decoration by warriors. Particular rituals and festivities were held in Tláloc's honour in the months of *ATLCA-HUALO* and *TOZOZTONTLI*, at which time children were sacrificed on mountain tops; if the child cried it was considered a good sign, as the tears were a symbol of rain and moisture in a dry land.

Tláloc received victims of death by drowning, lightning and contagious diseases, including leprosy, into an earthly paradise called Tlalocán. In keeping with his more benevolent side, this "Place of Tláloc", was believed to be a garden of abundance and pleasure and, instead of being cremated (the normal death rite), such victims were buried with a piece of dry wood, which was believed to sprout abundantly with leaves and blossom in Tlalocán. (For an alternative interpretation, see *TEOTIHUACÁN SPIDER WOMAN*.) Tláloc's importance to agriculture and climate were further represented in his fourfold conception as the four world colours and cardinal directions. He was believed to keep four great clay jars, one for each earthly direction: from the jar for the east he dispensed life-giving rains to fertilize the soil, and from the other jars he poured forth death-dealing drought, frost and disease. (See also *CREATION & THE UNIVERSE*)

THE MASSIVE *carved block of the rain god Tláloc (or of his female counterpart or sister – the water goddess Chalchiúhtlicue) stands in front of the Museo Nacional de Antropología, Mexico City.*

TLALOCÁN, the mythical paradise of the rain god *TLÁLOC*.

THE TLÁLOCS, the gods of the four directional winds and cardinal points (two of whom were *NAPPATECUHTLI* and *OPOCHTLI*), were the dispensers of sustenance to humankind. At the beginning of time they had played a crucial role in bringing corn (maize) and other edible plants to humankind (see *TONACATÉPETL*) and continued to do so in the cycle of the seasons.

The *TEPICTOTON*, another manifestation, were the "little Tlálocs", gods of mountain rains.

TLALOQUE see *TLÁLOCS*.

TLALTECUHTLI ("earth lord") was one of the many central Mesoamerican deities to have dual gender (see *OMETEOTL*). Although perceived as having both male and female aspects, Tlaltecuhtli was usually referred to as female. She was the Earth Monster, portrayed as a huge, fat, toad-like beast possessing a wide mouth with two great protruding fangs, and feet armed with sharp claws. The Yucatecan *MAYA* pantheon included a similar earth beast, and the monster-toad image was frequently merged with another earth monster in the form of a colossal crocodile, whose wide, ridged back formed the world's mountain ranges. She was also the second of the 13 *LORDS OF THE DAY*.

Tlaltecuhtli swallowed the sun every evening as it set and regurgitated it in the morning at sunrise. She was said to consume the hearts of sacrificial victims and was therefore frequently carved on the undersides of the stone boxes called *cuauhxicalli* (literally "eagle house" or "eagle box") in which the heart and blood of the victims were placed after being torn from their opened chest cavities.

In the creation – or more correctly the re-creation – of the earth, it was Tlaltecuhtli who provided

TLALTECUHTLI, the fat toad-monster and foundation of the earth, is suitably placed to support the base of a Totonac pyramid-platform. (POSTCLASSIC PERIOD GULF COAST TOTONAC SITE OF EL TAJÍN.)

the raw materials. The process began when *QUETZALCÓATL* and *TEZCATLIPOCA* descended from their abode in the sky to see Tlaltecuhtli astride the world ocean. She greeted them ferociously and craved flesh to eat; not only were her jaws equipped with fangs, but her elbows, knees and other joints also had gnashing mouths. The appalled Quetzalcóatl and Tezcatlipoca concluded that the new world of the Fifth Sun could not possibly exist while such a monster survived, so they plotted to destroy her. Transforming themselves into two great serpents, one seized her by the right hand and left foot while the other seized her by the left hand and right foot and, in the ensuing struggle, they eventually succeeded in ripping her asunder – but not before she had torn Tezcatlipoca's left foot off his leg. The upper portion of her body became the earth and the remaining portions were thrown into the sky to create the heavens.

The other gods were not pleased with such summary action, however, and, in order to console the spirit of the dismembered earth

monster, they decreed that all the plants of the earth that are essential to the well-being of humans must arise from the parts of her body. Thus, her hair became the trees, flowers and herbs, while her skin provided the materials for the grasses and smaller flowers. Her eyes were transformed into sources for springs, wells and caves, while her mouth was the source of large caverns and the great rivers. Her nose was transformed into the mountains and valleys.

Mesoamericans declared that the sounds of the earth were sometimes the screams of Tlaltecuhtli in her death throes, or alternatively the sounds of her demands for human flesh and blood. Only the sacrifice of humans could quell her anger and ensure that the earth would continue to provide its sources of human sustenance; so, as with the demands of *HUITZILOPOCHTLI* and *TONATIUH*, the *AZTECS* were provided with more reasons to pursue their wars of conquest (see *XOCHIYAÓYOTL*).

TLALTÍCPAC ("earth"), in the tripartite *AZTEC* universe, represented the here and now, the visible, tangible present, the surface of the earth. It stood in juxtaposition to *TOPÁN* – "that which was above" – and to *MICTLÁN* – "that which was below".

TLAMIQUECHOLLI see *QUECHOLLI*.

TLAUIXCALPANTECUHTLI see *TLAHUIZCALPANTECUHTLI*.

THE TLAXCALTECA, also sometimes called the Teochichimeca, were one of the original seven *AZTEC* tribes from the legendary caves of *CHICOMOZTOC*. They migrated from northwestern Mesoamerica in the 12th century AD and eventually settled in the eastern Basin of Mexico, in Alcoluacán. Their patron deity was the god *MIXCÓATL-CAMAXTLI*.

In the 14th century they were driven to the south by the Tepanec, Culhua and México Aztecs, some migrating to Chalco and others over the eastern rim of the Basin into Tlaxcallán, the area of the present-day state of Tlaxcala. The México continued to attack them but never succeeded in conquering them and incorporating them into their empire. When the Spaniards arrived, the Tlaxcalteca eagerly joined them in their attack on the Aztec Empire.

TLAXOCHIMACO see *MICCAILHUITONTLI*.

TLAZOLTÉOTL, a central Mesoamerican earth goddess related to *CIHUACÓATL* and *COATLÍCUE*, was the goddess of desire and carnal love, and therefore of fertility. Her NAHUATL name translates literally as "goddess of filth", and in that sense she represented the consequences of lust and licentiousness, and, by extension, the purification and curing associated with diseases of sexual excess; in this aspect she had the alternative name of TLAEL-QUANI, which literally means "eater of excrement". She was patroness of the day OCÉLOTL, the 14th of the 20 days, was the fifth of the 13 LORDS OF THE DAY, and seventh of the nine LORDS OF THE NIGHT. She was also sometimes associated with the more primitive earth goddess TOCI. Other manifestations or associations for Tlazoltéoltl were with IXCUINAN and HUIXTOCÍHUATL and, in certain aspects, her MAYA counterpart was IX CHEL.

Tlazoltéotl was portrayed in the codices with a band of raw cotton and with two spindles or bobbins decorating her headdress. Sometimes, like the god XIPE TOTEC, she would wear the flayed skin of a human sacrificial victim, possibly to represent new birth from the womb. She was worshipped during the festival of OCHPANITZTLI along with CHICOMECÓATL (goddess of corn/maize) and TETEOINNAN (the old earth goddess).

Her ultimate origin was HUA-STEC, and she appeared in the AZTEC pantheon after their conquest of the northern Gulf Coast.

TLOQUE NAHUAQUE ("lord of everywhere"), an abstract concept, was a deity advocated by the TEXCOCAN king NEZAHUALCÓYOTL ("Fasting Coyote"). He/she was a representation of infinity ("he – or it – without beginning or end"), and the unknowable. In spirit he/she was genderless, a creator deity and the supreme force of the cosmos. He/she was invisible and, although worshipped like other gods and goddesses, there were no idol images of him/her in the temples.

Such an over-theoretical deity was far ahead of its time compared to the rest of the Mesoamerican pantheon, and Tloque Nahuaque was the closest approach ever made to monotheism in Mesoamerica (see also COQUI XEE, HUNAB KU and OMETEOTL). In deference to his people's feelings and beliefs, Nezahualcóyotl was careful not to neglect the conventional gods and goddesses. Acceptance and veneration of Tloque Nahuaque was not widespread, nor did it survive long after the king's death.

TOCHTLI ("rabbit") was the eighth of the 20 AZTEC day-names and one of the year-bearing days – there were 13 Tochtli years in a 52-year cycle (see also ÁCATL, CALLI and TÉCPATL). It had a favourable augury and its patron deity was MAYÁHUEL, associated with the moon and fertility; its orientation was south. The MAYA and ZAPOTEC equivalents were LAMAT and LAPA.

Calendrical dates and deity associations included: 1 Tochtli, for Mayáhuel as goddess of PULQUE; 2 Tochtli, for OMETOCHTLI ("two rabbits"); 7 Tochtli, for the earth goddess COATLÍCUE; and 400 Tochtli, for the pulque gods in general (see CENTZÓNTOTOCHTIN).

TOCI, "our grandmother", was an ancient earth goddess. It is possible that she was originally a goddess of the HUASTECS. A major AZTEC deity, she was closely associated with TETEOINNAN ("mother of the gods") and was sometimes called Tlallilyollo ("heart of the earth"). She was worshipped at the harvest festival of OCHPANITZTLI.

As an earth goddess Toci was the patroness of midwives and curers, and was also closely associated with the Mesoamerican sweat bath (temescal; see also QUILAZTLI). She was also clearly related to TLAZOL-TÉOTL-TLAELQUANI, and was often depicted with black facial markings and a cotton-spool headdress similar in appearance to those worn by these goddesses.

Toci was also associated with war. According to Aztec legend, when they were offered a daughter of the ruler of Culhuacán in a marriage alliance, the Aztecs sacrificed the unfortunate girl to their war god HUITZILOPOCHTLI, and flayed her as Toci. As a result of this act they incurred the wrath of the Culhua, who banished them to the marshes of the western lake shores.

TOHIL was a major deity of the highland Quiché MAYA of Guatemala, who was described in the sacred POPUL VUH text as the god who guided the Quiché during their migrations through Mesoamerica to the highlands. He made great demands for blood sacrifice of his people, and the Quiché obliged him by sacrificing some of their own as well as war captives. Tohil's principal temple was situated at Utatlán, the Quiché capital city.

TOLLÁN
see TOLTECS.

TLAZOLTÉOTL ("goddess of filth") or Tlaelquani ("eater of excrement"), originally a Huastec deity, was the goddess of sexual desire, excess and sin – the consequence of overindulgent lust.
(ILLUSTRATION FROM CODEX VATICANUS B.)

THE TOLTECS were a mingled group of *CHICHIMECA* tribes from the northwest of Mesoamerica who migrated into central Mesoamerica and ultimately into the Yucatán Peninsula in the ninth and tenth centuries AD. Their culture became a combination of more ancient *TEOTIHUACANO* (and other central Mesoamerican city-states), Gulf Coast and *MAYA* elements, mixed with distinctive Toltec elements.

According to *AZTEC* legend, the Toltec dynasty was founded by their heroic leader *CE TÉCPATL MIXCÓATL* ("One Flint Cloud Serpent"), who led his people from somewhere in northwest Mesoamerica into the Basin of Mexico, where they established the city of Culhuacán. He married a local Nahua woman and, shortly after his murder by a rival political faction his son, the future king *CE ÁCATL TOPILTZIN* ("One Reed Sacrificer"), was born. Although the mother died in childbirth, Ce Ácatl Topiltzin was raised in exile to avenge his father, which he did upon coming of age.

As leader of the Toltecs, Ce Ácatl Topiltzin led them out of the Basin of Mexico to found a new capital to the northwest at Tollán (Tula). Again, according to legend, renewed political rivalry developed between factions supporting the peaceful plumed-serpent god *QUETZALCÓATL* and the war advocate *TEZCATLIPOCA*. Renamed as Ce Ácatl Topiltzin Quetzalcóatl, the king was driven into exile and led his followers east to the Gulf Coast, and, according to *MAYA* legend, became *KUKULKÁN*, the heroic founder of Chichén Itzá.

Toltec religion included most of the major central Mesoamerican gods and goddesses, and was centred on human sacrifice to honour and appease the deities. Their warlike tendencies were greatly revered and emulated by the Aztecs, who clearly altered the histories to establish a dynastic relationship with the Toltecs. The Aztecs, as well as many other central Mesoamerican peoples, regarded the Toltecs as the inventors of almost all civilized things, from writing, art and medicine to metallurgy.

Archaeological evidence at Tollán and Chichén Itzá bears out an astonishingly close relationship between the architecture of the two sites, but also reveals much longer sequences of settlement and development at both sites than the legendary histories would indicate. Nevertheless, the connections between the two cities and the peregrinations of the Tolteca-Chichimeca and their leaders seem to have some basis in fact. The very name Tollán, meaning "place of the rushes", was also applied by Mesoamericans to Teotihuacán and to the Aztec capital *TENOCHTITLÁN*; and the Quiché Maya sacred *POPUL VUH* text recounts the story of journey from their highland Guatemalan kingdom, east to "Tulan", by which it seems they actually meant Chichén Itzá (whose ancient name, Uucil Abnal, means "Seven Bushy Place"). (See also *THE RITUAL BALL GAME*)

TONACATECUHTLI or Ometecuhtli, seen here as the male part of duality – Ometeotl. A remote concept, he dwelt with his female counterpart Omecíhuatl in Omeyocán, the highest of the 13 heavenly levels. (ILLUSTRATION FROM CODEX VATICANUS B.)

TONACACÍHUATL
see *OMECÍHUATL*.

TONACATECUHTLI
see under *OMETECUHTLI*.

TONACATÉPETL ("sustenance mountain") was where, in the *CREATION MYTH*, corn (maize) and other grains were stored. According to the *ANALES DE CUAUHTITLÁN*, after the creation of the Fifth Sun and of humans, the gods realized that they needed to supply the new race with sustenance. They therefore set about searching for a source of food for humans, and it was *QUETZALCÓATL* who espied a red ant running along the ground carrying a grain of corn. He asked the ant, *AZCATL*, where such a wonderful food was to be found, but the ant at first refused to tell. After much threatening, however, Azcatl agreed to show Quetzalcóatl the source, and led him to Mount Tonacatépetl. Quetzalcóatl changed himself into a black ant and followed Azcatl through a narrow entrance and deep into the mountain, to a chamber filled with not only corn, but also with many other seeds and grains. Quetzalcóatl took some of the corn kernels back to *TAMOANCHÁN*, where the gods chewed the corn and fed some of the resulting mash (*maza*) to the infant humans, whereupon they gained in strength and grew.

The gods then asked, "What is to be done with Tonacatépetl?" Quetzalcóatl tried to sling a rope around the entire mountain and haul it to a more convenient place on earth, but it proved too heavy even for him to move. So, rather than try to move the mountain, with its grains and seeds, to humankind, it was decided to scatter the grains and seeds from the mountain. The old diviners *OXOMOCO* and *CIPACTONAL* cast lots to determine how to do this, and the signs told them that the weak and diseased god *NANAHUATZIN* should break Tonacatépetl open. To do so he called upon the help of the four *TLÁLOCS*, the directional gods of the winds and the rains, and, crucially, of lightning. Tonacatépetl was duly split asunder, and the black, blue, red and white (or yellow) winds blew the grains and seeds across the land, while the rains watered them so that they grew where they fell. Humans were quick to take advantage of these renewable sources of food.

The Aztecs sometimes identified Iztaccíhuatl, a lofty volcanic cone on the southeastern rim of the Basin of Mexico, as Tonacatépetl.

TONALAMATL, a Mexican *Book of the Days*, was a ritual calendrical text written to record a *Tonalpohualli* or cycle of 260 named days and months. The text and pictures, known as a codex, were painted on deerskin or bark paper and folded as a screen-fold. For the elements of the *Tonalamatl* and *Tonalpohualli*, see the feature spread *ORDERING THE WORLD*, and *LORDS OF THE DAY* and *LORDS OF THE NIGHT*.

THE TONALTEUCTIN were the 13 Aztec *LORDS OF THE DAY*.

TONANTZIN ("little mother") was the *AZTEC* name for the benevolent manifestation of the goddess *CIHUACÓATL* in her role as earth goddess and mother of humankind (see *CREATION MYTHS*). In Aztec *TENOCHTITLÁN* a temple dedicated to Tonantzin stood on the site of the present-day Basilica of Tepeyac in Mexico City, the church that contains the shrine of the Virgin of Guadelupe, patron saint of Mexico.

TONATIUH, the central Mesoamerican sun god, was manifested as *Cuauhtlehuánitl* ("ascending eagle") and as *Cuauhtémoc* ("descending eagle"). His counterpart was *YOHUALTECUHTLI* (or *Yohual-tonatiuh*), meaning the "night sun". Especially for the México *AZTECS*, he was associated with the god of war, *HUITZILOPOCHTLI*, as the young warrior. In another manifestation he was *PILTZINTECUHTLI*, the youthful Tonatiuh and third of the nine *LORDS OF THE NIGHT*. His Zapotec equivalent was *COPIJCHA*.

Tonatiuh, the life-giving sun, was the present, the Fifth Sun of central Mesoamerican creation. He ruled the day *QUIÁHUITL* ("rain") and was fourth of the 13 *LORDS OF THE DAY*. Through his heat and thirst for human blood he gave strength and courage to warriors. It was to him – as well as to *TLALTE-CUHTLI* and to Huitzilopochtli – that frequent human sacrifice, carried to extremes by the México Aztecs, was required, and to whom the hearts and blood of the victims were offered. Daily he battled against the dark and was swallowed by the Earth Monster Tlaltecuhtli. Daily he accepted the spirits of slain warriors and escorted them across the sky to his paradise.

Tonatiuh himself was born as a result of the personal sacrifices of the gods: first *NANAHUATZIN*, who heroically leapt into the ceremonial fire and rose again as the sun – at first stationary – at the meeting of the gods and goddesses at *TEOTI-HUACÁN*; then the other gods and goddesses, who appeased Tonatiuh's demands for sacrificial blood by allowing *QUETZALCÓATL-TLA-HUIZCALPANTECUHTLI* to cut out their hearts and create *Nahui Ollin* (literally "four movement"), the sun of motion (see *CREATION MYTHS*).

The huge, intricately carved stone popularly known as the "calendar stone", discovered at the site of the Templo Mayor (Great Temple) in Mexico City (*TENOCH-TITLÁN*) in 1790, is believed by some scholars to represent Tonatiuh. Others hold that the central image represents his counterpart, the night sun Yohualtecuhtli or Yohualtonatiuh. Whichever aspect is portrayed, the symbolism of the sun and the cosmic forces of Mesoamerican mythology are manifest. The sculpted face of the stone is made up of a centre and series of ring-panels. In the centre is the sun, carved as a stylized human face. From his mouth protrudes the sacrificial knife and, in the first ring, to right and left of the face, two rounded arms form claws clutching human hearts. Some scholars have suggested that the stone was used flat, as a sacrificial platform upon which to stretch victims.

The remaining concentric ring-panels are filled with hieroglyphic signs. The first ring, framing the face, is the predicted date (*Nahui Ollin*) of the end of the Fifth Sun. The dates of the preceding suns – Jaguar, Wind, Rain (of Fire) and Water – are carved in boxes to upper left and right, and lower left and right, of the face. The second ring contains glyphs of the 20 *NAHUATL* day-names. Starting at top left, reading anti-clockwise, these are: *CIPACTLI* ("crocodile"), *ÉHECATL* ("wind"), *CALLI* ("house"), *CUETZPALLIN* ("lizard"), *CÓATL* ("serpent"), *MIQUIZTLI* ("death"), *MÁZATL* ("deer"), *TOCHTLI* ("rabbit"), *ATL* ("water"), *ITZCUINTLI* ("dog"), *OZOMATLI* ("monkey"), *MALINALLI* ("grass"), *ÁCATL* ("reed"), *OCÉLOTL* ("jaguar"), *CUAUHTLI* ("eagle"), *COZ-CACUAUHTLI* ("vulture"), *OLLIN* ("movement", or "earthquake"), *TÉCPATL* ("flint knife"), *QUIÁHUITL* ("rain") and *XÓCHITL* ("flower"). Next, a narrow ring has repetitive, decorative designs, and the final ring contains repeated symbols of turquoise and jade, the colours of the heavens, and symbols of the equinoxes and solstices. The outer border comprises two *XIUHCÓATL* (turquoise or fire snakes) that symbolize cosmic order, cyclicity and the present world. Their heads, adorned with appropriately elaborate headdresses, meet at the base, and at the top their tails flank a boxed glyph of the ritual date "13 Reed" – AD 1011, the "official" date of the start of the Fifth Sun. (*See ORDERING THE WORLD*)

TONATIUH "ascending eagle", the Aztec sun god and ruler of the Fifth Sun. On his back is the symbol for ollin (earthquake), which the Aztecs believed would destroy the world of the Fifth Sun. His image also occupies the central part of the great "calendar stone" (see ORDERING THE WORLD and DUALITY & OPPOSITION).

TOPÁN ("that which is above us") was part of the *AZTEC* tripartite universe, comprising *TLALTÍCPAC*, *MICTLÁN* and Topán. Topán included the skies and the heavens – the dwelling place of the gods and goddesses.

THE TOTONACS were a people of Postclassic Mesoamerica who inhabited the area of the present-day Mexican states of northern Puebla and northern and central Veracruz. The powerful early Postclassic Period city-state of El Tajín might have been their early capital but, by the 16th century, it was at Cempoala, more than 150 km (93 miles) to the south. They spoke a language belonging to the Macro-Mayan group.

Cempoala was among the first cities visited by the Spaniards and the Totonac were the first allies to Hernán Cortés in his campaign against the *AZTECS*.

TÓXCATL ("dry thing") was the sixth (or, in some sources, the fifth) of the 18 months in the *AZTEC* solar year, during which special ceremonies were held to honour *TEZCATLIPOCA* ("smoking mirror"). Preparations for the ceremony began a year in advance, when a young warrior, captured in battle, was chosen to impersonate the god Tezcatlipoca. For a year Aztec priests taught him how to conduct himself at court as a noble. He was given his own entourage to attend to his needs, including four chosen maidens who were themselves impersonating the goddesses *ATLATONAN*, *HUIXTOCÍHUATL*, *XILONEN* and *XOCHIQUETZAL*. He was taught to play the clay flutes and allowed to stroll the streets of *TENOCHTITLÁN* carrying a bouquet of flowers and smoking tobacco from a gilded reed pipe.

At the beginning of *Tóxcatl* his dress was changed for that of a warrior captain and he was symbolically married to the four goddesses. On the ceremonial day

he was praised by the king and nobles as a great man, and honoured with bouquets of flowers and ritual dances. Then, on the appointed day, he was taken with his wives and court by royal canoe to a small temple on the lake shore, where all but a few attendants abandoned him. He walked towards the temple playing his clay flutes and, as he mounted the temple steps, broke a flute on each step. At the top, where the priests awaited him, he was spread across the sacrificial stone, a priest holding each limb, while a fifth cut open his chest with an obsidian knife and extracted his heart. This month is also called *Tepopochtli* ("hill of little moisture").

The "Battle of Tóxcatl" or "Massacre of Tóxcatl" occurred in Tenochtitlán in 1520. Hernán Cortés had been welcomed somewhat reluctantly into the city by Moctezuma II Xocoyotzin, but had returned to the coast to confront an expedition, led by Pánfilo de Narváez from Cuba, that had been sent to arrest him. He left his lieutenant, Pedro de Alvarado, in command. As this was the month of *Tóxcatl*, the Aztecs proceeded with the festival. The Spaniards, uneasy at the noise and activities around their quarters, interpreted – or used as an excuse – the enthusiasm and exuberance of the gathered crowds of Aztecs as a threat, and impetuously attacked the ceremony as idolatry. According to Spanish chronicles, more than 8,500 unarmed Aztecs were slain in the ensuing fight.

TOXIUHMOLPILIA ("the tying of the years"), also referred to as the New Fire Ceremony or Sacred Fire Ceremony, was the intense and auspicious ceremony of the renewal and/or securing of the continuance of the present sun. It was the eve of the end of one 52-year calendrical cycle and the beginning of the next, a time of mixed fear and hope: unless the sun could be induced to rise again the next day, and the new fire could be rekindled, the end of the world was nigh.

All temple and household fires were extinguished and the idols of the gods in the temples were doused with water. Household effigies, cooking pots and implements, and the three traditional household hearth stones were discarded.

AT THE END of a successful Toxiuhmolpilia or "New Fire Ceremony", priests lit torches for runners to carry the renewed fire – and hope – to temples and households in Tenochtitlán. (CODEX BORBONICUS.)

Houses, courtyards and streets were swept free of debris. As darkness approached, people climbed onto rooftops and walls. Pregnant women and children covered their faces with *maguey*-leaf masks for protection against the demons of darkness; some sources state that women and children were confined indoors, and that pregnant women were hidden in huge corn (maize) storage jars. Children were kept awake for fear that if they were permitted to fall asleep they would be transformed into mice as a result of failing to witness the critical rite.

Priests, dressed as gods, climbed Mount Uixachtecatl (Uixachtlán) or Citlaltepec (the Cerro de la Estrella in the Mexico City precinct of Ixtapalapa) near the ceremonial centre of *TENOCHTITLÁN*, the *AZTEC* capital. At midnight, when the Pleiades (*Tianquiztli*) passed through the zenith and the star *YOHUALTECUHTLI* appeared in the centre of the sky, a selected captive

– no doubt intoxicated and feeling especially honoured – was sacrificed by opening his chest with a ceremonial obsidian knife and extracting his still-pulsating heart. In his opened chest cavity, a fire was kindled, and, if lit successfully, the cry went up – doubtless accompanied by huge relief and release from the tension of the moment – and runners with torches were despatched to dispense the new flame throughout the land in relays. Autosacrifice by ear-piercing and blood-letting was offered by all as penance and, as dawn broke, general rejoicing followed, including the renewal of discarded articles, the rekindling of the household hearths and temple fires, and even the start of new building projects.

If the fire in the sacrificial victim's chest should have failed to light, it was believed that darkness would engulf the earth, and that celestial monsters – the *TZITZIMIME* – would descent to devour it and all humankind.

TOZOZTONTLI ("short watch") was the fourth (or, in some sources, the third) of the 18 months in the *AZTEC* solar year, in which various rain, water and corn (maize) deities were propitiated, especially *TLÁLOC* (to whom flowers were offered) and *CHALCHIÚHTLICUE*, and *CENTÉOTL* and *CHICOMECÓATL*. Also in this month, the "flayed skin" ritual (see *TLACAXIPEHUALIZTLI*) was completed when the skins of human sacrificial victims were deposited in the "cave" Temple of *XIPE TOTEC* by alms-begging priests. It is also called *Xochimanalo* ("offering of flowers").

TYING OF THE YEARS see *TOXIUHMOLPILIA*.

TZAHUI see *DZAHUI*.

THE TZITZIMIME ("demons of darkness") were the stars visible only during a solar eclipse (see also *ITZPAPÁLOTL*). Naturally, to a

people to whom the sun god *TONATIUH* was a principal and life-giving god, they were seen as harbingers of dread and evil. According to the Aztec *CREATION MYTH*, one day the Tzitzimime would descend to the earth and devour humankind, thus ending the (present) age of the Fifth Sun. Ever-present and always threatening, although unseen, they engaged in a daily battle against the sun at sunrise and sunset.

TZITZIMITL, the *AZTEC* "grandmother" goddess in the sky, was the jealous guardian of the beautiful young virgin *MAYÁHUEL*, who became goddess of the *maguey* plant. She pursued Mayáhuel and the wind god *ÉHECATL*, who had abducted Mayáhuel down to the earth, and, finding the two lovers already united as the entwined branches of a tree, split the tree in two in her rage. This destroyed the branch representing Mayáhuel, the shreds of which Tzitzimitl fed to her demon servants, the *TZITZIMIME*. Éhecatl, however, was unharmed, and he resumed his former shape, gathered Mayáhuel's bones and planted them in a field, where they grew into plants. These were the *maguey* or *agave* (*Agave americana*), from which the white "wine", known as *PULQUE*, is made.

TZOMPANTLI, the skull rack, was a framework supporting poles for displaying the skulls of sacrificial victims – the skulls were aligned along poles inserted through holes drilled in their sides. Stone blocks were also carved in facsimile of these racks.

UAYEB GOD, a *MAYA* deity of misgivings and mishaps, was associated with the five ill-omened days (the *uayeb*) at the end of the solar calendar year (see *NEMONTEMI*). The Uayeb god was portrayed as an old man and also as the small atlante figures, made of stone, that supported stone shelves, plinths and benches, and he was associated with the *BACABS* and with the *PAUAHTUN*. His symbols included, of course, the number five, and he can be identified by a snail or turtle shell on his back. He was also a god of the underworld.

UEUECÓYOTL see *HUEHUECÓYOTL*.

UIXACHTECATL, or Uixachtlán, was one of the *AZTEC* names for Cerro de la Estrella in the Mexico City precinct of Ixtapalapa, near to the ceremonial centre of *TENOCHTITLÁN*, and the venue for the *TOXIUHMOLPILIA*, "the tying of the years", ceremony.

THE SKULLS of sacrificial victims were stacked on tzompantli *(skull racks) in rows, and also represented on huge block stone sculptures – as seen here at Tenochtitlán/Mexico City.*

UIXACHTLÁN see *UIXACHTECATL*.

UIXTOXÍHUATL see *HUIXTOCIHUATL*.

THE VEINTANAS were the 18 annual 20th-day feasts and religious ceremonies held over the course of the Mesoamerican 365-day solar year. Every eight years, an extra set of rituals known as the *Atamalcualiztli* was held, and every 52 years the New Fire Ceremony – *TOXIUHMOLPILIA* – was celebrated. Within the 260-day calendar cycle – *Tonalpohualli* (see under *TONALAMATL*) – were still more ceremonies. These were the "movable ceremonies", so called because they did not occur at the same time each year but changed their dates according to the seasons. (See also the feature *ORDERING THE WORLD*, and the individual entries for each month)

VUCUB CAME ("seven death"), was one of the leaders of the Lords of *XIBALBA*, the Quiché *MAYA* underworld (see *HUN CAME*).

X

VUCUB HUNAHPÚ ("seven Hunahpú") was one of the first-born of the human race – born of the "grandfather" *XPIYACOC* and of the "grandmother" *XMUCANÉ* – and the twin brother of *HUN HUNAHPÚ*.

VUCUB-CAQUIZ was a bird-monster in the Maya *POPOL VUH*. At the creation of the world he proclaimed himself both the sun and the moon. Along with his evil giant sons *ZIPACNÁ* and *CABRACÁN*, he was slain by darts from the blow-guns of the hero twins *HUNAHPÚ* and *XBALANQUÉ* in *XIBALBA*.

WARRIOR CULTS were an important feature of *AZTEC* society. The Eagle (sun) and Jaguar (earth) "knights" were two Aztec military orders or cults, though they had originated, or had first been formally organized, by the *TOLTECS*, whose military prowess was legendary, and revered by the Aztecs. Members of the orders were selected, high-ranking members of society. Eagle and Jaguar warriors worshipped the rising sun – *TONATIUH* – and the setting sun – *TLALCHITONATIUH*, respectively. Members of each cult dressed in appropriate costumes of feathered helmet and/or shirt, or jaguar skin. The rites of each mystical order involved special knowledge and initiation procedures, in which, according to the 16th-century chronicler Diego Muñoz Camargo, an aspirant was confined in the temple for 30–40 days to practise fasting and autosacrifice. One privilege was the right to take part in the gladiatorial sacrifice of princely war captives, called the *TLAHUAHUANALIZTLI*.

WORLD TREE was a concept closely allied to the Mesoamerican recognition of the terrestrial cardinal directions and the perceived directions of the Mesoamerican universe, together with assignments of colours, birds, animals, trees, types, day- and year-signs,

EAGLE AND JAGUAR warriors, once chosen for membership, underwent elaborate initiation ceremonies. These were usually held in special temple complexes, often in remote mountain-top locations. One of the most intact of these is the cult site of Malinalco on a cliff top near Tenancingo, northwest of Cuernavaca in the State of Mexico. Steps carved out of the living rock lead up to the main temple, inside which the floor is sculpted with a central eagle, and a jaguar is carved on the bench that runs around the room.

and auguries to the cardinal directions. The *MAYA* assigned particular day-names as "year-bearers" whereas the *AZTECS* assigned particular deities as "sky-bearers", and in both cultures these were linked to the cardinal directions.

In Aztec myth, *TEZCATLIPOCA* and *QUETZALCÓATL* transformed themselves into trees to support the sky (see *CREATION MYTHS*).

The Maya world tree, *Yaxché* or *Kapok*, was the *Ceibe*. *Yaxché* itself signifies "first" or "green" tree, both terms being appropriate: first in terms of a cosmic centre and green as the Maya colour associated with a central place. The great world tree was perceived to link the parts or levels of the universe, with its roots anchored in the underworld, its trunk linking the earth to underworld and heavens, and its

branches spreading into the sky. A similar image prevailed among the cultures of central Mesoamerica, and similar association with the underworld, the earth and the sky are described in several Aztec codices. Throughout Mesoamerica, the world tree was regarded as the central, or fifth, direction, and of equal, if not greater, importance than north, east, south and west.

XAMEN EK, or Ah Chicum Ek, *MAYA* God C, was the god of the North Star (*xamen* means "north"). He was often associated in the codices with *EK CHUAH*, the "black star" or "black warrior". He was portrayed with a distinctive snub-nose and black markings on his head, and is thus frequently associated with, or identified as, the *MONKEY-FACED GOD*; as such, he ruled the Maya day *CHUEN* ("monkey"). His glyph resembles the head of a monkey, and signifies "north". He was a benevolent deity, often depicted alongside *CHAC*.

As the North Star he was the patron and guide of merchants, whose long-distance trading networks were of such importance to Maya civilization (see also *THE OLD BLACK GOD*). In the latitudes of the Yucatán and Petén regions of Maya culture, the North Star is the star that holds its position throughout the year. Xamen Ek's intercession and goodwill were invoked by prayers and offerings of *pom* incense (the resin from the *copal* tree) at special roadside altars. His *AZTEC* counterpart was *YACATECUHTLI*.

XAQUIJA, the Valley *ZAPOTEC* sun god, was an alternative name for *COPIJCHA*.

XARATANGA, the *TARASCAN* moon goddess, was the daughter of *CURICAUERI* and *CUERAUÁPERI*. She was the goddess of the new moon, and of germination, fertility, growth and sustenance. An ancient goddess of agriculture, her cult was centred on the island of Jarácuaro in Lake Pátzcuaro. Her mother, Curicaueri, was the goddess of the old moon.

XBALANQUÉ was one of the hero twins of the Quiché *MAYA* of Guatemala. The sacred *POPUL VUH* text describes how he and his twin brother *HUNAHPÚ* were conceived by the spittle of their father, *HUN HUNAHPÚ*, and how they journeyed to the underworld to avenge the deaths of their father and uncle. (See also *TWINS & CULTURE HEROES*)

XIBALBA, derived from the root word *xib* (meaning "fear, terror, trembling with fright"), was the Quiché *MAYA* underworld (the Lowland Maya and *AZTEC* equivalents were *MITNAL* and *MICTLÁN*). In the sacred *POPUL VUH*, Xibalba was the scene of the adventures of the twin brothers *HUN HUNAHPÚ* and *VUCUB HUNAHPÚ*, who are defeated by the Lords of Xibalba, and then of the revenge taken by the hero twins *HUNAHPÚ* and *XBALANQUÉ*, who succeeded in defeating the lords.

Xibalba had many different levels or worlds within it, including the House of Gloom, the House of Knives, the House of Cold, the House of Jaguars, the House of Fire and the House of Bats. In the last of these, *Zotzihá*, the hero twins faced and passed a series of tests, and Hunahpú was temporarily beheaded by the bat-god *CAMA ZOTZ*. (See also *TWINS & CULTURE HEROES*)

XÍHUTL was the Nahuatl term for the 18 months of 20 days each (that is, 360 days) of the *AZTEC* solar calendar. The remaining five days were called the *NEMONTEMI*.

XILOMANALIZTLI

see *ATLCAHUALO*.

XILONEN,

XILONEN, an adolescent goddess, was a central Mesoamerican fertility deity, the goddess of young corn (maize) – both the plant and the cob. As such, she was closely related to the fertility goddess *CHICOMECÓATL* and in some ways a manifestation of the latter, or a continuity within the concept of fertility. Together with *CENTÉOTL* and *ILAMATECUHTLI* she formed part of the cycle from young and tender corn, through mature and ripe corn, to the old and withered plant. Xilonen was served by a special cult of young virgins in the *AZTEC* capital, *TENOCHTITLÁN*.

Xilonen was one of four Aztec goddesses – with *ATLATONAN*, *HUIX-TOCÍHUATL* and *XOCHIQUETZAL* – who were impersonated by virgins and who were wed for a year to a chosen young warrior, impersonating *TEZCATLIPOCA*, until his sacrifice at the festival of *TÓXCATL*.

XIPE TOTEC

XIPE TOTEC ("flayed one") was the central Mesoamerican god of springtime, an agricultural deity

XIPE TOTEC, the "flayed god" of spring, was probably of Olmec origin. Priests performed ritual dances in his honour wearing the flayed skins of sacrificial victims to symbolize renewal.

and patron of seeds and of planting. He was the Red *TEZ-CATLIPOCA* and was associated with the east cardinal direction. He was patron of *CUAUHTLI* ("eagle"), the 15th of the 20 *AZTEC* day-names, and was represented by the date *1 OCÉLOTL*. His three brothers in the Aztec pantheon were *HUITZ-ILOPOCHTLI*, *QUETZALCÓATL* and *TEZCATLIPOCA*.

Xipe Totec seems to have been of southern highland Mesoamerican origin, possibly ultimately derived from the ancient *OLMEC GOD VI*, or possibly among the *YOPE* of the southern highlands of Guerrero. He was especially honoured by the *TLAXCALTECANS*, and was also honoured by the *ZAPOTECS* and *MIXTECS* of the southern highlands and by the *TARASCAN* state. He was introduced to, and taken up by, only in Late Postclassic times, a few of the *MAYA* city-states, where his imagery appeared in the cities of Oxkintok, Chichén Itzá and Mayapán. Perhaps because of the long tradition of superb craftsmanship – especially metalwork – in the southern highlands of Oaxaca–Guerrero, he was also the patron god of metalsmiths and lapidaries.

He was a god closely associated with torture, and demanded a heavy toll in human sacrifice for his services in giving each year's crops a good prognosis. In the spring festival of *TLACAXIPEHUALIZTLI*, in the third month of the 365-day solar year, ceremonies to supplicate his

favour were held in which sacrificial victims were flayed (skinned) and priests then donned the skins to performed a dance (see also *TLA-ZOLTÉOTL*); the victims were war captives from the *XOCHIYAÓYOTL*, and the purpose was to evoke ancient fertility rites. The "bravest" captive was selected for the honour of being slain in the one-sided "gladiatorial sacrifice" called the *TLAHUAHUANALIZTLI*.

Statuary and masks of Xipe Totec are easily recognizable by their puffy appearance, with double lips and sunken eyes showing a priest in the hideous stretched skin of a victim; on full-body representations the skin is tied with string at the back. The act of donning the sacrificial victim's flayed skin symbolized the regeneration of plant life – the skin was regarded as analogous to the seed husk of the living plant – and flaying the sacrificed victim was considered a re-enactment of the plant's own yearly self-sacrifice of shedding its skin in the act of renewal. The victim's sacrifice was an act of penitential torture, a spiritual liberation, for in the Mesoamerican mindset, death by sacrifice was widely regarded as an honourable death, on a par with death in battle.

Through this association with death, Xipe Totec was linked with the underworld, *MICTLÁN*, and, by extension, it was he who sent dreadful illnesses to humankind, such as smallpox, the plague, skin diseases, scabs and blindness.

XIUHATLATL

XIUHATLATL ("turquoise spear-thrower") was the weapon and sign of office of the *OLD FIRE GOD* and related deities, such as *HUITZILOPOCHTLI*.

XIUHCÓATL

XIUHCÓATL ("turquoise serpent") was the coil of fire, the counterpart of *XIUHTECUHTLI*. In contrast to the benevolent serpent god, *QUETZALCÓATL*, Xiuhcóatl represented the power of fire and the dangerous forces of aridity and drought. In *AZTEC* mythology, the turquoise serpent carried the sun from its rise in the east to its zenith at noon, and, indeed, two such serpents are found encircling the great Aztec "calendar stone" discovered at *TENOCHTITLÁN* in 1790 (see *TONA-TIUH* and *ORDERING THE WORLD*). Turquoise serpents were also seen as an accoutrement of the deities *HUITZILOPOCHTLI* and *TEZCATLIPOCA*.

In their form as an "endless" circle, huge stone sculptures of Xiuhcóatl formed a wall (*coate-pantli*) or boundary around the sacred precinct of Tenochtitlán. A continuous row of them also forms the base of three sides of the great pyramid-platform of the Tenayuca, a city north of Tenochtitlán; and beside the north and south sides, two great coiled serpents are depicted sitting on platforms.

XIUHCÓATL, the fire serpent, could be represented in several forms: such as an endless ring of two serpents around the "calendar stone" of Tonatiuh, or as a double-headed turquoise serpent, as here.

XIUHPILTONTLI, literally "turquoise shield", was the general *NAHUATL* word for the sun.

XIUHTECUHTLI, or *HUEHUETÉOTL*, was the *AZTEC* name for the primitive Mesoamerican deity, the "Old One" and *OLD FIRE GOD*, who possibly originated in the Preclassic Period cultures of the Basin of Mexico and among the *OLMECS* of the Gulf Coast as *GOD I*. Among the *OTOMÍ* he was called *OTONTECUHTLI* and Xócotl. He was usually depicted as an old man, with wrinkled skin and toothless mouth, supporting a brazier on his head for burning incense. Patron of the day *ATL* ("water") and first of the nine Aztec *LORDS OF THE NIGHT* and of the 13 *LORDS OF THE DAY*, he was associated with the number three, symbolic of the three hearthstones

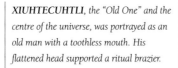

XIUHTECUHTLI, the "Old One" and the centre of the universe, was portrayed as an old man with a toothless mouth. His flattened head supported a ritual brazier.

of the traditional Mesoamerican household. His counterpart was *XIUHCÓATL*, the serpent of fire.

He was perceived as the great, ancient pillar of the world. His fire ran through the entire universe, beginning in *MICTLÁN* ("that which is below us") to *TOPÁN* ("that which is above us"), via the realm of the serpent goddess *COATLÍCUE* and the home fires of all the peoples of the earth. It was Xiuhtecuhtli who presided over the New Fire Ceremony (the *TOXIUHMOLPILIA*), when all household fires had to be extinguished and kindled anew, and who assisted the spirits of the dead in being absorbed into the earth. (See also *COLOURS & THE CARDINAL DIRECTIONS*)

XMUCANÉ was the highland Quiché *MAYA* creator goddess in the *POPUL VUH*, wife of *XPIYACOC* and the "grandmother" of the human race. Her sons were the twins *HUN HUNAHPÚ* and *VUCUB HUNAHPÚ*. Her Aztec equivalent was the goddess *OXOMOCO*.

THE XMULZENCAB were the *MAYA* bee gods of the *CREATION MYTH* in the sacred text of the *CHILAM BALAM*. Each was assigned to a cardinal direction and associated with a specific colour. A deity depicted in the murals at the fortified site of Tulum, on the east-

XOCHIPILLI, the Aztec "flower prince", was a youthful, benign god of pleasure and representative of summer. He is portrayed here bedecked with flowers, singing and accompanying himself with rattles (now lost).

ern coastal cliffs of Yucatán, and designated "the descending god", is interpreted by some scholars as a representation of a Xmulzencab. (See also *AH MUCEN CAB* and *THE BACABS*)

XÓCHILHUITL see *IZCALLI*.

XOCHIMANALO see *TOZOZTONTLI*.

XOCHIPILLI ("flower prince") was a benevolent central Mesoamerican deity. As the god of flowers and souls, and the symbol of summer, he was the benign and amiable manifestation of the young sun god *PILTZINTECUHTLI* – the youthful representation of *TONATIUH*, and the third of the nine *LORDS OF THE NIGHT*. He was closely associated, as well, with *CENTÉOTL* and, in the guise of Centéotl-Xochipilli ("corn-flower prince"), was seventh *LORD OF THE DAY*. He was the flayed flower god of souls, the red-faced personification of the spirit. Thus, penitence to Centéotl-Xochipilli was thought to ensure a regular supply of corn (maize). *AHUIATÉOTL*, the *AZTEC* god of voluptuousness, was another of his manifestations.

With his brothers *IXTLILTON* and *MACUILXÓCHITL*, Xochipilli formed a triumvirate of general good health, pleasure and well-being. He represented masculine fecundity and youth in terms of general gaiety, frolicking, playful mischievousness and even poetry. Little wonder, then, that he ruled the day *OZOMATLI* ("monkey"). *PULQUE* was consumed in large

quantities at ceremonies and festivals held to worship him and other gods of like mind. Alongside his sister/female counterpart *XOCHIQUETZAL*, he was popular among the *CHINAMPA*-dwellers of the southern and western lakes of the Basin of Mexico, especially Xochimilco. Statuary of him was decorated with flowers, garlands and butterflies.

Xochipilli appears to have superseded an earlier pan-Mesoamerican deity of the Preclassic to Classic Period, known as *THE FAT GOD*, who was worshipped especially in the Classic Period city of *TEOTIHUACÁN*. His *ZAPOTEC* equivalent was *QUIABELAGAYO*.

XOCHIQUETZAL, the sister/female counterpart of *XOCHIPILLI*, was the *AZTEC* goddess of flowering and of the fruitful earth. Her name literally means "feathered flower", "richly plumed flower" or, more poetically, "precious flower".

Xochiquetzal was the personification of love and beauty, of domesticity and flowers, and epitomized female sexual power. As the goddess of physical love, the Aztecs saw her as the giver of children. She was patroness to the *anianime* or *maqui*, the courtesans and lady companions of unwed Aztec warriors, and of silversmiths, sculptors, painters and weavers. In some regards she was related to *TOCI* and to *TLAZOLTÉOTL*, but unlike those goddesses, she remained ever young and beautiful. In the codices, she is depicted with two large plumes of quetzal feathers. She ruled the day *XÓCHITL* ("flower").

In myth she was the first wife of *TLÁLOC*, but was abducted by *TEZCATLIPOCA*. She was also associated with the underworld and was celebrated at festivals of the dead with offerings of marigolds. In legend she graced the earth with beauty and with the gifts of flowers and lush growth during the peaceful reign of *QUETZALCÓATL* and the world of the Second Sun.

Xochiquetzal was also one of four Aztec goddesses – along with *ATLATONAN*, *HUIXTOCÍHUATL* and *XILONEN* – who were impersonated by virgins and who were wed for a year to a chosen young warrior, impersonating *TEZCATLIPOCA*, until his sacrifice at the festival of *TÓXCATL*. The human Xochiquetzal was herself sacrificed and flayed, and her skin put on by a priest who pretended to weave at a loom while craftspeople dressed in monkey, jaguar, puma, dog and coyote costumes danced around him. The worshippers completed this gruesome ritual by confessing their sins

XOCHIQUETZAL, "feathered flower" or "precious flower", personified beauty, physical love, female sexual power and fertility. She was the first wife of Tláloc and the sister/female counterpart of Xochipilli.

to Xochiquetzal's idol through bloodletting from their tongues and achieved atonement through a ritual bath.

XÓCHITL ("flower") was the last of the 20 *AZTEC* day-names; it had a neutral augury and its patron deity was *XOCHIQUETZAL*, the "precious flower". The *MAYA* and *ZAPOTEC* equivalent days were *AHAU* and *LAO* or *Loo*.

Calendrical dates and deity associations included: *1 Xóchitl*, for the corn (maize) god *CENTÉOTL*; *2 Xóchitl*, for the feast day of merchants; *5 Xóchitl*, for *MACUILXÓCHITL*, god of pleasure; *7 Xóchitl*, for the sun; and *10 Xóchitl*, for the war god of the city of Huaxtepec, in the present-day state of Morelos, south of the Basin of Mexico.

XOCHITOCA see *IZCALLI*.

THE XOCHIYAÓYOTL ("Flowery War"), initiated by Tlacaélel, the *CIHUACÓATL* (co-ruler) of Moctezuma I Ilhuicamina in the 15th century, was a ritual tournament set up especially to supply victims for sacrifice. They were mock combats, not intended to kill, although warriors often did die. An ongoing state of belligerence between the México *AZTECS* of *TENOCHTITLÁN* and their neighbours, especially against the stubborn and recalcitrant *TLAXCALTECAN* state to the east of the Basin of Mexico, provided captives for sacrifice to *HUITZILOPOCHTLI*, god of war and of the sun, who demanded regular, frequent

blood sacrifice as nourishment. His chosen people seem to have gone out of their way to secure regular supplies of sacrificial victims (as well as for empire-building and economic domination). Indeed, it was considered more honourable to capture an enemy for sacrificial purposes than to kill him outright in battle. The souls of warriors who died in these "wars" were taken and protected by the god *TEOYAOMIQUI*.

The bound and hapless victims were handed over to the priests at the foot of the Templo Mayor (the Great Temple) in Tenochtitlán, from where they were dragged up the steps, stretched across the sacrificial stone and their chests sliced open with an obsidian knife. The heart of the victim was wrenched out, the corpse flayed and the limbs dismembered. Allegedly, pieces of the flesh were sent down to the rulers and nobility to eat, while the heart was sometimes consumed by the priests. As well as human sacrifices, priests offered Huitzilopochtli flowers, incense and food, and adorned his idol with wreaths and garlands.

XÓCOTL see *OTONTECUHTLI*.

XOCOTLHUETZI see *HUEYMICCAILHUITL*.

XÓLOTL ("dog animal") was the *AZTEC* name for the god of Venus as the evening "star", who pushed the sun down into the darkness each night. He was a manifestation or twin of *QUETZALCÓATL-TLAHUIZCALPANTECUHTLI* (Venus as the morning "star"). He ruled *OLLIN* ("movement" or "earthquake"), 17th of the 20 day-names, and was often portrayed with a dog's head with a burst eye, set on a human body with backward-turned feet. By extension, he was thus the god of deformity and misfortune (his burst eye has been interpreted as a sign of penitence). In one version of the *CREATION*

XÓLOTL, the "dog animal", represented Venus as the evening "star", who pushed the sun down into darkness at the end of each day.

MYTH, Xólotl acted as Quetzalcóatl's companion and dog guide to the underworld, when he visited *MICTLÁN* to collect the bones of the people of the world of the Fourth Sun. In another variation, it was Xólotl who brought back a bone to the gods, who sprinkled it with blood and caused it to give birth to a boy and a girl. Xólotl then raised the children on thistle milk, and they peopled the world of the Fifth Sun.

Xólotl was also the name of a legendary *CHICHIMEC* leader (see *CHICHIMECA* and *OTOMÍ*). (See also *DUALITY & OPPOSITION*)

XONAXI GUALAPAG see *XONAXI QUECUYA*.

XONAXI HUILIA see *XONAXI QUECUYA*.

THE RITUAL BALL GAME

THE MESOAMERICAN BALL GAME was as much a ritual as it was a sport, and features in both myth and legend – for example in the tale of Hun Hunahpú and Vucub Hunahpú. Stone-clad ball courts formed an integral part of ceremonial complexes, and many cities had several courts. Versions of the game, using dirt ball courts, spread to native cultures beyond Mesoamerica – northwards into the US Southwest, and eastwards to the Caribbean Antilles. The game originated in the Preclassic Period and, by the middle Classic Period, it had become a state cult in which human sacrifice played a vital part, with the losing team or captain as the victim. It was especially important to the Warrior Cults.

BALL PLAYERS were frequently portrayed in several media, including ceramics (left) and stone (above). Ceramic models of players come from the Island of Jaina in the Gulf Coast region and the Maya frequently included sculptured stone panels of players on the their ball courts and other buildings. Both players shown here are Early Postclassic Period in date and show the typical gear worn by players for protection – belts, waist and hip pads, knee and wrist pads, and fancy headdresses.

ALMOST EVERY *Mesoamerican city had one or more ball courts. One of the most famous ball courts, and one of the largest, is that of the Maya-Toltec city of Chichén Itzá (above). On either side of the court, mounted vertically in the walls were two stone rings – the goals. The earliest known ball court was at the Olmec site of San Lorenzo, and the Olmec are thought to have invented the game. Rules varied from culture to culture, area to area, and through time; in most games, the object was to knock the rubber ball through the ring using only the body – not the hands – to manoeuvre and hit the ball.*

A FAMOUS SCENE of ritual sacrifice (above), at the culmination of a Classic Period ball game, is one of six bas-relief carved panels lining the two sides of the South Ball Court at El Tajín (one of seven courts in the city). It depicts two priests on either side of the unfortunate victim (probably the captain of one of the teams), holding him down and ready to slice his chest open with an obsidian sacrificial knife. To the left of the scene rises death, represented by a skeleton.

Z

XONAXI PEOCHINA COYO
see *BENELABA*.

XONAXI QUECUYA
was the Valley *ZAPOTEC* goddess of the dead and the underworld who, along with her husband *COQUI BEZELAO*, was special to the city of Mitla. Her Sierra Zapotec and Southern Zapotec names were respectively Xonaxi Gualapag and Xonaxi Huilia.

XOO
("earthquake") was the 17th of the 20 *ZAPOTEC* day-names and one of the year-bearing days – there were 13 *Xoo* years in a 52-year cycle (see also *CHINA*, *QUIJ* and *PIJA*). The *AZTEC* and *MAYA* equivalent days were *OLLIN* and *CABAN*.

XPIYACOC
was the highland Quiché *MAYA* creator god in the *POPUL VUH*, husband of *XMUCANÉ* and the "grandfather" of the human race. His sons were the twins *HUN HUNAHPÚ* and *VUCUB HUNAHPÚ*. His *AZTEC* equivalent was the god *CIPACTONAL*.

XQUIC,
the ill-fated daughter of one of the Lords of *XIBALBA* (the underworld), was the mother of the hero twins *HUNAHPÚ* and *XBALANQUÉ*. After the brothers *HUN HUNAHPÚ* and *VUCUB HUNAHPÚ* had been defeated by the Lords, and Hun Hunahpú's severed head hung in a calabash tree, she came to see the tree and asked herself aloud if she should pick one of the fruits. The head, overhearing her, informed her that the "fruits" were only a crop of skulls. Nevertheless, Xquic requested a fruit, whereupon Hun Hunahpú spat into her hand, thereby impregnating her. When her father demanded to know the identity of her lover, she denied any sin and escaped his wrath by travelling up to the surface to her mother-in-law *XMUCANÉ*. Xmucané rejected her at first, but then tested the truth of her claim to be Hun Hunahpú's wife by bidding her to collect corn (maize) from the field

of her half-brothers-in-law, *HUN BATZ* and Hun Chouen, knowing that there was only a single corn plant in the field. Xquic nevertheless returned with a great load of ears, which proved her claim to Xmucané. Despite this, Xquic's twin sons Hunahpú and Xbalanqué were not well received by Xmucané, and their half-brothers remained jealous. (See *TWINS & CULTURE HEROES*)

YÁCATA
was the name for a *TARASCAN* temple. In the Yácatas, perpetual fires to the sun god *CURICAUERI* were kept burning by specially designated priests. The centre of the cult, the great temple complex at the capital Tzintzuntzan, comprised a huge rectangular platform, some 425 by 250 m (465 by 273 yards), upon which stood five *yácata* platforms, each one T-shaped in plan, with a large circular extension at the base of the stem.

YACATECUHTLI,
or Yiacatecuhtli, ("he with the pointed nose") was the *AZTEC* patron of merchants, and the god of their "guild", the *pochteca*. He was portrayed with, and symbolized by, a bamboo staff and a fan. He was worshipped especially by the citizens of Cholula and Tlatelolco, both city-states in the Basin of Mexico before the founding of the Aztec capital at *TENOCHTITLÁN*. Tlatelolco later became the home and great central marketplace of the

Aztec Empire. His *MAYA* equivalents were *EK CHUAH* and *XAMEN EK*.

YÁOTL
was the general *AZTEC NAHUATL* word for "enemy", or the malevolent aspect of certain Aztec gods. (See *HUITZILOPOCHTLI* and *TEZCATLIPOCA*)

YAQUI-TEPEU
see under *TEPEU*.

YAXCHÉ
see under *WORLD TREE*, and *COLOURS & THE CARDINAL DIRECTIONS*.

YEAR-BEARER
see under *WORLD TREE*, and *COLOURS & THE CARDINAL DIRECTIONS*.

YIACATECUHTLI
see *YACATECUHTLI*.

YOHUALTECUHTLI,
or Yohualtonatiuh, literally "Lord of the Night", was the counterpart to the sun god *TONATIUH*, and therefore the "night sun". He was the representative of both the sun and Venus as they joined in the underworld to end each daily cosmic cycle. Yohualtecuhtli was identified as the star appearing in the centre of the sky at midnight among the Pleiades, initiating the crucial sacrifice of the *TOXIUHMOLPILIA*. In general he represented darkness, midnight and cyclic completion, and was regarded as the central world direction (as opposed to the four cardinal directions).

THE TARASCAN YÁCATA, like their language, was unique in Mesoamerica, emphasized here in the round base of the temple platform.

The huge, intricately carved stone popularly known as the "calendar stone", discovered at the site of the Templo Mayor in Mexico City in 1790, is believed by some scholars to represent the night sun Yohualtecuhtli rather than Tonatiuh.

THE YOHUALTEUCTIN
were the nine Aztec *LORDS OF THE NIGHT*.

YOHUALTONATIUH
see *YOHUALTECUHTLI*.

THE YOPE,
or Yopi, were a people in the southern highlands region known as Yopitzingo, in what is now the Mexican state of Guerrero. The cult of the "flayed one", *XIPE TOTEC*, possibly began in this region.

YUM CIMIL
("Lord of Death"; *cimi*, "death"), was an alternative name, used especially in Yucatán, for the *MAYA* god *AH PUCH*.

YUM KAAX
("Lord of the forests") was an alternative name for the *MAYA* agricultural deity known as *AH MUN*.

ZAC CIMI
see *THE BACABS*.

ZAC PAUAHTUN
see *THE PAUAHTUN*.

ZAC XIB CHAC
see *THE CHACS*.

THE ZAPOTECS
("Cloud People") were the peoples who settled in the southern highlands of

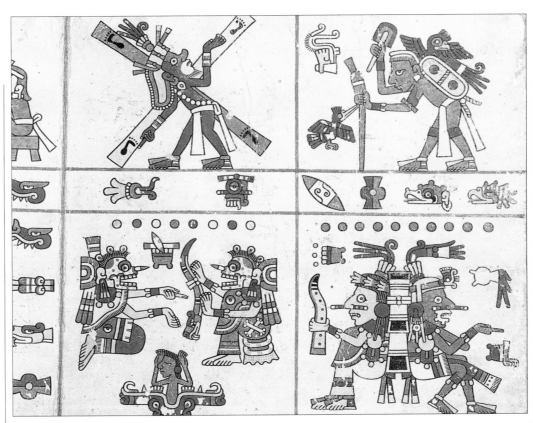

YACATECUHTLI, "he of the pointed nose", Aztec god of merchants, is portrayed carrying a crossroads with footprints. To his right, a merchant holds a staff and fan of his profession and carries a bundle of quetzal birds. (ILLUSTRATION FROM THE CODEX FEJÉRVÁRY-MAYER.)

central Mesoamerica, in and around the Valley of Oaxaca (in the present Mexican state of that name). Their civilization was centred on the mountain plateau site of Monte Albán, which dominated three converging valleys below it (collectively called the Valley of Oaxaca). They spoke one of the variations of the Oto-Zapotecan language groups.

In the Preclassic Period, agricultural communities in the valleys grew to a point where there was increasing competition for control of the region and its resources. Long-distance trade links had been established with the OLMECS of the Gulf Coast. A deliberate alliance appears to have been established among the local élite, which resulted in the construction and maintenance over several hundred years of a huge ceremonial "capital" and centre on the plateau overlooking the three principal valleys of the region. This site, Monte Albán, was begun about 500 BC and endured as a ritual centre, residential city and burial place for Zapotec kings for more than 1,000 years until the Zapotec state crumbled and the site was all but abandoned by about AD 800. The site was later recognized as a sacred place by the MIXTEC inheritors of power in the region, and used as a burial place for Mixtec kings as well.

At the height of Zapotec power, the rulers of Monte Albán commanded a kingdom that enjoyed long-distance trade networks throughout Mesoamerica and included diplomatic relations with the TEOTIHUACÁN "empire" in the Basin of Mexico and with several MAYA city-states. Throughout the Classic period, the Zapotecs domi-nated the southern highlands, while the Teotihuacanos dominated the central and northern regions of Mesoamerica, and also penetrated beyond the Zapotecs, to establish relations with several Maya cities themselves. Each site maintained an enclave of its own citizens as merchants and artisans in the other's city.

Zapotec civilization supported a large population in towns and villages throughout the Valley of Oaxaca and in and around Monte Albán itself on terraced residential suburbs, including at least 15 elite palaces around their own plaza compounds. At its most populous, from c. AD 400 to 700, it has been estimated that 25,000 people lived in Monte Albán. The reasons for Monte Albán's collapse are uncertain, but its coincidence with the collapse of Teotihuacán indicates that there was widespread economic implosion and a rise in city-state rivalry.

THE ZAPOTEC GODS present

a bewildering verbal maze of names. Although it is as full as the pantheons of other Mesoamerican cultures, it includes gods and goddesses for the same purposes and natural forces. In one view, all the deities of the Zapotecs represent parts of one great wholeness, comprising one god with numerous manifestations. Although the names vary, the creator deities and gods and goddesses of earth, sun, rain, war, love and death can be grouped into those of the Valley Zapotec (in the Valley of Oaxaca and its environs), the Sierra Zapotec (to the north of the Valley) and the Southern Zapotec (to the south and east, towards the Isthmus of Tehuantepec). Many cities had their own patron deities, and the characters of most Zapotec gods resembled those of deities for similar forces occurring elsewhere in Mesoamerica.

ZEE, or *Zij*, ("serpent") was the fifth of the 20 ZAPOTEC day-names; the AZTEC and MAYA equivalent days were *CÓATL* and *CHICCHAN*.

ZIJ ("serpent") see *ZEE*.

ZIP was the Yucatecan MAYA god of the hunt, particularly associated with the hunting of deer.

ZIPACNÁ, an evil giant in the Maya *POPOL VUH*, was the first son of *VUCUB-CAQUIZ* and brother of *CABRACÁN*; he was destroyed with them by the hero twins *HUNAHPÚ* and *XBALANQUÉ* in *XIBALBA*. Zipacná was so mighty that he could lift mountains. He once fooled 400 warriors into thinking that they had killed him, but, as they celebrated their victory, he rose and destroyed their house around them, crushing them to death (after which the warriors became stars in the night sky). He suffered poetic justice at the hands of the hero twins, who lured him deep into a mountain cave by offering him his favourite dish, a succulent crab, and then pulled the mountain down and buried him within it.

ZOTZ ("bat") was represented by the MAYA glyph of the leaf-nosed vampire bat. He was a main feature of the name glyph for the Maya city of Copán, and also the name for the royal house of the Cakchiquel Maya in the Guatemalan highlands (for example, King Ahpozotzil, literally "Lord Bat"). (See also *CAMA ZOTZ*)

ZOTZIHÁ ("House of Bats") was one of the levels of *XIBALBA*, the Quiché MAYA underworld.

CHRONOLOGY

15,000–2500 BC
ARCHAIC PERIOD
This period began with people migrating into the New World across the Bering Strait land bridge. This migration was made possible by a lower sea level when much water was locked up in glacial ice. There is some evidence that this migration may have been dated *c.* 15,000 BC. The earliest incontrovertible evidence of humans in Mexico is dated *c.* 7500 BC at Iztapan.

7000 BC Populations first established.

c. **5000 BC** Corn (maize) cultivation became more widespread and numerous village-farming communities were established throughout Mesoamerica.

2500–100 BC
PRECLASSIC PERIOD
This period saw the first cultural developments to warrant the term civilization. Villages grew in size and population, and the construction of special buildings among ordinary dwellings indicates the beginnings of religious ceremony.

c. **1200 BC** THE OLMEC civilization of the central and southern Gulf Coast began to erect ceremonial architecture and to construct monumental sculptures with iconography that depicted deities, cosmology and symbols of rulership. The civilization lasted until *c.* 400 BC.

600 BC At this time, THE ZAPOTECS, in the southern highlands, were also building ceremonial buildings and using iconography – calendrical symbols came into use around this time.

500 BC The Zapotec mountain city and ceremonial centre of Monte Alban was established. The city appears to have come about as a deliberately cooperative effort by the towns of the valley. Monte Alban was at the height of its power and influence *c.* 700 BC to *c.* 400 BC. After the decline of the Zapotec dynasty it was later used by THE MIXTECS, who took over power in the region, as a ritual centre.

100 BC–AD 300
PROTOCLASSIC PERIOD
Complex urban-based cultures began to flourish all over Mesoamerica. Long-distance trade and diplomatic and military contact spread pan-Mesoamerican religious themes, raw materials and artefacts among these cultures.

c. **100 BC–AD 100**
A number of ceremonial centres of stepped stone temple platforms were constructed at Cuicuilco and at TEOTIHUACÁN in the southern and northeastern Basin of Mexico, respectively, and at lowland Maya sites such as Tikal and many others.

c. **AD 50** The city of TEOTIHUACÁN grew in power and began to dominate the Basin of Mexico and expand its economic "empire" throughout much of central Mesoamerica and into the Maya area.

AD 300–900
CLASSIC PERIOD
During this period the city of TEOTIHUACÁN dominated central Mesoamerica and grew to become the largest and most populous city, with an economic empire extending throughout Mesoamerica.

Maya ceremonial cities, such as Palenque, Chichén Itzá, Tikal, Copán and scores of others, flourished throughout eastern and southern Mesoamerica at this time. Maya hieroglyphic writing reached a high level of complexity and reveals the names of Maya cities, rulers and deities. Classic Period Maya cities were never united into a single empire or confederation, but hieroglyphic inscriptions record the temporary alliances and conquests of numerous rulers and cities. Monte Alban still dominated the Oaxaca Valley and Southern Highlands region.

AD 300 The city of TEOTIHUACÁN was at the height of its size and powers.

AD 650 The city of TEOTIHUACÁN began to decline.

AD 692 Approximate start of THE MIXTEC dynasty in the southern highlands, inheriting Zapotec cities.

c. **AD 700** At Xochiacalco, there is evidence to suggest that there may have been a gathering of priests and "astronomers" from the Maya, Zapotec and central Mesoamerican cities to synchronize and standardize their calendars.

AD 900–1521
POSTCLASSIC PERIOD
This period began with the virtual abandonment of many Classic Period Maya cities, along with Monte Alban and TEOTIHUACÁN, many of which had suffered periods of decline in the century and a half before AD 900.

c. **1100** One of the most important Chichemec groups entered the Basin of Mexico, led by legendary chief XOLOTL. (CHICHIMECA was a general term used by THE AZTECS for the nomadic hunter-gatherer people of the northern deserts.) The Chichimeca founded the city of Tenayuca in the northern Basin, and their descendants later joined the Acolhua Aztecs on the eastern lake shores to establish a capital city at TEXCOCO.

c. AD 900–1250

New cities sprang up to dominate the regions of Mesoamerica. To the north-west of the Basin of Mexico, Tula (ancient TOLLÁN) dominated northern and central Mesoamerica, as climatic change shifted the northern limits southward. At about the same time Chichén Itzá in Yucatán rose as a ruling city remarkably similar to TOLLÁN in what appears to be a sort of Toltec "empire" of strong military alliance between north and south.

c. AD 968 THE TOLTEC city of TOLLÁN (Tula) was founded.

1011–63 Reign of legendary ruler EIGHT DEER TIGER CLAW of MIXTEC cities of Tilantongo and Tututepec.

c. 1100 MÉXICA Aztecs left the north of Mexico and travelled southwards in search of new lands.

1168 Chichemec people destroyed the city of TOLLÁN and Toltec power came to an end.

1250–1521
LATE POSTCLASSIC PERIOD

The Toltec and Chichen Itzán powers waned, while THE AZTECS rose to power in the Basin of Mexico from their capital at TENOCHTITLÁN, and began their conquests of central Mesoamerica. By c. 1500 THE AZTECS dominated almost all of central Mesoamerica from the Gulf of Mexico to the Pacific coast, and they continued to expand to north and south. Territorial frontier established

in northwest with Tarascan Kingdom.

At this time, THE MAYA population shifted north in Yucatán Northern Lowlands, establishing new Maya city-states, such as Mayapan and Tulum.

The kingdom of the Tarascans, in the northwest of the Basin of Mexico, and the Tlaxcaltecan state to the east of the Basin, managed to hold out staunchly against any Aztec attempts to conquer them.

c. 1300 THE MIXTEC civiliz-ation was thriving at Oaxaca, southern Mexico.

1325 TENOCHTITLÁN was founded on an island at the centre of Lake TEXCOCO, central Mexico.

c. 1400 THE AZTECS con-quered THE MIXTECS.

1468 THE AZTECS set up the Triple Alliance.

1519 Hernán Cortés and about 500 Spanish soldiers landed at Vera Cruz. Despite its wealth and power, the Aztec empire was only about a century and a half old. Many of its subjects resented Aztec domination and were eager to grab any opportunity to rebel. Cortés wasted no time in taking advantage of this internal ferment. He used his knowledge of the predicted return of QUETZALCÓATL (the plumed serpent god) in the guise of a bearded man from the east, to ignite the turmoil into open rebellion. He quickly gained hundreds of thousands of native allies and overthrew the Aztec Empire.

1520 Battle/Massacre of TOXCATL. Cortés had been welcomed rather reluctantly into the city of TENOCHTITLÁN, by the emperor Moctezuma II. Shortly afterwards, Cortés left the city to confront an expedition from Cuba, and left his lieutenant in charge. THE AZTECS continued with the important festival of TOXCATL. The Spaniards were made nervous by the crowds and the noise and activities of the festival around them. They interpreted this as threatening, or pretended to find it so, and so attacked the crowds at the ceremony. According to the Spanish chronicles of the time more than 8,500 unarmed Aztecs were killed.

1521 The city of TENOCHTITLÁN was besieged and captured, and the Aztec dynasty overthrown by Hernán Cortés.

POST-COLONIZATION

After the collapse of the Aztec and Maya civilizations, the populations were decimated but their traditions and culture survived.

1525 The Spanish took con-trol of Aztec lands.

1527 Maya lands fell under Spanish rule.

1535 Mexico became a Spanish colony.

1554–1558 The POPUL VUH was written. It was a sacred book of the Quiché Maya of highland Guatemala. The manuscript was discovered in the early 18th century, and was then lost, but not before it had been copied and translated. It provides a detailed description of Maya cosmology and the story of the Hero Twins.

1790 The so-called "calendar stone" was found in what is now Mexico City, but was the ancient city of TENOCHTITLÁN, a MÉXICA Aztec city. On it is carved the foundation date of TENOCHTITLÁN, encircled by rings depicting the Aztec calendrical symbols for the days and months, and a two-headed sky serpent.

1978 One of the most spectacular finds – Templo Major in Mexico City (on the site of Tenochtitlán's central ceremonial precinct) – a huge carved stone portraying COYOLXAUHQUI, the Aztec moon goddess.

BIBLIOGRAPHY

Aveni, Frank (1980) *Skywatchers of Ancient Mexico*. University of Texas Press.

Benson, Elizabeth P. (ed.) (1981) *Mesoamerican Sites and World Views*. Dumbarton Oaks, Washington, DC.

Berdan, Frances F. (1982) *The Aztecs of Mexico: An Imperial Society*. Holt, Rinehart & Winston, New York.

Berrin, Kathleen, and Esther Pasztory (eds) (1993) *Teotihuacan: Art from the City of the Gods*. Thames and Hudson, London and New York/The Fine Arts Museums of San Francisco.

Bierhorst, J. (1990) *The Mythology of Mexico and Central America*. Harper & Row, New York.

Bierhorst, J. (1992) *History and Mythology of the Aztecs: The Codex Chimalpopoca*. University of Arizona Press.

Blanton, Richard E., Gary M. Feinman, Stephen A. Kowalewski and Linda M. Nichols (1999) *Ancient Oaxaca: The Monte Albán State*. Cambridge University Press.

Boone, Elizabeth H. (ed.) (1970) *Ritual Human Sacrifice in Mesoamerica*. Dumbarton Oaks, Washington, DC.

Bray, Warwick (1968) *Everyday Life of the Aztecs*. Batsford, London.

Broda, Johanna, David Carrasco and Eduardo Matos Moctezuma (1987) *The Great Temple of Tenochtitlán: Center and Periphery in the Aztec World*. University of California Press.

Brotherston, Gordon (1982) *A Key to Mesoamerican Reckoning of Times: The Chronology Recorded in Native Texts*. British Museum Occasional Papers, 38, London.

Brotherston, Gordon (1995) *Painted Books from Mexico: Codices in UK Collections and the World They Represent*. British Museum Press, London.

Brundage, Burr Cartwright (1979) *The Fifth Sun: Aztec Gods, Aztec World*. University of Texas Press.

Burkhart, Louise M. (1985) *The Slippery Earth: Nahua Christian Moral Dialogue in Sixteenth-Century Mexico*. University of Arizona Press.

Carrasco, David (1990) *Religions of Mesoamerica: Cosmovision and Ceremonial Centers*. Harper & Row, San Francisco.

Carrasco, David (1991) *To Change Place: Aztec Ceremonial Landscapes*. University of Colorado Press.

Caso, Alfonso (1958) *The Aztecs, People of the Sun* (trans. Lowell Dunham). University of Oklahoma Press.

Clendinnen, Inga (1991) *Aztecs: An Interpretation*. Cambridge University Press.

Collis, John, and David M. Jones (1997) *Blue Guide Mexico*. A & C Black, London/W. W. Norton, New York.

Conrad, Geoffrey W., and Arthur A. Demarest (1984) *Religion and Empire: The Dynamics of Aztec and Inca Expansionism*. Cambridge University Press.

Diehl, Richard A. (1983) *Tula: The Toltec Capital of Ancient Mexico*. Thames and Hudson, London and New York.

Durán, Fray Diego (1971) *Books of the Gods and Rites* (trans. Fernando Horcasitas and Doris Heydon). University of Oklahoma Press.

Durán, Fray Diego (1971) *The Ancient Calendar* (trans. Fernando Horcasitas and Doris Heydon). University of Oklahoma Press.

León-Portilla, Miguel (1963) *Aztec Thought and Culture*. University of Oklahoma Press.

León-Portilla, Miguel (1980) *Native American Spirituality: Ancient Myths, Discourses, Stories, Doctrines, Hymns, Poems from the Aztec, Maya, Quiche-Maya, and other Sacred Traditions*. Paulist Press, New York.

McEwan, Colin (1994) *Ancient Mexico in the British Museum*. British Museum Press, London.

Matos Moctezuma, Eduardo (1988) *The Great Temple of the Aztecs: Treasures of Tenochtitlán* (trans. Doris Heydon). Thames and Hudson, London and New York.

Miller, Mary Ellen, and Karl Taube (1993) *The Gods and Symbols of Ancient Mexico and the Maya: An Illustrated Dictionary of Mesoamerican Religion*. Thames and Hudson, London and New York.

Muser, Curt (1978) *Facts and Artifacts of Ancient Middle America*. Dutton, New York.

Nicholson, Henry B. (1971) "Religion in Pre-Hispanic Central Mexico", in Robert Wauchope, Gordon Ekholm and Ignacio Bernal (eds.), *Handbook of Middle American Indians*, vol. 10, pp.395–446, University of Texas Press.

Nicholson, Henry B. (ed.) (1976) *Origins of Religious Art and Iconography in Preclassic Mesoamerica*. University of California Press.

Pasztory, Esther (1983) *Aztec Art*. Harry N. Abrams, New York.

Porter Weaver, Muriel (1993) *The Aztecs, Maya, and their Predecessors: Archaeology of Mesoamerica* (3rd ed.). Academic Press, San Diego.

Rostas, Susanna (1992) "Mexican Mythology", in C. Larrington (ed.), *The Feminist Companion to Mythology*. Pandora Press, London.

Sahagún, Fray Bernadino de (1950–69) *General History of the Things of New Spain* (trans. Arthur O. J. Anderson and Charles F. Dibble). University of New Mexico Press.

Saunders, Nicholas J. (1993) "Mesoamerica", in Roy Willis (ed.), *World Mythology: An Illustrated Guide*, pp.234–49. Duncan Baird, London.

Scarborough, Vernon, and David R. Wilcox (eds) (1991) *The Mesoamerican Ballgame*. University of Arizona Press.

Schele, Linda, and Mary Ellen Miller (1986/1992) *The Blood of Kings: Dynasty and Ritual Maya Art*. Kimbell Art Museum & George Braziller, Fort Worth, Texas/Thames and Hudson, London and New York.

Sharer, Robert J. (1994) *The Ancient Maya* (5th ed.). Stanford University Press, California.

Siméon, Rémi (1885/1984) *Diccionario de la Lengua Nahuatl o Mexicana* (trans. from French Josefina Oliva de Coll). Siglo Veintiuno, México, DF.

Soustelle, Jacques (1955/1961) *Daily Life of the Aztecs on the Eve of the Spanish Conquest* (trans. Patrick O'Brian). Stanford University Press, California.

Soustelle, Jacques (1979/1985) *The Olmecs: The Oldest Civilization in Mexico* (trans. Helen R. Lane). Oklahoma University Press.

Spence, Lewis (1923) *The Gods of Mexico*. T. Fisher Unwin, London.

Spores, Ronald (1984) *The Mixtecs in Ancient and Colonial Times*. Oklahoma University Press.

Taube, Karl (1983) "The Teotihuacan Spider Woman", in *Journal of Latin American Lore*, 9 (2), pp.107–89.

Taube, Karl (1992) *The Major Gods of Ancient Yucatan*. Dumbarton Oaks, Washington, DC.

Taube, Karl (1993) *Aztec and Maya Myths*. British Museum Press, London.

Tedlock, Dennis (trans.) (1985) *Popul Vuh: The Definitive Edition of the Mayan Book of the Dawn of Life and the Glories of Gods and Kings*. Simon and Schuster, New York.

Townsend, Richard F. (1992) *The Aztecs*. Thames and Hudson, London and New York.

Townsend, Richard F. (ed.) (1992) *The Ancient Americas: Art from Sacred Landscapes*. The Art Institute of Chicago.

Whitecotton, Joseph W. (1977) *The Zapotecs: Princes, Priests, and Peasants*. Oklahoma University Press.

GENERAL READING

Brotherston, Gordon (1979) *Image of the New World: The American Continent Portrayed in Native Texts*. Thames and Hudson, London and New York.

Coe, Michael, Dean Snow and Elizabeth Benson (1986) *Atlas of Ancient America*. Facts on File, New York and Oxford.

Willis, Roy (ed.) *World Mythology: An Illustrated Guide*. Duncan Baird, London.

PICTURE ACKNOWLEDGEMENTS

The publishers are grateful to the agencies, museums and galleries listed below for kind permission to reproduce the following images in this book:

AKG: 20cl Biblioteca Nacional, Madrid; 20tl, 25cl Museum für Völkerkunde, Berlin; 27cl Österreichische Nationalbibliothek, Vienna; 34bc; 54tr; 57bl SMPK Museum für Völkerkunde, Berlin; 57c; 64tcl; 67tr; 67bl British Museum, London; 80 Bibliothèque Nationale, Paris; 86r Museo Nacional de Antropologia, Mexico City

Ancient Art and Architecture: 22br; 29br; 30; 35tl; 35br; 45bc; 52br; 69r; 70; 84tr; 85tr

Andes Press Agency: 21br Museo Nacional de Antropologia, Mexico City; 45tl; 63; 74bc; 76

The Bridgeman Art Library: 10 Museo Casa Diego Rivera, Mexico; 25tr Museo Nacional de Antropologia, Mexico City; 26bl Royal Geographical Society, London; 27tr Museo Casa Diego Rivera (INBA), Guanajuato, Mexico; 37tr Royal Geographical Society, London; 44br; 55br, 66 British Museum, London; 67cr Biblioteca Apostolica Vaticana; 83tl Museo Nacional de Antropologia, Mexico City; 87t

Grażyna Bonati: 13bl; 65br

Sylvia Cordaiy: 23bl; 32br; 42tc; 51cl; 73cl

ET Archive: 11, 19br National Library, Mexico City; 20br Archaeological Museum, Copan, Honduras; p22tc, 23cr National Library, Mexico City; 23tl; 24tr; 27br Anthropological Museum, Merida, Spain; 41tc National Library, Mexico City; 41br Antochiw Collection; 44tl National Library, Mexico; 45tr Archaeological Museum, Copan, Honduras; 48bl;

51br, 53tr National Library, Mexico City; 55tl; 57b; 58br, 59tr National Library, Mexico City; 60br; 61tl Archaeological Museum, Mexico City; 61br Antochiw Collection; 67tl; 67cl; 67br; 71tl, 75tc, 77, 78 National Library, Mexico City; 85bl Archaeological Museum, Mexico City; 86l Archaeological Museum, Copan, Honduras

Michael Holford: 39br Museo Nacional de Antropologia, Mexico City

Hutchison Library: 40tr Museo Nacional de Antropologia, Mexico City

David M. Jones: 64tr; 73tl; 73tr; 73cr; 82

Panos Pictures: 51tl

South American Pictures: 12; 13tr; 14; 16 Chris Sharp, Museo Nacional de Antropologia, Mexico City; 19tl; 28br; 29tl; 31tl; 31br; 32tc; 47br; 48tc; 60tcl; 60tr; 62; 65tc; 72; 73bl; 75br; 81; 87b; 88

Mireille Vautier: 24tl, 24bl, 28tc, 38bl, 50bl, 71br National Library, Mexico City

Werner Forman Archive: 18 British Museum, London; 21tl Private Collection, New York; 26r St. Louis Art Museum, US; 33br Liverpool Museum, UK; 36 Museo Nacional de Antropologia, Mexico City; 37cr; 37cl Biblioteca Universitaria, Bologna, Italy; 39tl Dallas Museum of Art; 43 David Bernstein, New York; 46 Museum für Völkerkunde, Basel; 47tl

Museo Nacional de Antropologia, Mexico City; 47tr Anthropology Museum, Veracruz University, Jalapa; 47bl Museum für Völkerkunde, Berlin; 49tl Museo Nacional de Antropologia, Mexico City; 49tr British Museum, London; 55ct Anthropology Museum, Veracruz University, Jalapa; 57r; 74tl Biblioteca Universitaria, Bologna, Italy; 79bl, 79bc Museum für Völkerkunde, Basel; 83br British Museum, London; 84bl Museo Nacional de Antropologia, Mexico City; 89 Liverpool Museum, UK

H

INDEX